FROM FEARFUL TO
FEAR FREE^{SM}

Marty Becker, DVM
Lisa Radosta, DVM, DACVB
Wailani Sung, PhD, DVM, DACVB
Mikkel Becker, KPA CTP, CBCC-KA, CDBC, CPDT-KA, CTC

Health Communications, Inc.
Deerfield Beach, Florida
www.hcibooks.com

**Library of Congress Cataloging-in-Publication Data
is available through the Library of Congress**

© 2018 Fear Free, LLC

ISBN-13: 978-07573-2079-8 (Paperback)
ISBN-10: 07573-2079-1 (Paperback)
ISBN-13: 978-07573-2080-4 (ePub)
ISBN-10: 07573-2080-5 (ePub)

Publisher: Health Communications, Inc.
      3201 S.W. 15th Street
      Deerfield Beach, FL 33442–8190

Author photos pages 222–223: Joel Riner/Quicksilver Photography (Dr. Marty Becker), Courtesy Dr. Lisa Radosta (Dr. Lisa Radosta), Jeff Paulson (Wailani Sung), Jane Sobel Klonsky/Project Unconditional (Mikkel Becker)

CONTENTS

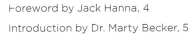

Foreword

Animals have always played an important role in my life. When I was eleven, I started volunteering with our local veterinarian, cleaning cages. I also started a mini-farm on my parents' property in Tennessee with my brother and sister, raising pigs, goats, chickens, and horses. I even brought a donkey to college with me and marched him in the homecoming parade! Animals are my life, no matter what species or size. However, there is nothing that can compare to the meaningful relationships I've had over the years with my dogs.

My first pets as a child were two Collies named Lance and Vandy. They taught me so much and led me toward a career path by which I am still truly inspired every day. After I graduated college, my wife, Suzi, and I continued to work with animals, and I went on to become the director of the Central Florida Zoo and then the Columbus Zoo, where I've have spent the last thirty-eight years. Animals of all kinds have been a central part of my life at work and at home. Suzi and I have always emphasized the importance of caring for our family dogs while raising our three daughters, Kathaleen, Suzanne, and Julie. The girls always had a dog in the house—whether it was our Old English Sheepdog, Daisy, our Mastiff, Ben, our Golden Retriever, Brass, or our yellow Labrador Retriever, Tasha, you didn't have to look far until you found a four-legged friend.

Our family dogs were always treated as members of the family, for better or for worse! And I truly believe that pets, dogs in particular, have a way of teaching us about so many things—constant care, responsibility, loyalty, unconditional love, and inevitable loss—that serve as a gentle introduction to the parallel experiences we all have as humans.

Dogs are called man's best friend for a reason: they provide humor, companionship and love—some of the things we need most. However, we sometimes overlook the things that our furry friends need in return. Dogs can suffer silently from a variety of issues because effectively communicating with our pets is one of the most difficult hurdles to address. Don't you wish your dog could just open his mouth and speak the same language as you? He could tell you when he was in pain, when he was hungry or nervous, or when he just wanted to play. Instead, we must rely on a variety of context clues and observations about our pets to point us in the right direction.

One of the biggest issues dogs can face is fear. Fear of the veterinarian, fear of bad weather, fear of abandonment, and even fear of loud noises, such as fireworks or a car backfiring, are all common issues that dogs experience. Fear is overlooked in many dogs simply because we, as pet parents, don't know the signs. However, every pet owner knows how mentally and physically painful it can be to witness his or her dog struggle with an unknown ailment.

I am thrilled that my friend Dr. Marty Becker, along with Mikkel Becker, Dr. Wailani Sung, and Dr. Lisa Radosta, came together to write *From Fearful to Fear Free*, which addresses not only your dog's issues with fear but also your own well-being as a concerned pet owner. Most of the time, your dog's fear is not your fault; it is a product of genetics and environment. And while your dog's contentment is important, you also can't forget how important it is, as his owner, to live without feeling shame or guilt.

I have been lucky to have meaningful connections with animals all my life. I feel even luckier to be able to continue to learn new things around every turn. *From Fearful to Fear Free* provides a variety of positive-reinforcement pointers, training tips, and easy-to-follow techniques to improve the well-being of both you and your furry friend. I hope that by the end of this book, you will be able to look back and see the wonderful journey you and your dog have taken together and perhaps make some adjustments to your interactions that further improve your relationship.

—*Jack Hanna*, Director Emeritus, Columbus Zoo and Aquarium; Host, *Jack Hanna's Into the Wild* and *Jack Hanna's Wild Countdown*

Introduction

With this book, I've authored or co-authored twenty-five books that have sold around eight million copies. Three of them were *New York Times* bestsellers. And I've never written a book that I felt was so important for every pet owner to read.

My reason is simple: You should read this book because your pet can't. Dogs *need* their owners to understand the information in this book so they can help their beloved pets live not just healthy, but also happy, lives.

This isn't a recycled version of the same health and training information covered in many other books (including some of mine!). It features some amazing new information and is the definitive source on helping pet owners remove fear, anxiety, and stress (FAS) from their pets' lives, and it gives positive, proactive ways to keep dogs happy and calm.

We call it "the calm instead of the storm," both literally and figuratively. That's because pets do **not** have to suffer FAS from thunderstorms and other noises, ranging from Fourth of July fireworks to alarms, gunshots, and vacuum cleaners. The same goes for separation anxiety, the pet equivalent of what a human child feels at being lost and separated from family in the bowels of a mall, at a large fair or festival, or on a camping trip.

To ease that suffering means that we, as veterinarians and as pet owners, can no longer ignore FAS but instead must realize that emotional distress is not only damaging in itself, but it also causes physical damage to pets and undermines their health, happiness, and longevity. There are proven tactics and tips in this book that can help your pet become independent and relaxed while you're away at work or play. We also showcase dozens of holistic solutions for FAS, including "chill pills," calming music, pheromones, compression garments, and therapeutic massage.

Know that we practice what we preach when it comes to our mandate to consider sedation as a first option, not a last resort. That's why we also give you some specifics on how to talk productively with your pet's veterinarian about proven prescription solutions for stubborn or chronic emotional problems. This book also taps into the decades of experience of the coauthors to provide proven solutions for doggy fears ranging from fear of people or other dogs to fear of inanimate objects, including the exam table at the vet's office and the vacuum cleaner at home.

The four coauthors bring a combined eighty-eight years of postgraduate, in-the-trenches experience working directly with fearful animals and the people who own them. The group includes two highly respected boarded veterinary behaviorists (of only seventy-four in the United States), a popular dog trainer with four other books and hundreds of articles on training to her credit, and me, a veteran veterinarian. Although I've been appearing on television for more than twenty years, I don't just play a veterinarian on TV; I still practice at North Idaho Animal Hospital in Sandpoint, Idaho, and routinely deal with fearful pets and fearful pet owners.

We call all corners of the United States home, but we are in one unified huddle when it comes to giving a voice to suffering pets who deserve happiness. While we don't speak a lick of Labrador, we know the meaning of canine body language, vocalizations, and other signs of happiness or stress, and we give that knowledge to you in this book so that you can become the master of your dog's well-being.

—*Dr. Marty Becker*

PART I

YOUR DOG'S BRAIN:

WHAT'S REALLY GOING ON IN THERE

FEAR AND **ITS EFFECTS**

Do you remember the first time you felt severe fear? It was probably when you were a young child, and we're not talking a Halloween-mask "boo!" Maybe your mother disappeared behind a rack of clothes in a store, and you didn't know where she was. Maybe you saw a shadow on the wall in your darkened bedroom. Or maybe you were frightened by the approach of an ominous stranger.

Fear is a universal reaction experienced by every species, including dogs. It's an emotional response caused by an encounter with anything, real or anticipated, that appears to be a threat: the disappearance of a loved one, the unknown, or something that experience teaches will cause pain (syringe + needle = ouch!).

Whether we are human or canine or some other species, our bodies experience changes in brain and organ function when we are afraid. When we are faced with danger, whether obvious or anticipated, our bodies spring into action. We breathe more rapidly, our heart rate increases, and our muscles tense up, right down to the thousands of individual hair follicles. In the blink of an eye, these physiological reactions alert the brain to the presence of a threat. Body and mind go into self-defense mode, commonly referred to as "fight or flight"—prepare for a live-or-die battle or run for your life!

Fear helps humans and animals survive by allowing them to recognize danger and take

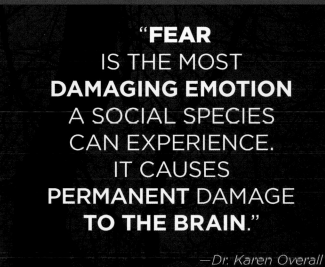

"**FEAR**
IS THE MOST
DAMAGING EMOTION
A SOCIAL SPECIES
CAN EXPERIENCE.
IT CAUSES
PERMANENT DAMAGE
TO THE BRAIN."

—*Dr. Karen Overall*

action, whether it's to freeze in place, hide, run away, fidget (bark or run in circles), or stand and defend themselves (or at least look and sound as if they could). It's an instinctive protection system, but it can also cause inappropriate responses that make life miserable for fearful pets and their people. Not just uncomfortable, which is bad enough, but damaging physiologically and emotionally. In short, think PTSD (post-traumatic stress disorder) for pets.

When fear or anxiety takes over a dog's life, it can become impossible to take him to the veterinarian or groomer, have him ride comfortably in the car, go for a walk around the neighborhood, leave him home alone, or have friends or family visit. A fearful dog may become aggressive, destructive, or withdrawn. He may become physically ill with vomiting or diarrhea when he is placed in a situation that he fears, or he may refuse to eat at all. That's no way to live—for you or your dog! That's why it is vital that we take the necessary steps to

Fear Factor

You may remember seeing a news story circulating on social media about a woman who jumped out of a moving car, leaving her nine-year-old child in the backseat. What motivated her to abandon her child in such a dangerous situation? An innate (and potentially deadly, in this case) fear of spiders. While backing out of her driveway, the woman saw a spider in her car, and her first instinct was to escape from it. Her fearful reaction to the spider was so intense that she simply reacted. That fear overcame the normal instinct of a mother to protect her child. Now, if rational people can respond this way when they are afraid, it's easy to understand how our dogs might also exhibit fear in situations or circumstances in which they have no control.

—*Dr. Wailani Sung*

reduce or remove the triggers for anxiety and fear in when they arise in animals' lives and vow to always travel along a path that moves both pets and humans from fearful to Fear Free.

THE ELEMENTS OF FEAR

We are fortunate to be living in a time when we have a better understanding of brain chemistry as it relates to fear than we had in the past. Understanding and recognizing a dog's fear and anxiety—or the potential for those emotions—helps us increase his comfort level in stressful situations as well as help him cope with his stress in constructive ways. But first, let's take a look at how fear works.

Your dog's fear response begins when information is sent from the sensory cortex. This is where the brain receives the signals from the outside world. For example, when your dog hears the can opener, this information is transmitted to the auditory cortex, causing him to anticipate delicious food.

Neurochemicals, such as epinephrine and norepinephrine, put the body on high alert. In an instant, they speed up the heart rate, increase blood flow to the muscles, dilate air passages for better lung capacity, and release glucose for energy.

Cortisol, known commonly as the stress hormone, is a natural steroid that increases

blood sugar, enables the brain to make better use of glucose, and increases availability of substances that repair body tissue. Cortisol suppresses nonessential body functions—such as the digestive, reproductive, and immune systems—that might hamper a fight, flight, freeze, or fidget response. It also communicates with areas of the brain that control fear. In normal amounts, cortisol plays an important role in fighting stress as well as regulating other facets of good health, such as weight, tissue structure, and skin condition.

The body's response to this influx of hormones occurs rapidly, without conscious thought or action. The rush of neurochemicals and hormones throughout the body and brain aid in what is called memory consolidation and retrieval in a part of the brain called the medial prefrontal cortex. In short, your dog remembers very well what happened to him when he was scared. When he is back in that situation again, his body will be able to access that memory quickly. He will remember that incident, which caused him fear and rocked his entire body, more clearly than he will remember the half hour you spent teaching him how to high-five the weekend before.

While, in the wild, this type of memory can save an animal's life (i.e., there's a predator in that area so I should avoid going there) as he goes about his daily activities, this avoidance mechanism can mean that a pet doesn't receive proper veterinary or preventive care, putting his health (and, by extension, his human's health) at serious risk.

Their recall ability is what helps dogs know how to react to a threat, but it can also be what gets them into fear-related trouble. As you probably know, dogs are extremely observant. They spend their lives watching us and are good at learning from experience and observation. This movement from the

Brain Anatomy: Amygdala

The amygdala is a small, almond-shaped part of the brain that receives information from all of the sensory systems in the body. Think of it as a processing and distribution center for environmental stimuli, turning sights and sounds into emotional responses. The signals are then broadcast to other parts of the brain, such as the hypothalamus (panting, trembling, increased blood flow to muscles), brainstem (fight, flight, freeze, fidget), and cerebral cortex (emotional experience). When a dog is frightened, on the surface we see only that he is hiding under a chair, trembling, but major events have occurred inside his body, altering the way he feels emotionally and physically and ensuring that he will never forget that particular experience.

—Dr. Lisa Radosta

Anticipating **Fear**

Dogs can be very perceptive. I have had many owners tell me that their dogs know the route to the veterinary hospital. When the owner turns down certain streets, the dog immediately starts to pant and shake. Some dogs become so anxious and fearful that they won't even jump out of the car or walk into the veterinary clinic and must be carried inside. If a dog is too fearful, sometimes the owner needs the veterinary staff to make a human barrier and slowly walk up behind the dog to get him to move toward the clinic entrance. How sad is that? Think about how it makes the staff of the veterinary clinic feel. It also doesn't set the dog up for a happy veterinary visit.

Other dogs associate any car ride with visits to the veterinary clinic. They won't jump in the car, or they pace, pant, whine, or bark for the entire duration of the car ride. Some dogs vomit during the car ride or as soon as they arrive at the destination. I have had several patients who even defecate or urinate during the car ride. That's unpleasant for both dogs and owners.

These reactions aren't limited to visits to the veterinary clinic. Many dogs exhibit fear and anxiety during car rides because they may have generalized fear or anxiety of the unknown. Where are we going? Is it going to be fun or scary? It's not easy to explain to your dog that he doesn't have to be scared.

—*Dr. Wailani Sung*

recliner means mom is going to the bathroom, whereas this seemingly same motion means we're going for a walk. Puppies' first lessons on responding to threats come from their mother, and they quickly pick up additional fear reactions as they interact with other dogs, other animals, and with humans (especially those who can unintentionally inflict pain or fear, such as members of the veterinary team). Once acquired, reactions to fear are not easily forgotten and may intensify with experience.

WHEN AND HOW FEAR STARTS

We think of fear as something that develops with experience, but fear can be genetic, starting in the womb. Canine behavior is complex, affected by both genetic and environmental factors. Genetics create a puppy's behavioral template, but his environment and experiences in utero, after birth, and growing up all influence the expression of behaviors. This is why feral dogs on reservations or in parts of the world where they live on the periphery of humanity (because of religious taboos, fear of rabies, or not enough homes) can be more difficult to integrate into a household; for them, almost every motion or noise could be a death threat.

For instance, what a mother eats can affect her offspring's taste preferences. If the mother experiences a physical or psychological trauma or is malnourished during pregnancy, the puppies' development, including their response to stress, can be negatively affected. The pups may not be as friendly or learn as quickly as pups whose mother had better care.

An example of a heritable fear is noise phobia, such as fear of thunderstorms, fireworks, or gunshots. Research shows that herding breeds, Border Collies in particular, tend to be especially predisposed to this type of fear, suggesting that a genetic component is at work. Many dogs with noise phobia have parents, siblings, or other relatives with the same problem.

Fear can also be environmental. A fear of strangers or people in uniform who "invade territory" (think delivery people), for instance, may develop from lack of positive exposure during the sensitive period for socialization from three to fourteen weeks of age. Early negative experiences, such as being threatened or attacked by an aggressive dog, may also set fear in motion. Even an accident or illness at an early age (a

Are They
the Same?

Fear, anxiety, and phobias are often lumped together, and dogs experiencing them may have similar physiological signs, but each has a distinct definition.

Fear is an emotion caused by the presence of danger. An extremely large and aggressive dog or an accelerating vehicle is charging toward me. It triggers an immediate response in the brain—specifically, the amygdala—to the perceived threat.

Anxiety is nervousness or apprehension regarding an anticipated threat. The best example is pulling up in front of the veterinary clinic. Think dogs can't anticipate? Think again. A dog is quite capable of making the association that the last two times he went for a car ride, he was taken to the veterinarian's office, where he experienced unpleasant things.

A phobia is an extreme, persistent, and abnormal fear of something. Usually, there's no reasonable explanation for the existence of a phobia. The fear associated with a phobia is so strong that it affects quality of life or ability to function. A dog who is phobic about fireworks, for instance, may tremble, cry, or hide under the bed. Some go into full-blown panic mode and try to escape by jumping through a window, chewing through a door, or going over a fence and running away.

Fear Figures

Hate taking your pet to the vet? You're not alone. Statistics show that the frequency of veterinary visits is down, with one major factor being the animal's perceived emotional stress about the visit combined with the stress the owner feels as a result. A study shows that just thinking about taking an animal to the veterinarian is stressful for 26 percent of dog owners, and 38 percent say their dog hates going to the vet's office. In another study, 51 percent of owners said their pet dislikes going to the veterinarian, up from 45 percent in 2010. In the same study, 38 percent of owners agreed with the following sentiment: "Just thinking about taking my pet to the veterinarian is stressful." That's up from 30 percent in 2010. Fear is a real concern when it means pets can't get regular healthcare.

—Dr. Marty Becker

painful fracture, skin laceration, or near-death experience from parvovirus) can affect a pup's future development and behavior, with the potential to cause behavior problems such as aggression, fear of strangers, and separation anxiety.

It's not unusual for dogs with one type of fear or anxiety to exhibit those emotions in other situations as well. For instance, dogs with noise or thunderstorm phobias are more likely to also suffer from separation anxiety.

CONSEQUENCES OF FEAR

To a certain extent, stress is beneficial because it aids survival, but as we know from human medicine, too much stress leads to physical and emotional problems. Unnecessary fear has physical, mental, emotional, and behavioral drawbacks and affects overall quality of life.

Fear has physiological effects: increased blood pressure, elevated stress hormones, lowered immune system, reduced coping ability. A stressed and fearful animal is more prone to disease and infection because rising cortisol levels suppress his immune system. He may suffer digestive upset, such as vomiting and diarrhea. One study found that dogs suffering extreme stress and fear have shorter life spans.

Fear creates powerful negative associations for an animal. Over time, emotional reactions to even mild fear can become stronger if the reactions are not addressed effectively. When a dog's efforts to communicate with us by lowering his tail, hiding, jumping (seeking higher ground), barking, or otherwise exhibiting stress, fear, and anxiety fail, he may try to find other ways to tell us that he needs help. A puppy, for instance, may growl at the veterinarian or technician by the third

The Scent of **Fear**

We humans typically have a pretty weak sense of smell, at least compared to dogs. Chemically, there's a lot going on in the world that goes completely unnoticed by us, but scent is one of the ways that dogs, other mammals, and insects react to and spread knowledge of a threat.

When they encounter something dangerous, animals emit what are called alarm pheromones, chemical signals that alert others of the same species that something wicked this way comes. These alarm substances may cause the animals to freeze, defend themselves, or take off to a safer spot, depending on the situation and, of course, the species. While humans may secrete pheromones, scientists have not yet specifically identified any.

visit when he anticipates a vaccination. He may urinate or defecate on himself or cry out. Traumatic experiences, such as a painful, bleeding toenail or a jerk from a choke chain for growling at the vet tech, become fixed in the dog's mind. Dogs remember negative experiences; like us, their brains are wired to readily recall strong emotional experiences.

Fearful dogs can be more difficult to handle or may even become aggressive. They may bite, scratch, or otherwise act in a panicked manner, running the risk of injuring themselves, their owners, or the veterinary staff and making necessary veterinary care a struggle. The dogs' fear limits who may work with them and what care or treatments they may receive.

In extreme cases, the pet may be unable to receive care or treatment without sedation.

Take Bear, for instance. The two-year-old Chihuahua/Yorkie mix has been banned from numerous grooming shops. He gets his nails trimmed only while under sedation at the veterinary clinic.

For owners of dogs like Bear, veterinary care is more expensive, inconvenient, and time-intensive, not only in the cost and time spent administering sedation but also in the dog's recovery time. When pets require sedation for simple and necessary procedures such as nail trims, the expense and effort limit the regularity of the procedure. Unnecessary fear bleeds into other areas of a dog's life, causing him to be uncomfortable in such situations as meeting new people, being groomed, or having his paws handled.

Even if a pet's fearful behavior is manageable in the beginning, it's not likely to improve

without help. We might hope that our dog will "grow out of it," but most often that is not the case. Dogs who are anxious and fearful generally escalate and may show aggression if not helped.

Using force may seem like the only solution. Why can't the dog just tough it out? Maybe you've been able to do that when you were afraid, so why can't your dog? The truth is that you have a much higher cognitive ability than your dog. In addition, most of us aren't able to tough it out! We get sedation at the dentist, avoid roller coasters, and stay away from snakes. Imagine if you were scared of snakes, and someone held you down and dumped a box of snakes on you. That would be petrifying! Now, imagine that during this ordeal, a person is jerking on your neck or raising their voice to you. Do you feel less scared? Of course not. And neither does your dog.

Force only perpetuates and heightens the cycle of fear, reducing the dog's trust in his human caregivers. Just because you can hold a puppy down to trim his nails doesn't mean you should. It damages the human–animal bond and reduces your pet's trust in you. And some dogs will eventually get large enough that they can successfully resist force and even become aggressive in response. Others may be so fearful that they flee in the face of treatment, risking injury to themselves and others.

Once developed, a fear or anxiety response can be mounted in the absence of the original stimulus as events become chained together in the dog's mind. For example, if the dog rides in a car only when he goes to the veterinarian, the car ride can become linked with the veterinarian's office. This association is so strong that the car itself elicits the same stress reaction that the veterinarian's office typically causes, even if the car ride is to someplace pleasant.

Animals who were driven somewhere and abandoned may have a similar fearful response to a car ride, even if it's for a pleasurable purpose. The fear reaction may include crying, panting, yawning, licking their lips, drooling, or having diarrhea.

While normal fear has benefits because it protects our dogs from harm and teaches them to avoid certain threats, it can take over their lives if it becomes overwhelming. An abnormally fearful dog is unhappy and unhealthy, and his owner is equally unhappy.

DOGS DON'T HAVE TO BE AFRAID

Building confidence and fearlessness starts at home. Of course, it's ideal if your puppy gets a Fear Free start right from the get-go, but even older dogs can benefit from changes in their environment and their owners' actions. Let us introduce you to what a Fear Free environment—home, veterinary hospital, or other pet-centric locale—looks, sounds, smells, and feels like for a dog.

Imagine that your home is as comfortable for your dog as it is for you. He has a den, such as a crate or kennel, where he can retreat for some quiet time, away from curious toddlers or noisy teenagers playing raucous video games. He has fresh water, puzzle toys filled with his daily ration of food so he can go on a nonlethal hunt, and squeaky and chew toys to indulge his love of pouncing, tugging, and gnawing. There are few or no scented candles or potpourri to overwhelm his sensitive nose. When no one is home, the stereo or TV is tuned to the sounds of nature or DOGTV.

Outdoors in the fenced yard, your dog has another den, such as a doghouse or covered kennel run, where he can go to be protected from the elements. If he wants, he has a place

where he can dig and bury treasure or make himself a nice, cool bed in the dirt or sand. He has fresh water, and he's free to follow the sun's path as it makes its way across the yard. He can take his time as he checks his "pee mail" and then deliberate over the ideal spot to deposit his feces (instead of the Chinese feng shui, think "dung shui").

Your dog is relaxed because he lives with people who are predictable and loving. They work hard to remove, reduce, or manage situations that cause him anxiety or fear, such as noises, separation anxiety, and conflicts with other animals in the home. They pay attention to his body language, vocalizations, and habits so they can tell whether he is happy and calm or anxious and fearful. Even better, they know how to reinforce calm or happy behaviors and

What Is That **Thing?**

Sometimes, because of previous negative experiences, the mere sight of certain items can cause dogs to show fear and instantly lose trust in a caregiver. I had one patient who was friendly and approachable throughout the consultation. We were able to pet him and have him perform his training cues for food rewards. I was able to look into his eyes, ears, and mouth without a problem. He was happy to let me feel all his lymph nodes and gently palpate his abdomen. But as soon as I pulled out the stethoscope, the dog immediately lowered his body, flattened his ears, barked at me, and jumped 5 feet back. I immediately became the "monster" in his eyes. It took ten minutes of targeting exercises before he would approach; however, he would not let the stethoscope touch his body.

I had another patient who was happy to approach and take treats and even allow me to pet him, but the owner warned that the dog was usually aggressive during physical examinations. When the owner took out the dog's basket muzzle, the dog instantly barked and lunged at me, even though I was sitting several feet away and had made no attempt to approach or touch him. The simple act of bringing out the muzzle caused the dog to think something bad was going to happen to him.

—Dr. Wailani Sung

ameliorate fearful or anxious behaviors. They not only provide his basic needs—food, water, shelter, veterinary care—but they indulge his genetic exuberance by providing many enrichment activities, such as toys, exercise, training, and play. They know that play is the Fear Free barometer: when a dog is feeling happy, healthy and calm, he plays!

I LOVE THE VET!

At a Fear Free veterinary hospital, relaxation begins in the parking lot. The owner may check in via phone from the car or in person in the lobby while the pet waits in the car. There's no waiting in the stewpot of stress called the waiting room. Instead, dog and human are ushered right away to the privacy of an exam room or may choose to wait in the comfortable familiarity of their vehicle until the veterinarian can see them.

Dogs at this clinic are greeted with their favorite treats by all the staff they encounter.

Depending on the dogs' temperaments, staff members either toss the treats to the dogs or hand the treats directly to the dogs. Petting and play are on offer, too, but always with canine body language in mind: no direct eye contact or facing the animal head-on. Staff speak in low, calm tones of voice and never abruptly reach for animals.

The scale is set in the floor and covered with a nonslip rubber mat or carpeting so the pet doesn't even know he's getting weighed. A small dog in a carrier can be placed on a scale in the exam room while still in the carrier. Later, when the dog is out of the carrier, the vet tech weighs the carrier separately, allowing him or her to calculate the dog's weight in an unobtrusive manner.

The exam room is quiet, except for calm, classical music designed for dogs. Pheromone plug-ins emit an aroma that's calming to some dogs (they think Momma must be in the room) but unnoticeable by humans. A nonskid mat or carpet on the floor or exam table provides a secure and comfortable surface for the dog to stand or lie on. Comfortable bench seating allows owner and dog to sit next to each other if they want.

When the owner notifies the clinic in advance that his or her dog is anxious or fearful, this pet may have the luxury of coming in during specific times designated for timid dogs, such as the first appointment of the day. The appointment has extra time built in to allay the pet's fear. The technician tosses treats while taking the dog's history. This not only helps create a positive experience for the pet but also allows the technician to gauge the animal's demeanor and mood. Does he take the treats and eat them? If not, he is beyond his stress threshold. If he does take the treats, the technician begins to help him form positive associations with being in the room and works to build a relationship with him.

When the pet appears comfortable, the technician takes vital signs: temperature, pulse, and respiration. If the pet is uncomfortable, and if the pet is healthy, the tech may decide to skip taking his temperature. Some dogs, when offered tasty treats such as liver paste, squeeze cheese, or peanut butter, may not mind the procedure at all. If the animal protests, the technician should stop the procedure and allow the pet to calm down. The veterinarian can get the vital signs later, during the exam.

At every step of the visit, the entire veterinary team looks after the dog's emotional and physical well-being. Everyone wants him to be happy and relaxed before moving on to diagnostic procedures or treatments. If sedation is a better option for a particular dog, it's a first resort, not a last resort.

Any type of Fear Free environment, from home to grooming shop to pet-supply store, incorporates these types of techniques. Both

pets and owners should feel comfortable, welcome, calm and relaxed.

BENEFITS OF FEAR FREE HANDLING AND CARE

First experiences set up how a dog will respond to care and handling in the future. In a best-case scenario, they introduce him kindly to what he can expect.

Ensuring that a dog has many positive experiences helps outweigh the inevitable unpleasant experiences. Think of it as an emotional bank account, with more positive deposits than negative withdrawals. The goal is to minimize bad experiences by making them as nonaversive as possible. As owners, veterinarians or other caregivers, we can't always prevent negative experiences , but if they happen inadvertently or are unavoidable—such as discomfort or pain from a procedure—the positive balance can help the dog recover more quickly with less likelihood of lasting trauma.

We always make note of what caused calm behavior or fearful behavior and work to increase the former and decrease the latter. For example, if a pet is more relaxed when examined on the floor of the exam room, if a certain gentle control method worked best, and if the pet enjoyed one treat in particular, all of those things will happen on his next visit. We have an emotional well-being record to go along with the medical health record.

It's not trial-and-error or hit-and-miss; it's a long march of removing or reducing fear and anxiety triggers and increasing things that calm. For example, if a pet has a serious negative reaction to the prick of a needle for vaccinations, antibiotics, or blood draws, we might use a topical anesthetic, such as lidocaine, to numb the skin before pricking it. When a pet has low-stress veterinary or grooming visits, daycare or boarding stays, walks around the neighborhood, or visits

Nervous **Tics**

Maybe you're just a little nervous about something. You bite your fingernails, twirl your hair, shift in your seat, laugh tentatively, or tap your fingers on a surface. These are all minor signs of stress.

But go for a walk in the woods and see what happens when you encounter a snake. Your heart races, and your palms get sweaty. You may jump back, freeze, or become shaky. When you see a threat, your body responds before your conscious mind catches up and recognizes that the snake is at a safe distance from you. Or that it's not a snake at all, but a stick.

Fear of flying might cause similar signs. You may be so anxious that not even chocolate or wine can help calm you down. You take the medication your doctor prescribed, but it's too late. Once you've reached a heightened state of fear, medication is less likely to have a beneficial effect.

Anxious or fearful dogs go through a similar array of signals. If they are a little nervous or excited, they may yawn, lick their lips, pant, avert their gaze, hide, groom themselves, shake themselves, look away toward an exit, or whine. More extreme fear can cause them to freeze or initiate a fight-or-flight response (e.g., bite or lunge at a person or leap off an exam table). They may also experience physiological effects, such as panting or yawning. For a dog who is fearful of new people, an approaching stranger can cause the same kind of fear as when you see a snake. The dog's nervousness progresses according to the perceived level of threat and factors such as distance, duration, intensity, and his ability to move away.

—*Mikkel Becker*

to relatives' homes, the result is a higher likelihood of success each time you repeat these activities.

When dogs are less fearful about veterinary visits or being handled by groomers or others, there's a lower risk of injury to the dog and all people involved. That means that the dog can receive healthcare, training, and grooming on a regular basis because these tasks are less stressful for the dog, the owner, and everyone else. The pet, pet owner, and the care providers will all have a better experience. Early intervention in health, behavior and care problems is more likely to happen. Regular veterinary care and early intervention in health and behavior problems increase the likelihood of successful treatment and reduce the cost of treatment.

Reducing fear has positive effects beyond the ability to take the pet to the vet or groomer. When a pet has a positive experience in a potentially frightening situation, it increases his confidence and improves his ability to adjust to change, welcome new experiences, and accept interactions with different people. The great news is that after decades of research and almost a decade of intense focus, we have cracked the code of what causes fear and anxiety for most dogs in general and can drill down to find out what negatively and positively affects each individual dog. When armed with a good medical and emotional history, utilizing proven products and techniques will extinguish anxiety and fear and promote calm. Committing to looking after both the physical and emotional health of pets, we can move them from fearful to Fear Free.

RECOGNIZING **FEAR, ANXIETY,** AND **STRESS/ RECOGNIZING** CALM

Fear and anxiety are two different emotional states. Fear is a normal response to a threat, while anxiety is anticipation of a response. Stress is a general term referring to the result of any physical, mental, or emotional demand on the body or brain. In this chapter—and throughout this book—we are talking about all three.

Our dogs can't talk to us, but we can learn to interpret their body language, and often that's just as good. A flick of the ear, a roll of the eye, or the speed of a tail wag can tell us almost everything we need to know about

a dog's emotional state, which is especially important when it comes to recognizing the early, subtle signs of fear, anxiety, and stress. Knowing those signs can help us keep our dogs on the "relaxed, happy, or only mildly tense" end of the spectrum—as much as possible, at least. When we notice signs of fear, anxiety, or stress early on, it's much easier to intervene than when a pet is already at the stage of fight, flight, freeze, or fidget. Once fear, anxiety, and stress have progressed to panic, they are much more difficult to address.

Consistency **Counts**

Among my patients are many dogs who suffer from lack of consistency in their lives, including dogs who have been rehomed several times, dogs whose owners have changed homes multiple times, and dogs whose owners have frequent changes in their schedules. They usually exhibit anxious and destructive behavior, often leading to full-blown panic attacks when their owners are absent because they may believe the owners will never return. Even changes that occur uncommonly, such as an owner's return to work after a hiatus or a long vacation, can be enough to cause a pet to become anxious about being left alone.

When these dogs are left in the care of a pet sitter or boarded when their owners go on vacation, all they know is that their owners are gone and there is no assurance that they will return. The resulting panic causes a physical change called the stress response, resulting in signs such as pacing, drooling, and excessive vocalization. Sometimes, these behaviors continue for only a brief period of time after the owner leaves, but other dogs perform them throughout the entire time the owners are absent.

Some dogs will eliminate inappropriately and chew or scratch at windows or doors. I have had several patients scratch enough to force themselves through windows that were barely open and subsequently fall out of two- and three-story buildngs. One two-year-old neutered Australian Shepherd mix became so frantic when left alone that he would jump on furniture and kitchen counters. One day, he turned on the kitchen stove and set the house on fire. Luckily, he and his canine housemate were rescued by the fire department. Even though there was another dog in the home, it wasn't enough to ease his fear of being abandoned.

—*Dr. Wailani Sung*

In general, dogs can be fearful because they have inherited the tendency through traumatic experience and through the influence of learning. Anything in the environment when an animal is fearful, anxious, or stressed can become a trigger for that emotional state. That includes you. Dogs can pick up on the body language and tone of voice of their people. Your anxiety about taking your dog to the vet or groomer or seeing an unknown dog approach travels right down the leash to your dog and activates his own fearful, anxious, or stressed reaction.

Dogs react to our body language as well. They can read smiles and frowns. You may have heard advice against comforting a fearful dog. It's not wrong to help a dog through his fear, but it's important to stay calm so he can pick up on your attitude.

Finally, some pets are simply born fearful, just as some people are genetically programmed to be short. For instance, German Shepherds and English Springer Spaniels are common study subjects for researchers because of the high incidence of fear or aggression seen in those breeds. That is genetics, not human influence.

WHAT CAUSES FEAR?

Fear travels many paths to a dog's brain. For instance, it can result from lack of socialization. Socialization is the positive exposure to many different people, other animals, sounds, sights, and experiences that a puppy needs early in life, between three and sixteen weeks of age, to help

be the root of a dog's fear. Dogs who have suffered traumatic injuries, such as being hit by a car, can react fearfully, even if you are trying to help them.

Diseases or conditions later in life, such as hypothyroidism, orthopedic diseases, certain tick-borne diseases that cause joint pain, or loss of vision or hearing can also cause dogs to be fearful. For instance, a dog with painful joints may react fearfully when touched or when he thinks he will be touched.

A veterinary exam can often be instrumental in uncovering a cause of fear. Any time your dog seems fearful, anxious, or stressed, it's important to let your veterinarian know so he or she can rule out potential medical causes of fear and anxiety. These causes can include painful arthritis, ingestion of a toxic substance that is causing unusual behavior—pressing the head against the wall, for instance—or conditions such as thyroid disease or a brain tumor.

Lack of companionship, communication, or normal activities may play a role. Dogs are highly social animals. When they lack interaction with people or other animals, when their attempts to communicate are misunderstood, or when they are unable to behave normally (no opportunity to chew or dig, for instance), they can become anxious, stressed, or fearful.

A final factor is heredity, which is an underlying factor in many cases referred to veterinary behaviorists. Acknowledging this is important to understanding why fear, anxiety, and stress can't always be fixed like a dent in a car or a broken television.

RECOGNIZING FEAR, ANXIETY, AND STRESS

Noticing fear, anxiety, or stress early on is important. When you can do that, it allows

him become a well-rounded adult dog who takes new things in stride.

Lack of consistency in life is another source of fear, anxiety, and stress. We might see this in dogs who are passed from family to family or who are abandoned to shelters or the streets. When their lives aren't predictable, it's no surprise that dogs can develop fearful, anxious, and stressed behaviors.

Of course, frightening experiences, such as being attacked by another animal or being startled by the boom and crack of thunderstorms, gunshots, or fireworks, can trigger fear as well. That's one of the reasons it's vitally important for puppies to meet friendly dogs and people, have positive experiences with veterinarians and other caregivers, and become accustomed to unexpected loud noises during the critical socialization period of three to sixteen weeks of age.

Like frightening experiences, painful illnesses or injuries, especially early in life, may also

Wag the Dog

We often hear that a wagging tail means a dog is friendly, but that's not the whole story. With the way that a dog holds his tail and the speed at which he wags, dogs communicate a range of feelings, from aggression to relaxation to welcome. You might even say they're tattle-tails!

Even more fascinating, the direction in which your dog's tail wags may reveal how he feels about you, according to a study from Italy published in 2013 in *Current Biology*. The study showed that when dogs were attracted to or wanted to approach a person or stimulus, their tail wagged mainly toward the right. Dogs who were fearful or wanted to withdraw from a person or stimulus wagged mainly toward the left. Here's what you should know about the tell-tale tail:

- Tail height offers important insight into a dog's state of mind. A tail held high may signal that a dog is feeling alert, excited, or confident. A dog who holds his tail lower than normal or tucks it tightly to his body may be afraid, submissive, tired, or in pain.

- Beware of a dog whose tail is rigid or stiff and held high. The hair on the tail may stand on end, making the tail look bigger. This dog is aroused or agitated and may react to whatever catches his attention, whether that's a person, a dog walking down the sidewalk, or a cat crossing the lawn.

- The curly tail of a dog such as a Pug becomes even more tightly wound when the dog is tense. The existing curl in the tail tightens as the dog becomes more aroused, eventually curling over itself. In these dogs, a tensed tail can indicate excitement or aggression. When a curly-tailed dog is relaxed, the tail may unwind and go straight. A loose tail may also signal that he's tired or not feeling well.

- The speed and style of a tail wag also indicates a dog's attitude. A sweeping tail wag that moves from side to side at the height of the dog's normal tail carriage suggests a happy, relaxed dog. A tail beating back and forth with gusto at a neutral level signals an exuberant, joyful dog. This dog's hind end may be wiggling with his tail rotating like a helicopter blade.

- Remember that while a friendly dog may not wag his tail at all, a tense dog may. A dog who's feeling insecure usually holds his tail low, flicking it back and forth slightly or swiftly. This type of wag may indicate deference or that the dog is feeling conflicted and may bite. A tail held high with the tip wagging very quickly is a sign of high arousal. Dogs who display this body language signal have their brain neurochemistry turbocharged and may bite.

- Of course, how a dog holds his tail varies with each dog's tail type and height. Siberian Huskies and Alaskan Malamutes, for instance, have curved tails that float over their backs, while Whippets and Greyhounds normally carry their tails low.

- It's fun—and often important—to be able to read a dog's tail lingo, but don't forget to look at his overall body language to get the full story. Your knowledge of your dog's personality as well as the surrounding environment or circumstances can help you determine if your dog feels happy or threatened, scared or relaxed.

—Mikkel Becker

you to remove your dog from a stressful or frightening situation before his reaction escalates to escape or aggression. It also helps you prevent your dog from becoming chronically stressed, which can affect his physical health and emotional well-being.

A head-to-tail scan of your dog's body can give you significant clues that he's feeling uncomfortable in a particular situation. First, know your dog. What does your dog look like when he is stressed? Does he pant, pace, or scan his surroundings? Does he freeze and become stiff, glancing at you and showing the whites of his eyes? In a fearful, stressed, or anxious dog, the whites of the eyes may be more noticeable because the dog's body and head are stiff, but he keeps his eyes focused on what is scaring him. Some dogs have an intense or direct stare with dilated pupils (big, glazed eyes). Still other dogs avoid eye contact with people or other dogs, or they blink more frequently than normal.

Note the ears. Your dog may perk erect ears up higher or lay them back close to or flat against his head. Dogs with floppy ears may move them back slightly from their normal position, a subtle motion that's not as easy to notice as the carriage of upright ears.

An anxious, fearful, or stressed dog may close his mouth tightly or pull his lips back in a tense grimace. He may pant excessively. You may notice that his whiskers are erect and that the whisker beds appear more pronounced. His next step may be to growl, snarl, snap, or bite. Other vocalizations that can signal distress are barking, whimpering, and whining.

Look at your dog's stance. If he's stressed, he may stand in one place and lift a front paw or shift his weight away from whatever is causing him concern. He may turn his head and body away or lower his body in an attempt to make himself look harmless.

Change in activity level is another signal. Anxious, stressed, or fearful dogs may freeze,

Signs of **Fear in Dogs**

It's easy to overlook signs of fear in dogs. Some of them are obvious (screaming, for instance), but, too often, the signals of fear, anxiety, or stress may be subtle or may simply look like normal behaviors if you're unaware of what you're looking for.

The following examples of body language and behavior can help you understand when your dog is telling you that he's frightened, anxious, or stressed. Not every dog will show all of these signs, but if you notice any of them in your dog, it's time to look around and see what might be causing fear.

- Acting clingy
- Acting excessively or unusually alert
- Avoiding eye contact
- Barking
- Biting
- Blinking or squinting
- Cowering
- Curling his lips
- Defecation
- Dilated pupils
- Drooling
- Ears lowered or flattened
- Freezing or walking slowly
- Furrowed brows
- Growling
- Hard stare with dilated pupils

- Hiding
- Licking lips
- Lifting a paw
- Lips pulled back
- Mouth closed tightly
- Mouth pursed forward
- Mouthing, nipping, or snapping
- Pacing
- Panting
- Raised hackles (hair stands on end)
- Refusing treats or grabbing them
- Rigid forward stance
- Running away
- Screaming

- Self-grooming (licking or scratching)
- "Shaking off"
- Sniffing or appearing distracted
- Sudden heavy shedding
- Sweaty paws
- Trembling
- Tucked tail
- Turning away so that the body forms a "C" shape
- Turning head
- Whining
- Whiskers erect
- Yawning

—Dr. Marty Becker

refusing to move. On the opposite end of the spectrum, they can become hyperactive, appearing on edge and ready to react defensively.

The sooner you recognize a dog's fear and take steps to reduce or eliminate the cause altogether, the more confident and comfortable your dog will be with you. He will start to look to you to help him when he is fearful, anxious, or stressed instead of escalating to panic or aggression.

FEAR IS INDIVIDUAL

Fear, anxiety, and stress look different in every dog. One may be hyperactive, bordering on hysteria, while another shakes and quakes and a third looks sleepy or shuts down altogether. Some become silly and puppylike in an attempt to turn away actual or perceived aggression by presenting themselves as harmless.

An individual dog's progression of fearful behaviors occurs on a spectrum as well. Some may begin by trying to avoid the fearsome person, animal, or situation. If avoidance doesn't work, they move on to other tactics, which may include becoming puffed up, ready to use defensive aggression; becoming fearful and cowering or hiding; or progressing to all-out panic and attempting to escape.

Ruby's Story

Ruby, a six-month-old German Shepherd Dog, had shotgun pellets in her when she was found. Not surprisingly, she was fearful of people. In her new home, she would hide under the bed, unwilling to come out.

Jim, Ruby's owner, had been advised to push her to meet new people by using the leash to drag her in front of him instead of letting her hide behind him. That made her even more afraid.

I worked with them to teach Ruby (and Jim) that she had a choice about meeting people. She was never forced to approach anyone and could move away when she wanted to.

One of the greatest moments of progress was when we discovered that Ruby was calmer when she was with another dog. Seeing the other dog interact positively with people gave her confidence and a feeling of security.

Surprisingly, Ruby did well in a class setting because she loved other dogs so much. Their presence helped to gradually countercondition her to the presence of humans and gain a greater acceptance of people in general.

—*Mikkel Becker*

When determining whether a dog is fearful, it's important to put body language in context. This means looking at what is normal for an individual dog as well as what his entire body is doing. As mentioned, the dog's tail height, ear type, and ear carriage all play a role.

Looking at the situation as a whole is essential to correctly reading a dog's body language. For example, a dog who is licking his lips in one situation may be expressing fear or anxiety; in another context, however, he may simply be anticipating a treat. Other dogs lick their lips when they feel nauseous. As you evaluate body language, pay special attention to behavior that seems out of character for your dog.

TYPES OF FEARS, ANXIETIES, AND PHOBIAS

What scares dogs? Well, of course, anything can, especially if it is unexpected or something the dog has never encountered before. We most commonly see dogs who are suffering from the following fears.

NOISE AND THUNDERSTORM PHOBIAS

Up to 20 percent of dogs of all ages and breeds suffer from noise phobias so severe that their people seek professional help for them, according to veterinary behaviorist Bonnie Beaver in her book *Canine Behavior: A Guide for Veterinarians*. Thunder and fireworks are usually the most common causes of noise phobias, but dogs can develop a fear of any sound: the rustling of a plastic garbage bag, the beep of a microwave oven, or the whirr of a ceiling fan. Terry M. Curtis, a veterinary behaviorist at the University of Florida College of Veterinary Medicine, recalls one client whose dog was afraid of the sound of the toilet paper roll.

Sometimes, dogs become fearful of loud noises after a specific event, such as sudden or unexpected exposure to gunshots, loud trucks or buses, a smoke detector going off, or a severe thunderstorm. In other cases, their fear develops gradually from multiple exposures to the frightening sound over time. For instance, a dog who is afraid of fireworks or thunderstorms can become more afraid with each Independence Day celebration or thunderstorm season.

Fears of loud or unexpected noises are triggered by what's called the "orienting response," the brain's mechanism for being aware. When dogs (or humans) hear certain sounds, the brain instantly processes the sensory input to determine whether it signals danger. Sensitivity to sound is instinctive to all dogs, but dogs who tend to be anxious are more likely to develop noise phobias.

While any breed or mix can develop a noise phobia, it appears to have a genetic component in certain dogs, such as Border Collies and other herding breeds. They may have a greater tendency toward this type of fear.

Thunderstorm phobia is a complex fear. It encompasses sound, changes in barometric pressure and ionization, darkening skies, the presence of wind and rain, and the flash of lightning, making it one of the most difficult noise phobias to manage. Interestingly, dogs with noise or thunderstorm phobia may also exhibit separation anxiety. Their response to noises or storms may worsen if they are alone when they experience the fearsome situation.

SEPARATION ANXIETY

If your dog pees or poops in the house, chews up furniture, destroys doors or windows, or barks nonstop when you're not at home, he may be suffering from separation anxiety, a behavior problem that affects an estimated 20 to 25 percent of dogs.

A dog with separation anxiety is unable to cope with being left alone. He may have been given up to a shelter or rescue group by previous owners; endured a traumatic event, such as a severe thunderstorm, while alone; or simply never learned the skill—and it is a skill—of being independent from his owners. When left to himself, he may drool, pace, lick himself

PTSD Affects **Dogs, Too**

Like people who have endured traumatic events, dogs can suffer from post-traumatic stress disorder (PTSD). It's an extreme fear response triggered by a sight, sound, or smell that evokes the memory of the original event, even if that exact sight, sound, or smell wasn't present during the original experience.

Dogs with PTSD act depressed, apathetic, and unhappy. They are often unwilling to play or eat. Others may try to hide or escape, sometimes to the extent of injuring themselves. One such dog was Rocky, a 70-pound brown dog with a black nose and perfect black eyeliner. One of his ears stood up and one lay flat. He had a purple cast on his hind leg where he had broken his tibia—a large bone in the lower leg—after jumping from a second-story window when his owner wasn't home.

As soon as I entered the room, Rocky greeted me happily and then promptly fell asleep, snoring loudly as his owner and I talked. At that time, the doctors and nurses at the hospital where I worked carried phones with a walkie-talkie feature. My phone alerted, and Rocky jumped up, his pupils widely dilated. He was panting heavily, as if he had run a marathon. He immediately jumped into his owner's lap, almost knocking her into the wall, as he scratched frantically and whined loudly.

We never discovered the source of Rocky's original trauma, but we were able to identify the sounds that induced his signs of PTSD. Treatment was ultimately successful.

—Dr. Lisa Radosta

FEAR OF STRANGERS

The sudden or unexpected appearance of someone they don't know can send some dogs into a frenzy of barking and growling, even if they are normally friendly. This antagonistic response to strangers—a visitor carrying a suitcase up the stairs or a deliveryperson in uniform holding a box, for instance—is a type of fear aggression, although it is often mistaken for offensive or territorial aggression. The behavior is especially likely to occur if the dog feels trapped or cornered (e.g., if he is on leash when the stranger approaches), or if he is surprised by the person's presence. Owners of this type of dog may describe their dogs as cautious, nervous, or shy.

raw, break housetraining, bark excessively, or refuse to eat or drink. Separation anxiety can be frustrating, but behavior modification and, often, medication can help.

Any person who frightens a dog—from bearded men to people wearing hats or kids on skateboards—can elicit an aggressive

Back-Door **Dog**

Not every fear of the veterinary clinic has its origins in a bad experience with the veterinarian. Sometimes it begins at the front door or in the waiting area. Early in my career, when I was practicing at Twin Falls Veterinary Hospital in Twin Falls, Idaho, a Brittany named Trigger would come in for routine vaccinations. Nowadays, veterinary hospitals require pets to be on leash or in carriers when they come through the front door, but back then, it wasn't uncommon for well-trained working or hunting dogs such as Trigger to go everywhere off leash. As Trigger walked through the door of the hospital, he was attacked by a massive unneutered Labrador Retriever named Drake, who was also off leash. Drake had always been Mr. Mellow, so this attack was unexpected and seemingly unprovoked.

Unlike some fights that are all gnashing of teeth, snarling, and body scuffles with no real biting, this one was fangs bared, teeth chomping, mouth around Trigger's throat. Drake was unharmed, but we had to sew up a couple of lacerations on Trigger under anesthesia.

After this incident, Trigger was terrified of the veterinary practice in general and of the front door and waiting area specifically. He would pant, salivate, and shake as he approached the hospital entrance when his owner brought him in for various preventive measures, to be treated for minor injuries, or to be boarded from time to time.

In the 1980s, none of us knew anything about anxiety, fear, and stress in dogs, but we started having Trigger's owner bring Trigger in through the back door of the practice. That did the trick, provoking no negative response at all from Trigger.

—Dr. Marty Becker

Happy's Tale

When he underwent temperament testing in the shelter, Happy, a German Shorthaired Pointer, was described as a "resource guarder." He would use aggressive behavior to protect his food whenever people approached. After adoption, Happy's behavior changed dramatically, which is not an uncommon response to a change of environment. But it wasn't for the better.

In his new home, Happy was petrified at mealtime. As his new owner prepared the food, he would act excited and hungry, but as his owner moved to give it to him, he would run away with tail tucked and body held low. His owner would find him in the next room, hiding or cowering. Sometimes it would take him hours to get up the courage to eat. When Happy did eat, he acted extremely fearful.

Perhaps something extremely negative happened to Happy at mealtimes in his previous home, but we'll never know the real reason behind his behavior. The best we could do was to start him off with a clean slate. We changed his associations with mealtime by using various games, such as feeding him by hand, putting his kibble inside food puzzles, scattering kibble on the ground for him to find, feeding him out of bowls that were made of a different material than his previous bowls, and adding canned dog food to make his meals more appetizing.

—Mikkel Becker

response. Some dogs are afraid of people of a specific gender or ethnicity, while others may fear active young children. If a dog lives with someone who doesn't have visitors frequently, the appearance of a passel of relatives at the holidays can give him pause.

Dogs who are afraid of people are often thought to have been abused at some point, especially if nothing is known of their past. That's possible, but, in most cases, fear of strangers—stranger danger—can probably be chalked up to lack of socialization at an early age. It can also have a genetic basis, passed on by parents who are shy or fearful. Sometimes we may never know the source of the fear, but we can work to reduce it through behavior modification, fear-reducing medications, and other techniques.

FEAR OF OTHER ANIMALS

Dogs who have been attacked by other dogs or who have a negative experience when meeting animals such as cats or horses for the first time may experience this type of fear. Heck, wouldn't a cat's hisses and claws or a horse's size scare you if you didn't know anything about the other animal?

Sometimes this fear manifests itself only when a dog encounters strange animals in person. If they've been attacked by another dog, they may exhibit fear only toward dogs of that breed or color or size, or they may generalize their fear to all other dogs.

Still other dogs take exception to animals they see on television as well. They growl ferociously at images of lions, tigers, elephants, camels, cats, and other dogs.

It's not unusual for fearful dogs to go on the offensive when they see "the enemy." At the sight of a cat in the window or other dogs in the neighborhood, a fearful dog growls, barks, and lunges, often leading his people to believe that he is aggressive, not fearful. More classic signs of fear in the presence of strange animals are trembling, panting, whining, or trying to run away.

In a perfect world, a puppy will have positive early experiences with many different animals—dogs, cats, horses, or any other animals that he is likely to meet. That gives him a foundation to build on so that when he eventually meets an animal who's not so friendly, the encounter won't set him back.

FEAR OF PLACES

Who doesn't know of a dog who trembles in fear as the car pulls into the parking lot of the veterinary clinic? We've certainly encountered them in our practices. Other dogs may have the same reaction to going to the groomer or boarding kennel. A crowded environment, elevator, car, park or other area where he's had a bad experience can also elicit a fearful reaction.

This type of fear, also referred to as situational fear or sometimes as agoraphobia (literally "fear of the marketplace," if you recall your ancient Greek), may be seen in dogs who don't get out much.

Such a dog spends all his time at home except for the occasional visit to the scary place. Or the problem develops after the dog has a frightening experience and associates it with the place where it occurred.

The owner of one Chihuahua mix decided against boarding her dog when she saw the little dog's fearful reaction to the noise in the kennel. The dog had been adopted from a shelter, and the surroundings may have seemed similar to her. A Cavalier King Charles Spaniel who had previously enjoyed his walks around the neighborhood became reluctant after being attacked by a loose dog. Walks in other areas weren't a problem, though.

Counterconditioning or desensitization may help dogs with situational fears. Younger dogs are more likely to respond better to treatment than older dogs, but any dog may benefit from a patient owner who has the help of a board-certified veterinary behaviorist.

FEAR OF OBJECTS

You never know what might set off a dog's fear radar. Seemingly innocuous items, such as hats, coats, canes, wheelchairs, walkers, umbrellas, and piles of bagged leaves, as well as scarier items, such as Mardi Gras masks or pictures of fierce-looking creatures, have all been known to send dogs into frenzies of barking. More timid dogs may try to run and hide. Any item that startles a dog can become an object of fear to him. He may be afraid of

Calm Canines

What we all want to see—in our own dogs, our practices, and out in public—are confident, relaxed, happy dogs. What do they look like? Here's what to look for:

- The mouth may be loosely closed or slightly open. It may look as if the dog is smiling.
- Eyes may range from slightly squinty to rounded and relaxed.
- Ears are held forward and slightly to the side. They may twitch or rise up at the sound of something interesting.
- If the dog is accepting a treat or giving a kiss, he may lower his ears or move them back, a normal, friendly gesture.
- The tail wags with wide, sweeping motions or loose, circling movements.
- The tail is held at a comfortable height, more or less even with the back (a dog may hold his tail slightly higher when he is interested in a treat or toy you are holding in your hand).

Once you start to tune in to your dog's body language, you'll be fascinated by all the ways he communicates with you. And just as talking to the people we love brings us closer to them, understanding what your dog is saying to you can help improve and strengthen your relationship with him.

it because it makes you look different (think cowboy hat or crutches or walker) or because he's never seen you walk into the house carrying a Christmas tree. The object might move erratically or make a sound he doesn't expect. Maybe he ran into the sliding glass door and now doesn't want to go near it.

Often, an owner can manage a dog's fear simply by avoiding the objects in question, but sometimes the objects are a part of a dog's daily life—grocery bags, doors, a leash, a collar—and avoidance is impossible. In cases like this, dogs may need medication and behavior modification for effective treatment.

FEARS OF UNKNOWN CAUSE

Profound fear and withdrawal for no apparent reason is known as idiopathic fear. The word *idiopathic* comes from the Greek words "idios" (meaning "one's own") and "pathos" (meaning "suffering"). In medical terms, we use the word to refer to any condition that has no obvious cause.

A dog with idiopathic fear may have a fearful response of unknown origin to people, sounds, unexpected movements—you name it. When he encounters the person or situation that frightens him, he may slink fearfully out of the way, run and hide, or refuse to come when called. Often, he doesn't even like to be looked at.

Idiopathic fear has been noted in certain dog breeds, including the Siberian Husky, German Shorthaired Pointer, Chesapeake Bay Retriever, Bernese Mountain Dog, Great Pyrenees, Border Collie, and Standard Poodle. There appears to be a strong familial component in these breeds, with the likelihood of a genetic influence.

FEAR AND **FORCE:** **RECIPE FOR** DISASTER

As much as we love our dogs, they can be prone to behaviors that get on our nerves from time to time. But before you blame your dog for annoying behaviors such as excessive barking, acting unruly on leash, or bolting in the opposite direction when you call him, consider that there may be reasons your dog behaves the way he does—and some of those reasons may have to do with you or other humans in his life.

THE HUMAN CONNECTION

Even with the best intentions and training tactics, a dog owner may unintentionally interact with his or her dog in ways that undermine good behavior and create confusion in the pet's mind. This can lead to a stressed dog who doesn't behave appropriately.

Most pet owners do their best to curb unwanted (we're not going to call it "bad," because all too often it's perfectly normal behavior for a dog) behavior, but it is possible that you are contributing to continuation of the very behaviors that you would like to stop. Dogs are as affected by our behavior as we are by theirs, so as much as your dog's behavior might stress you out, consider that your behavior may be causing him stress as well.

A Wet **Greeting**

Your puppy or even your adult dog urinates every time he walks into the local pet boutique, even though he likes the people there. He does the same thing when visitors enter your home. This embarrassing (to you) behavior can be caused by excitement or by submissive behavior.

Excitement-based urination isn't an unusual behavior in puppies. Puppies have little control over their bladders, and it's not unusual for them to pee a little when they're excited to see someone.

Submissive urination is another matter. In this situation, the dog hunkers down and releases urine as he greets someone. The message? He is fearful, anxious, or stressed about his interactions with that person and wants to make it clear that he's not a threat.

Puppies often outgrow excitement-based urination, but insecure or fearful dogs may continue delivering a leaky greeting into adulthood.

—Mikkel Becker

Now, that's not to say that you're entirely responsible for the way your dog acts. Factors such as genetics, early environment, and inadvertent learning through experiences outside your control can all contribute to his behavior. Nonetheless, human-related factors can greatly affect a dog's actions.

Whether or not we realize it, our dogs are learning every moment. Most of a dog's learning takes place outside of structured training sessions. Dogs of all ages and life stages can learn new behaviors through training, but most behaviors are shaped in regular, everyday moments. Even dogs who have not had a single formal training session have been trained—albeit inadvertently—by people and the environment through day-to-day interactions and experiences.

Human-directed factors, such as a dog's daily environment and routine, work together to either set up a dog for success or make him more likely to display undesirable behavior. For example, when the UPS driver delivers a package, the dog barks like crazy and the driver leaves the package and then drives away. The dog thinks, "Wow! I am really good at scaring

that guy away. I will do that next time, but louder!"

THE ROLE OF FEAR, ANXIETY, AND STRESS

When fear, anxiety, and stress come into the picture, they bring trouble right along with them. Fearful, anxious, or stressed pets don't simply cower and whine. They may actively take steps to protect themselves from whatever is causing their emotional distress. Those steps can include urinating submissively (a form of appeasement or an expression of fear),

Types of **Punishment**

In psychological terms, punishment takes two forms: positive and negative. Positive punishment sounds like an oxymoron, doesn't it? But what it means is that you are actively doing something to your dog or to his environment that he doesn't like in an effort to decrease the frequency of a behavior in the future. The term "positive" in this sense is mathematical, meaning that you are adding something aversive, not that the punishment is in some way "good." Examples of positive punishment include verbal reprimands; tossing a rattle can; jerking a leash; using a choke, prong, spray, or electronic collar; and shaking, hitting, or kicking an animal.

The idea behind positive punishment is that the punishment or correction is severe enough that it outweighs any motivation on the dog's part to perform the behavior. Too often, however, the punishment has unwanted and unexpected effects. One example is the dog whose owners enclosed their yard with an underground electronic fence, which delivered a shock to the dog if he got too close to the boundary. After just one shock, the dog no longer had any desire to go into the yard. The owners had to drag him outside by the collar, at which point he would drop onto the ground. His fear of going into the yard diminished over time, but he never wanted to stay outside for long.

Negative punishment is the removal or withholding of something the dog likes. For instance, you ask your dog to lie down. If he doesn't comply, he doesn't get a treat or praise or the opportunity to play with his favorite toy. Taking away attention when a dog does something you don't like is another form of negative punishment. Let's say that the dog jumps up on you. Turning around and walking away is negative punishment. So is walking away when he nips you with sharp puppy teeth.

Dogs like our attention—not to mention treats and toys—so when we withhold those things, it's a form of punishment. When negative punishment is administered consistently, dogs learn to decrease the behavior that caused the loss of the reward.

Although the term "negative punishment" sounds unpleasant, the technique can be effective in certain situations without being unkind. In general, use negative punishment and do your best to avoid positive punishment.

growling or biting, or just getting the heck out of Dodge.

When a dog is punished for such behaviors, often because his fear, anxiety, or stress isn't recognized, the result is even more stress and confusion. Punishing a dog whose behavior is caused by fear increases the risk that he will become aggressive toward the person punishing him or the person with whom he is interacting. Sometimes a dog will turn on the dog next to him and show aggression when punished by his owner. If you aren't sure if a dog's behavior is caused by fear, anxiety, or stress, it's always better to seek a way other than punishment to deal with the problem.

Your first reaction when your fearful pet urinates inappropriately, behaves aggressively or runs away may be to get mad. You may yell at him or jerk on the leash or even swat his rear in an attempt to get him under control and express your displeasure. But as instinctive as those responses may seem, it's essential to avoid punishment.

What do we mean by the word "punishment," and why is it not the best reaction? You're probably wondering how else you're going to let your dog know that his behavior isn't acceptable. Let's look at the use of punishment in dog training and how it can affect behavior.

WHAT IS PUNISHMENT?

Punishment is anything that is intended to make a behavior decrease. The application of punishment includes everything from yelling at your dog to hitting him. We've all experienced punishment at some point in our lives. It's the rare person who has never been spanked by a parent, had a privilege taken away, been "grounded" or given a "time out," been written up at work or even fired, or received the silent treatment from a spouse or child. These are all examples of different types of punishment.

HANDS ON—IN A BAD WAY

With dogs, punishment is often physical. New-puppy owners used to be advised to swat the puppy with a rolled-up newspaper when he did wrong or to rub his nose in the mess if he peed or pooped in the house. We know now that those techniques aren't effective and may even worsen problems by causing dogs to do their dirty work in secret, or worse, fear their owners, but old methods die hard. Other types of physical corrections include leash pops with choke chains, the use of prong collars, or the use of electronic collars, also called remote or shock collars.

An electronic collar delivers a quick, painful electric shock to the dog's neck. In the hands of most of us, who lack perfect timing, this type of collar can be a method for abuse, thus increasing fear, anxiety, and stress. Many dogs react poorly to electronic collars, becoming scared of the environments in which the collars were used and refusing to enter certain rooms or their backyards. Some redirect their feelings by biting or attacking nearby animals, while still others become afraid of their owners.

Shock Gone Wrong

When the dog entered my consultation room, his big German Shepherd ears were pulled to the side and his tail was down and tucked. He whined, paced, panted, and licked his lips as I talked to his owners.

This highly anxious and fearful one-year-old neutered dog was reactive toward people and other dogs on walks. His owners had taken the advice of a trainer who recommended the use of a shock collar. When the owners started using the shock collar, the dog still did not pay attention to them, continuing to bark and lunge at people and dogs. The trainer instructed the owners to keep increasing the intensity of the shock. At higher levels of shock, the dog became even more reactive, barking louder and pulling harder. He also began to react to people and other dogs when they were at a greater distance from him. His bubble of safety went from 10 feet to across the street to as soon as he could see the person or dog, sometimes several hundred feet away.

I have had other patients whose owners used shock collars on walks. When the owners administered shocks for their dogs' aggressive behavior toward people or other animals, the dogs redirected their aggression by biting the owners.

—Dr. Wailani Sung

well as the individual dog. Some dogs are highly responsive to even mild verbal corrections while some others ignore them. Still others shut down when spoken to harshly.

HEAD GAMES

"Flooding" is forcing an animal to stay in a situation that causes him to panic, such as being in the presence of many other dogs (at a dog park, for instance), taking treats from strangers when he's afraid of them, having to listen to the sounds of fireworks or thunder played over and over, or being dragged across a slippery floor when he's unfamiliar or uncomfortable with the surface. It's similar to throwing a person who's afraid of water into a swimming pool and expecting him or her to overcome that fear.

Flooding can be extremely damaging to the dog's psyche, escalating fear, anxiety, and stress and damaging the human-animal bond. For flooding to be effective—which it rarely is—the dog must stay in the circumstance until he is calm. What usually happens instead is that the dog either becomes sensitized to the stimulus, causing increased fear, anxiety, or stress, or demonstrates learned helplesssness.

Unfortunately, once the dog is in a full-blown panic attack or is overwhelmed by fear, anxiety, or stress, he is unable to calm himself. Instead, the dog has yet another horrible experience with the person, place, or thing, causing him to panic even more in the future.

The other behavior pattern displayed by dogs who are being flooded is learned helplessness. This is one of the saddest states of mind possible for a dog. In this situation, the dog simply lies

Two of the factors that make shock collars so detrimental to the well-being of dogs are the severity of the correction and the inevitable poor timing of the owner. For example, let's say you are using a remote collar to stop your dog from jumping on visitors. He jumps, and you hurry as quickly as you can to press the button that delivers a shock. Whoops! You weren't fast enough, and you shock him as his feet hit the floor.

What did you just hurt your dog for? Not for jumping. That's right—you corrected your dog for the behavior that you want: having all four feet on the floor. This is extremely common and undermines the relationship you want to have with your dog.

THE VOICE

Dog owners commonly use verbal corrections as well. They range from the harsh "No! Bad dog!" to a firm "No" to the use of a calm neutral sound such as "uh uh"—sometimes referred to as a "no reward marker." The effectiveness of verbal corrections depends on factors such as the person's tone of voice, skill, and timing as

Shocking **Behavior**

I first met Jojo in a class I was teaching for people with reactive dogs. All of the dogs in this class showed aggression when walked on a leash.

Jojo was a muscular 90-pound white Boxer. He was absolutely fabulous to look at and behaved the way any good Boxer should. As soon as he saw someone at home, he would wiggle his butt and begin his happy dance. But that wasn't his response when he saw dogs, skateboarders, bicyclists, or joggers when he was being walked on a leash.

Whenever he saw any of those things, he exploded. His hair stood up (piloerection) and he reared up on his hind legs and growled ferociously, barking and pulling toward the person or dog. His behavior was frightening.

Jojo's owners reported, as many owners do, that their dog did not signal at all before becoming aggressive. This is a common complaint, and generally I can find body language signals that precede the aggressive behavior, allowing the owners to intercede prior to the outburst. In this case, the only body language signal I could note was that Jojo's pupils dilated (the black part of the eyes enlarged, indicating a stress response) just before he showed aggression. There was no way for the owners to intervene. There just wasn't enough time.

With some questioning, I found the cause. As is generally the case, Jojo's owners had tried lots of things to alter his behavior prior to coming to class. One of the things they had tried was a shock collar. Each time Jojo would show signs of aggression, such as stiffening his body or raising his head or even letting out a low growl, the owners would press the button and deliver a shock.

They had used the collar for only a couple of weeks, but the effect was permanent. They had punished those early warning signals of aggression, causing them to decrease in frequency. In other words, by using the shock collar when Jojo was signaling that he might become aggressive, the owners had made those signals vanish and thus created a dog who exploded like a bomb with little warning.

What the owners hadn't treated was Jojo's underlying fear of other dogs or people approaching quickly on strange-looking objects. The fear lived on, but Jojo couldn't tell anyone.

Jojo improved, but it took months of behavioral treatments in the clinic and medication to lower his arousal level.

—Dr. Lisa Radosta

Shock collars are powerful tools, but not necessarily in a good way. Their use can have serious repercussions for dogs and handlers. Dogs trained using shock collars are at a higher risk of developing negative associations with people or places as well as increased fear, anxiety, stress, avoidance behaviors, and aggression.

—Mikkel Becker

down and gives up. He can no longer process the psychological distress or fight against it; instead, he simply gives in to whatever fear, punishment, shock, or other negativity comes his way. Never flood your dog.

HOW PUNISHMENT CAN BACKFIRE

How you interact with your dog and the training you provide can either work for you and your dog or work against you. Punishment can worsen your dog's manners and hinder your ability to change his behavior. Using coercion, force, or pain can cause fear and stress in a dog, leading him to resist training, or it can even result in learned helplessness, which causes a dog to stop trying. Punishment has been shown to increase aggression and conflict-related behaviors in dogs. Worse, it can harm your relationship with your dog.

One of the ways in which punishment damages your relationship is when you focus on eliminating a behavior you dislike instead of encouraging or rewarding the behavior you want. Following are some reasons that this effort can be ineffective or counterproductive.

TIMING MISHAPS

One reason positive punishment is problematic is because it's really difficult to deliver correctly and effectively. To administer positive punishment in a way that the dog will understand requires perfect timing, perfect execution, and absolute consistency.

An effective punishment must be delivered within one-half to one second of the misbehavior and before the dog offers another behavior, as well as every time the dog performs the unwanted act. Owners

How Dogs Use **Negative Punishment**

As I watch my ten-week-old English Cocker Spaniel puppy play with my three-year-old neutered German Shepherd Dog mix, I am reminded again of how learning works on a daily basis. At first, when the puppy played too roughly, becoming excited or biting too hard, my older dog became more pushy and rough with the puppy. The puppy gave back what he got. He learned to jump faster and bite harder. When my shepherd mix, who had no previous experience playing with puppies, decided to back off and move away when the puppy became more rambunctious and out of control, the puppy calmed down more quickly. He learned that the rough behavior led to his play partner's moving away and ignoring him. When the puppy approached my adult dog in a calmer manner to solicit play, the adult dog reengaged in play behavior.

This is typical behavior seen in wolf packs and other canine social groups. If one pack member exhibits inappropriate behavior that another member does not "like" or want to be exposed to, then that pack member moves away. A canine mother uses this approach with her young when the puppies try to nurse and the mother is trying to wean them. She moves away and prevents access to her teats rather than biting or attacking her puppies.

—Dr. Wailani Sung

usually dole out the punishment too late—minutes or even hours after the misdeed—the punishment is often too broad for your dog to pinpoint what he did wrong.

INCONSISTENCY

Dogs need guidance from the people in their lives regarding the behavior and manners that people expect of them. Expectations, consequences, and structure must be as consistent as possible. For instance, you can't punish a dog for sleeping on the bed one night and then allow him to cuddle with you on your pillow the next night because your mood or circumstances have changed. Well, you can, but your dog will be really confused unless you set specific guidelines, such as letting him on the bed only in response to a particular command.

By the same token, all family members, plus anyone else who interacts with the dog, must be consistent in the training terms they use. Everyone needs to use the same cues and commands for the same behaviors, such as "Down" to mean "lie down" and "Off" to mean "don't jump on me" or "get off the sofa" instead of using "Down" and "Off" interchangeably.

Dogs need consistent consequences for behavior as well, such as a reward for listening, sitting, or otherwise complying with a command. If that doesn't happen, the positive behavior will disappear. This also applies to managing unwanted behaviors. Actions such as pulling on the leash or jumping up must go unrewarded by everyone. If even one person in the dog's life rewards an unwanted behavior, even if it's just once, and even if it's inadvertent, the negative behavior will persist.

It's important as well for everyone in the household to know and follow the rules that pertain to the dog. It's unfair for the dog to have the rules change from person to person.

Kids, Dogs, and **Punishment**

Parents and grandparents, take heed: children often emulate the actions of adults, even if warned not to. That means that a child will model a parent's yelling, scolding, or physical intimidation toward a dog. When a child copies the punishment techniques he witnesses, there is a good chance that the dog will react with aggression toward the child. This is an excellent reason to follow what one trainer calls "the eleventh commandment"—never hit your dog.

If something is OK with one person and not another, it's confusing to the dog. The more predictable a dog's life is, with clear boundaries and rewards only for certain behaviors, the better behaved the dog is likely to be.

LEARNING THE WRONG THING

Think about rubbing a dog's nose in a potty accident. The dog doesn't associate the punishment with the behavior of peeing or pooping in the house. She doesn't learn to do

her business outdoors. Instead, she might learn that it's a bad idea to void in front of people. The dog may become conflicted around people, whom she sees as unpredictable, and start to hide from them when she goes to the bathroom, making the habit of going in the house even more difficult to break.

Punishment may temporarily stifle a behavior, but it doesn't teach the dog what to do instead. Either the behavior recurs and possibly even escalates or the dog replaces it with another equally irksome behavior.

IGNORING THE PUNISHMENT

Dogs can rapidly become accustomed to a particular punishment and begin to ignore it. Think of that classic Far Side cartoon depicting what we say to dogs ("OK, Ginger, I've had it! Stay out of the garbage or else!") and what dogs hear ("Blah, blah, blah, Ginger.")

That's not too far from the truth when it comes to how your dog adapts to punishments such as yelling, a squirt from a water bottle, a jerk on the leash, or a shock from a collar. It means that the punishment must increase in frequency or intensity over time to have any effect. It also risks the dog's making negative associations with the punisher as well as with objects or people in the vicinity when the dog is punished.

MAKING PROBLEMS WORSE

If you have a fearful, anxious, or stressed dog, punishment can worsen his behavior. When a dog is punished for growling or barking, he can no longer give a warning signal to show that he is uncomfortable in a particular situation. He remains highly aroused, agitated, or fearful. Unable to use his innate warnings, such as snarling, he may escalate more quickly into aggressive and dangerous behaviors, such as biting.

WHY PEOPLE USE PUNISHMENT

Pet owners and dog trainers may have many reasons for relying on punishment when they discipline dogs. They may believe it's a way of establishing themselves as the dog's boss. They may believe it's more effective than positive reinforcement or that it's the right thing to do because they've seen trainers on television use those techniques. They may believe that a dog knows when he has done wrong and thus is deserving of punishment. Or they may simply be frustrated and resort to it because they don't know how else to respond to a dog's unwanted actions. Let's take a look at whether these beliefs stand up to examination.

Is Your Dog Really Dominant?

Too often, certain dogs are labeled as "dominant," but that term is a misnomer. Dominance is not a personality trait; it's a situation-specific behavior between two individuals. In my experience as a trainer, dogs who are thought to be dominant in many cases are actually extremely insecure and fearful; in other words, they are the opposite of dominant. Behaviors commonly considered as signs of dominance, such as humping, frequently stem from insecurity or hyperexcitability.

Pet owners who say their dogs are dominant often feel justified in using harsh training methods, such as "alpha rolls" and prong collars, but these tactics do little to encourage positive long-term behavior changes and can often cause a dog to fear his owner.

—Mikkel Becker

BEING THE ALPHA

Do dogs want to dominate us? A once-popular theory that has now been discredited is that dogs need to see their humans as "pack leaders," or "alphas," in the relationship, but there is no scientific evidence to support the notion that there must be an "alpha" in a dog-human relationship. In fact, asking a person to dominate a dog can push the dog out of his comfort zone and result in aggressive behavior by the dog.

Being a good owner or dog handler is not about being the alpha and ruling your dog with an iron fist. It's about instilling discipline and creating a relationship with your dog. Dog trainer Steve White, who has handled and trained patrol and narcotics dogs for military, county, and city law enforcement agencies, likens it to turning your dog into a disciple by making yourself worth following. That means choosing an approach that makes you more interesting to your dog than the environment around him. Rather than pushing the dog around, you develop a partnership with him.

ARE DOGS SPITEFUL?

Dogs don't behave inappropriately by choice. Your dog behaves the way he does not because he's mad at you for leaving him alone during the day or because you were late feeding him one night but because a particular behavior is natural to him or is being reinforced by your response.

While dogs have emotions and complex thought processes, their reasoning is different from that of humans. To truly act out of spite, your dog would have to share your view of right and wrong and use that shared moral code to guide his behavior. Dogs don't operate that way: they are motivated by outcomes, not morals.

That seemingly guilty behavior your dog exhibits after he does something you consider bad? It's a reaction to your behavior and has nothing to do with repentance. Your dog acts submissive and frightened in an attempt to appease his unhappy human. He doesn't understand why you're unhappy, especially if the action that caused your anger— chewing up your Manolos, for instance— occurred hours before you came home and discovered the ruined shoes.

WHY AVOID PUNISHMENT?

We don't advise avoiding punishment because we're big softies. Science shows that punishment not only can be ineffective but also can also lead to unintended consequences, such as aggression. A 2009 study published in the journal *Applied Animal Behaviour Science* found that dogs were more likely to respond aggressively when owners used physical punishment or rough handling, such as hitting or kicking, forcing the dog to release an item or lie down, performing an alpha roll, staring or growling at the dog, or shaking the dog. Further research reported in the journal found that use of aversive methods, such as prong or choke collars, yelling, electronic or spray collars, electronic fences, and physical punishment more than doubles the risk of aggression toward people outside the home and nearly triples the risk of increased aggression toward family members.

CRIME AND PUNISHMENT

Positive or physical punishment can increase any negative associations the dog may have. It doesn't teach him what to do and can add an element of anxiety to an already scary situation. For instance, when we punish dogs for behavior such as growling, it may stifle the outward signs of anxiety but not the underlying emotions. This is often what leads to the dog who "bites out of nowhere."

Punishment doesn't work unless it's bad enough to stop the behavior, and that varies from dog to dog. A stern "No" is enough to stop some dogs in their tracks, while others ignore it completely. And the more a dog is punished, the more punishment it takes for him to respond to it. In other words, the dog becomes resistant, which causes the owner to become frustrated and then punish the dog more severely. It's a never-ending cycle.

As we've mentioned, while physical or positive punishment may relieve an owner's

Does **Physical Punishment** Work? Science Says **No**

Multiple studies in human children have found that spanking increased aggressive responses. The results of the studies have so consistently shown the negative effects of corporal punishment that the American Academy of Pediatrics rejects spanking, saying that it is no more effective than other means of discipline, that its effectiveness decreases with use, and that it is associated with increased aggression in preschool and school-aged children. The main thing punishment does is give parents an outlet for anger.

What does this have to do with dogs? It's important because when it comes to things like learning words, recognizing objects, and understanding certain concepts, dogs are thought to have comparable mental capacity or learning ability as two- to three-year-old children. It's not inconceivable to think that they would respond to physical punishment in a similar manner; in fact, this has been shown in a University of Pennsylvania survey of 140 owners who used confrontational or aversive methods with their dogs. Meghan E. Herron, lead author of the study, said, "Our study demonstrated that many confrontational training methods, whether staring down dogs, striking them, or intimidating them with physical manipulation does little to correct improper behavior and can elicit aggressive responses."

What to Do **Instead**

Instead of punishing your dog, refocus your mind on what you want your dog to do. Working with the whole family, reward your dog for the behaviors you like. Rewards can include treats, toys, praise, or a favorite activity, such as a game of fetch or tug.

Set your dog up for success by limiting his ability to make poor choices. That means putting trash, dirty laundry, or other enticing items out of his reach or restricting him to certain areas of the home until he develops appropriate house manners.

Don't punish your dog for being a dog. Chewing, digging, barking, and chasing are all natural canine behaviors. Give your dog a proper outlet for his instincts by finding ways to replace unwanted behaviors with acceptable ones.

For example, if you have a problem chewer, channel that natural behavior by offering desirable alternatives, such as a treat cube or a hard rubber toy with a hollow interior filled with goodies. End digging in the yard by creating a designated doggie digging pit. Put a stop to barking by teaching your dog to "speak" and "be quiet" on cue. Channel prey drive with toys or devices that mimic the predatory chase and turn it into a game.

Pay up. Too often, I see people expecting their dogs to obey simply to please the owner. Would you work for free at your job just because it pleased your boss? I didn't think so.

It's true that a simple "good dog" and a pat on the head is a reward for many dogs, but when it comes to ignoring major distractions or learning a behavior that takes extra effort on the dog's part, praise and petting may not be enough. I frequently see pet owners delivering little or no reward for behavior that requires the dog to have significant self-control. As a result, the desired behavior becomes less reliable, or the dog stops doing it entirely.

When you ask your dog to perform a difficult behavior or to do the behavior in a highly distracting or emotionally laden situation, give immediate and substantial rewards. Choose a reward that has value for your dog, whether that is a special treat, a game of tug, or the chance to play off leash in a protected area.

—Mikkel Becker

frustration over a dog's behavior, it doesn't help the dog understand what he should be doing instead. The main thing the dog learns is that people are crazy and unpredictable. What he doesn't learn is an acceptable alternative behavior.

You might succeed once through the use of punishment or force to get your dog to do what you want or need him to do, but you'll likely find that it's a hollow victory. Your dog will be even more difficult to handle the next time, and he may even be completely untouchable after a bad experience.

You want your dog to trust you to keep him safe and know what's best for him. Veterinary behaviorist Ilana Reisner says that dog owners who choose kinder training methods live with dogs who not only have good social skills but also are happier, more resilient, and more visibly confident.

The bottom line? Physical and positive punishment and force may seem faster or easier, but in the long run they're less effective and not worth the risk to your relationship with your dog.

REWARDS
FOR THE **WIN**

Who doesn't love getting a reward? Whether it's a pat on the back, a box of chocolates, or a trip to Tahiti, we all glow when we are recognized or rewarded for a job well done.

Dogs are the same way. Giving a reward to a dog is a way to communicate to him that he's done a good job, whether he sat promptly, retrieved a ball, or found a hidden scent. You can reward your dog for something you've asked him to do or for something he's done on his own that you'd like him to repeat in the future.

If you are of an age to remember old-school training techniques, such as swatting a dog on the rump with a rolled-up newspaper or giving him a leash pop with a choke chain, you may have the idea that training with rewards—known as "positive reinforcement"—is some sort of New Age, feel-good gimmick. But reward-based training has a long history. It has been demonstrated to be effective both in the trenches with trainers and—more important—in the realm of science.

THE SCIENCE BEHIND REWARDS

Scientists Ivan Pavlov and B. F. Skinner are among those who made famous the benefit of using rewards and positive associations to

The Power of **Rewards**

In general practice, I saw many sweet and friendly dogs, but others were anxious and fearful about going to the veterinary clinic. One was a seven-year-old neutered male Boxer who started barking at me as soon as I entered the room. I ignored him and started talking to the owner. After three to five barks, the Boxer would stop to take a breath. When he did, I would say "Good quiet" and toss a treat in his direction without looking at him. It took about five treats before he caught on that he received a reward when he was not barking. As he went longer and longer between periods of barking, I gave him more treats. That was how we established a relationship.

Treats furthered the Boxer's owner's ability to interact with him. She had been unable to place a basket muzzle on him, but I showed her how to guide his nose into the muzzle using liver paste on a tongue depressor.

It took three visits before I was able to treat him like a normal dog, meaning that I was able to palpate him all over and listen to his heart without him barking and lunging at me. We still placed a muzzle on him because he was very nervous, but he never tried to bite me because while I was giving him a "massage," the owner was feeding him tasty treats as a reward for not barking or behaving aggressively.

For the dog, receiving rewards was powerful because he was able to work toward a goal during the examination: "What can I do to earn the treat?" It made a scary situation less scary for him. For me, it was rewarding to see him change from a dog who required three to four people to restrain him to one whose owner could give him treats with only one technician lightly restraining him during an exam.

—Dr. Wailani Sung

Find Your Dog's **Currency**

Often, clients tell me that their dog should work for them because he loves them. They also say that their dog doesn't really like treats when stressed. While it is true that the appetitive response—which makes your dog want to eat or play—can be suppressed by the fear, anxiety, or stress response, often we can motivate dogs by finding the right reward.

When I have these conversations with clients, it reminds me of my residency at the University of Pennsylvania. I left a well-paying job as a primary-care veterinarian to enter residency in veterinary behavioral medicine. Residents don't get paid very much and, as a result, I had to give up one of my favorite hobbies: shoe shopping.

At the time, my husband had a blue Harley-Davidson motorcycle with orange piping. He loved that motorcycle and wanted nothing more than for me to ride on the back. Although I didn't think twice about getting on my horse and heading onto the trails in the Pennsylvania hills, I was petrified of the motorcycle. I was not getting on it.

He said that he loved me. "That is lovely," I said, "but I am not getting on that thing." He offered me a fancy dinner, a ride to my favorite botanical garden, and a new motorcycle jacket. I said no, no and no.

Then, one chilly spring day, he called me down to the driveway. I can still feel the chill on my face—the power of classical conditioning. He was standing in his bike leathers next to his shiny motorcycle. On the back was an open sport pack—the motorcycle equivalent of a car trunk. He looked at me with a smile and said, "I can fit two shoe boxes in here." I was scared out of my mind, but I got on that motorcycle and went to get those shoes!

My husband had found my currency: the one thing that would entice me to overcome my fear and ride his bike with him. That is what I encourage owners to do. Find your dog's currency. Keep trying to find that magical reward that will overcome all fears.

—Dr. Lisa Radosta

change an animal's behavior and emotions. Pavlov found that, over time, animals make associations with previously neutral stimuli, such as a bell, and positive stimuli, such as food. The dogs made these associations without conscious effort, and the associations were so powerful that the dogs in the experiment salivated as if there was food in front of them when they heard the bell. This phenomenon is called "classical conditioning."

Skinner's experiments explored ways to get animals to increase or decrease the frequency of certain behaviors depending on the consequence of that behavior. For example,

he taught lab rats that pulling a lever resulted in a treat appearing in front of them. This is called "operant conditioning."

Classical conditioning is the pairing of a neutral stimulus (something in the environment) with an involuntary response, such as salivation, fear, or relaxation, until that stimulus elicits the emotional or involuntary response. Operant conditioning links the action that your dog performs with a reward or consequence. If the behavior is rewarded, your dog will repeat it. If the behavior is punished, the dog will perform it less frequently.

Classical and operant conditioning can be combined to train dogs and other animals by way of positive reinforcement—in other words, rewards. By pairing rewards and positive consequences with a stimulus, such as giving high-value treats to a dog every time he sees another dog he was once unsure of, a trainer can change the dog's response from fear or aggression to joyful anticipation each time he sees that particular dog. This change in the dog's association with the stimulus—in this case, a particular dog—results in the desired behavior change in the dog—from, say, barking at the other dog to sitting peacefully at his owner's side.

THE RESULTS OF REWARDS

Using reward-based training has a number of benefits. Rewards change a dog's baseline emotion and focus. They let a dog know you like a particular behavior. They create a positive association with a particular environment, experience, or person. They build confidence and coping ability.

Nelson's **Story**

Nelson, a bright-eyed and happy twelve-week-old Yorkshire Terrier, had always behaved nicely on walks. He and his owner walked in a group every day with someone whose dog barked at other dogs on leash, which caused Nelson to become anxious about walks when other dogs came around. As Nelson got older, he would become upset at the sight of other dogs while on walks and begin to bark himself. He also started barking at the dog next door. During these episodes, Nelson's owners couldn't get his attention. Nelson was even reluctant to take treats that he loved.

I worked with them on teaching Nelson new behaviors in the presence of other dogs. Previously, he had learned that barking and lunging ended with the other dog moving away, reinforcing the barking and lunging. We taught him that when he exhibited calm behaviors in the presence of other dogs, they moved away from him. He learned to turn his head away or sniff the ground instead of barking, growling, and lunging.

When Nelson behaved calmly, his owner marked it with a "Yes" or a click and then jogged back 2 to 10 feet with him and gave him a reward. His owner then rewarded him for performing another behavior, such as looking at his owner or sitting.

Nelson became able to approach on leash again to the point where he was interested but not upset at the sight of the other dog. There, his owner repeated the exercise. Over time, Nelson was able to get close to other dogs without becoming anxious.

In the yard, Nelson learned to go to his owner when he saw the neighbor's dog. Soon it turned into a fun game to come to his person rather than bark when he saw the other dog.

—Mikkel Becker

Another benefit of rewards is that the entire family can use them, from young children to seniors. Rewards don't require the use of force, only creativity and good timing.

HOW AND WHY REWARDS WORK

Animals form associations between actions and consequences. These associations influence the frequency of certain behaviors. For instance, a friendly puppy may sit calmly at his owner's side when a person approaches. If the person then reaches down and pets the puppy while he's sitting, his calm behavior has been rewarded. He'll probably repeat it.

If a puppy is fearful and a stranger pets him while he's sitting next to his owner, the behavior of sitting quietly for a stranger will be punished. In other words, if he is afraid, people petting him is uncomfortable, not rewarding. If he gets petted every time he sits to meet a new person, he will begin to sit less often

in the future because he views being petted as a punishment. That's why it's extremely important to know your dog's body language and emotional state so you can predict how he will behave.

On the other hand, if a person approaches, and the puppy sits calmly at his owner's side and is ignored, the puppy may get antsy when he doesn't get attention. In frustration, he may bark. When he barks, the person or owner may reach down and pet him. This teaches the puppy that sitting quietly doesn't work to get attention, but barking does. The barking behavior will increase in the future. Meanwhile, he has not been rewarded for the sitting behavior, so it will decrease in the future.

Dogs are always learning, even beyond puppyhood, so it's important throughout the dog's life to reward behavior you like when it occurs. Behaviors that are not rewarded will fade away.

It's also important to be aware of whether the desirable behavior is self-rewarding. When a behavior is self-rewarding, no other reward is necessary to keep the behavior strong. A good example is chasing squirrels. For dogs, chasing squirrels is fun all in itself. No treat needed.

If you teach a sit using treats, you may be able to decrease the number of treats once your dog understands the behavior. For the behavior to remain consistent, though, positive results must follow the sit frequently enough to make it worth the dog's effort. For instance, if your dog gets excited when you come in the house, and you ask him to sit, you should follow

Treat Delivery

There's more to giving a treat than just handing it out. The direction of the reward matters. This is especially true when luring your dog. What do we mean?

Let's say you want to keep your dog's focus on you. You would give the treat in such a way that it's close to your body and holds your dog's attention.

You may want your dog to approach a certain area or object, such as the scale at the veterinary clinic. In that case, toss the treat toward that area or station yourself near the object and give treats when he approaches.

If you need to lure your dog to go to the scale (or other frightening object), start with the treats right next to your dog's foot. Keep them only a few inches apart and continue to reward him the entire time that he is on the scale as well.

To have him get comfortable in a room or in the presence of other people, toss treats just far enough to get your dog moving. This helps him investigate at a pace that's comfortable for him.

through with something your dog enjoys, such as petting, treats, or a game of fetch. The most powerful way to deliver rewards once your dog understands a behavior is through variable reinforcement (more later in this chapter).

It's also important not to accidentally reward undesirable behaviors. Chasing your dog when he runs away from you at the park? He thinks that's a fun game. He'll want to do it again. Petting him when he jumps on you will cause him to jump on you each and every time you come home.

Instead, work to teach him what you want from him in a particular situation. You may need to teach him some alternative behaviors that are more rewarding for both of you. Sometimes, doing what he wants instead of what you want may simply be more fun for him. You need to figure out how to make yourself more exciting so that he wants to, say, come when you call instead of running with the gang at the park or digging in the yard. It may be helpful to consult a professional to help you achieve your goals.

HOW AND WHAT TO REWARD—EMPHASIZE THE POSITIVE

Besides teaching new behaviors, you can reinforce or reward behaviors just because you like them. If your dog views what you are doing as rewarding to him, he will offer those behaviors more and more.

For example, watch your dog throughout the day. When he is doing something that you like, praise him quietly, hand him a small treat, and walk away. Is he sitting at the window quietly instead of engaging in his usual behavior of barking at passersby? Give him a treat. Is he lying calmly in the lobby of the veterinarian's office? Give him a treat. Remember to reward early and often if your dog has fear, anxiety, or stress. The stress response will overwhelm the appetitive response (the one that controls your dog's desire to eat), so don't wait until your dog is scared to start rewarding him.

Rewards don't have to be treats, but they should be simple: a chance to sniff, access to furniture or a lap, or an opportunity to perform a favorite trick. Willy, a Pug, would perform a command just to get the OK to jump over his owner's leg or through her arms. For him, the "Jump" behavior was so much fun that it was rewarding in and of itself. Other dogs thrive on verbal praise. You may be surprised when you realize the many different ways you can reward your dog.

That Lightbulb **Moment**

"Their faces light up." That's a common phrase we hear in reference to children when they how to solve a math problem or understand a difficult concept. A dog's face seems to light up as well when he learns that he will receive a reward for performing a certain behavior. You'll see the joy in his eyes, his willingness to make eye contact, or his desire to move closer to you. His facial expression relaxes, and his brow is less furrowed and tightly drawn.

Some of my fearful patients are a bundle of nerves when they first walk into my consultation room. Even though we play calming music, have a diffuser sending out calming pheromones, and soft carpeting on the floor, just being in a new place is scary to a fearful dog. After one or two visits, his attitude changes. He immediately enters the room and approaches us because the last time he arrived, he received a reward for approaching us. Or he runs to the toy closet and sits in front of it because this behavior earned him a toy at his previous visit.

I love seeing dogs enter the veterinary clinic who are trembling with joy rather than fear at the sight of me. That's my reward.

—Dr. Wailani Sung

FOOD TREATS: BRIBE OR REWARD?

It's a common belief that using treats in training is bribery and that the dog won't perform a behavior unless he's offered a treat. That can certainly happen if training is done incorrectly, but it shouldn't and doesn't have to be that way.

Showing a dog that you have a treat in your hand to get him to perform a certain behavior is indeed bribery. There is nothing wrong with that! A bribe can get the job done in all kinds of stressful situations. For example, when your dog goes to the veterinarian's office to have his nails trimmed, you can "bribe" him with peanut butter so that he will be less stressed. In reality, you are actually distracting him from the nail trim, which he probably finds very stressful.

What if he is barking at the mail carrier at the window and you need to move him away from the window quickly, but he hasn't yet learned to come to you when called? Shake a treat bag or get closer to him and offer him a treat to persuade him to come toward you. When he gets to you, give him the treat. These

are all examples of using food as a distraction to help your dog stay calm and keep negative behaviors from getting worse.

Now, it is ideal to teach the dog to do the behavior first and then reward him with a treat from a treat jar or bag. This is the end goal. When you are in a situation where your dog is fearful, anxious, or stressed, do what you need to with food, even as a lure, to keep him from escalating.

Try to vary rewards with nonfood options, such as a game of fetch or tug. Other types of rewards include petting, going outside or for a walk, food puzzle toys, or being released from a heel and allowed to walk on a loose leash.

Once your dog learns a behavior, use a variable reinforcement schedule to ensure that he responds reliably. A random schedule of rewards means he never knows when the payout will come—sort of like a Las Vegas slot machine. This system helps keep dogs motivated.

A fun way to teach your dog to be more patient and polite is with a training game. Hide

Taming the **Canine Shark**

Giving a dog a treat should be a pleasant experience—for dog and person—but if you have a grabby dog, the exchange can seem more like feeding Jaws. Dogs who are nervous may take treats "harder" and nip fingers in the process. Though the behavior is not typically aggressive, it's still intimidating and unpleasant. Fortunately, there are some simple ways to help put an end to grabby behavior and encourage your dog to be gentle when taking a treat, toy, or other item. In hunting dogs, this is known as having a "soft mouth," and it's a behavior we should encourage in all dogs.

Start by ruling out any potential underlying causes, including fear, anxiety, frustration, or aggression. When a dog who normally takes treats and toys gently suddenly becomes more forceful and less discriminating with his teeth, it may be a sign that he is agitated by or afraid of something in the environment. If this is the case, seek immediate assistance from a professional, such as a veterinary behaviorist or a veterinarian who works with a positive-reinforcement trainer.

Most likely, though, your dog's grabby behavior is motivated by excitement and experience. He wants what you are offering and has learned that grabbing it from your hands is the fastest way to get it.

a piece of kibble, a treat, or a small toy inside your closed fist. Most dogs will paw or mouth at your skin to try to get the item. (If you have sensitive skin that is prone to scrapes or cuts, wear gardening gloves during this exercise.)

Offer your dog the treat in your closed hand, but ignore pawing and mouthing. Wait for a gentle touch of the nose, tongue, or soft part of the muzzle before opening your hand and rewarding him. Use a click or say "Yes" to mark the gentle touches, then either drop the treat so it lands on the floor or open your fist and offer it from the flat of your palm, as if feeding a horse. This teaches your dog that pawing and biting never work to get what he wants, but soft touches will.

If you are working with a fearful dog, be careful not to bend over or loom over him as you're giving a treat. He may become jumpy, startled, or aggressive if you accidentally get in his face. Try sitting so you are more at his level or drop or toss the treat.

The way you offer a treat can also influence how your dog behaves. If you hold a treat just out of his reach, it forces him to jump or stand on his hind legs to get it. While this is a good abdominal workout for him, it makes it more likely that he will snatch the item from you. This can create a cycle in which you anticipate the dog's reaction and pull away quickly, emphasizing the dog's need to move fast to get what you are offering.

To help prevent your dog from jumping up to get his treat or toy, place your hands just under or aligned with the level of his muzzle, rather than above his muzzle, to ensure that he can reach the treat without having to stand up on two legs. Be sure that everyone who gives your dog food, treats, or toys does so in a way that promotes and reinforces his taking it gently. Ask them to always offer the treat on a flat palm and to hold it low enough that the dog doesn't need to reach or jump.

When there are multiple dogs in a household, establish a routine for how rewards are given. Ask all the dogs for a calm behavior, such as a sit, and then hand out treats in a consistent order—smallest to largest or oldest to youngest, for example. This makes the situation more predictable for

Treats as Distractions

In situations where your dog's emotions are intense, such as when he is experiencing fear or excitement, the use of food rewards can help calm him down. Once he learns to be calm in the situation, though, phase out the food reward and offer an alternative reward for good behavior.

—*Mikkel Becker*

Tips on **Treats**

There are hundreds of brands of treats on the market. They come in different sizes for small, medium, and large dogs and different flavors (duck, mango, and coconut, anyone?) and they have different claims on their labels, including "premium," "gourmet," and "organic," which may or may not actually mean anything. You aren't limited to commercial treats, though. You can give various fruits, vegetables, and other foods that are both healthy and rewarding.

The best treats are highly aromatic, as well as small and soft, so they go quickly down the hatch. If you are giving a lot of treats, scale back the amount of food you give your dog at mealtime so he doesn't gain unwanted weight. And remember that treats don't have to be big to be effective. The size of a pea is just about right.

Here are some treat suggestions.

- Your dog's own kibble. Set aside a small percentage of his food to give as treats throughout the day. That way, part of his daily meal is earned as a reward, and you don't run the risk of adding a lot of extra calories to his diet. Keep in mind that for most dogs, this reward has the lowest value. Many dogs will not take kibble when they are fearful, anxious, or stressed.

- Fruits and vegetables. Blueberries, baby carrots, strawberries, and apples are among the healthy, low-calorie treats that many dogs enjoy. Berries are sweet, and apples and carrots have a satisfying crunch. Keep the pieces small to give you more bang for your produce buck. Avoid grapes or raisins, which can cause kidney failure in dogs.

- Warm deli meat, such as white-meat chicken breast or nitrate-free hot dogs, or part-skim mozzarella cheese. For most dogs, these are high-value rewards.

If your dog is on a limited-ingredient diet because of allergies or other health conditions, make meatballs with the canned version of your dog's food or ask your veterinarian if compatible treats are available.

If your dog doesn't take the treat that you offer him, he doesn't view it as rewarding in that situation, so try a different treat to find what he is willing to work for. Once you find the right treat for that situation, stick with it so that you don't teach him to wait it out to get a better treat.

your dogs and less competitive, which helps to eliminate aggression in the household.

If you see little improvement in grabbiness, even with training and a change of delivery tactics, or if you see signs of aggression or fear associated with the behavior, seek the help of a professional, starting with your veterinarian. For incorrigible grabbers who have a clean bill of health from the veterinarian, try delivering treats from a distance. You can do this by placing the treat on a wooden spoon or tongue depressor (using peanut butter as an adhesive) or squirting out squeeze cheese or liver paste with a reusable plastic camping tube, piping bag, or plastic storage bag with a hole cut in the corner. In an emergency situation, just toss the reward on the floor or ground. When your dog is fearful, the most important thing is to change how he feels. Just get the reinforcer to him.

Hand **Games**

When you play with your dog, avoid wrestling with your hands. That teaches him that putting his teeth on your skin is acceptable behavior, and it's not. When you play tug of war or fetch with your pooch, discourage teeth-on-skin behavior by ending a game immediately if teeth touch hands or skin.

—*Mikkel Becker*

By using food not simply for training but to change your dog's emotional state, you can help your dog to feel differently about the situations that scare him. Using rewards to train and countercondition him is scientifically sound, can bring lasting behavior changes, and provides a common language between dog and human. The result is a deepening of the human-animal bond.

PART II

FEAR FIGHTERS: HOW **SOCIALIZATION, TRAINING, AND BEHAVIOR MODIFICATION** CAN HELP YOUR DOG GO **FROM FEARFUL TO FEAR FREE**

SOCIALIZATION AND PUPPY **KINDERGARTEN**

The fight against fear begins at the moment of birth, when a puppy first experiences a gentle human touch, the security of suckling his mother and drawing in her scent, and the comfort of snuggling with his littermates. Day by day, he experiences new variations on these themes. The world unfolds as his eyes and ears open, he receives more human handling by different people, and he learns lessons about his world by watching his mother, interacting with the environment and the people in it and playing with his littermates.

All of these interactions help to form the puppy's personality and responses to the world around him. Exposure to the people, animals, and other things in the environment is called socialization. The sensitive period for socialization is during the first three months of life, in particular between the ages of three and sixteen weeks, depending on the individual dog or breed. During this period, more than any other in his life, small, even minor, experiences, good and bad, are likely to have a large impact. Once the socialization period has ended, it takes more effort to make sure that the puppy becomes confident in his environment. Puppies can continue to benefit from socialization through six months of age, but early experiences are the most powerful.

Each puppy is wired neurochemically and behaviorally in his own way. This genetic blueprint will influence how the puppy experiences the world, reacts to stimuli, and responds to socialization. Some puppies' minds are clean slates when they are born while others are predisposed to fear, anxiety, and stress.

Many factors completely outside of your control affect the likelihood that your puppy will be well adjusted or fearful. If your puppy's mother or father was fearful, he is likely to be fearful as well. This tendency may be in his genetic blueprint or might be learned from the parents as he watches them interact with the environment. If your puppy's mother was sick or deficient in certain nutrients when she was pregnant, your puppy is more likely to be fearful and more difficult to train when compared to a puppy whose mother was healthy and gave birth in a warm, comfortable environment.

Puppies who don't get the best start in life can be more difficult to socialize, showing fear more profoundly than those that do. Socialization is still important for these pups. The work that you will do beyond socialization will be of great importance to help this type of puppy lead a happy life.

Regardless of your puppy's hereditary predispositions, the best ways to help him be happy and confident in his environment is to expose him to many different positive experiences with people, friendly animals, and pleasant situations and places and to encourage him to explore his environment in an interesting, safe, and fun way.

WIRED TO LEARN

Puppies are born with all of the brain cells they will ever have. The extent to which the

Puppy Safety

As puppies grow, they explore with their mouths, just as human babies do. They don't know that something is unsafe or that it is expensive and not to be chewed. Provide a range of safe things for your puppy to chew on and keep your belongings where he cannot get to them.

puppy's brain develops depends in large part on the types of environmental stimulation he receives during his first three to four months of life. During this time, your puppy's brain is most receptive to learning new things. A dog's breed and individual personality can also affect his development.

Fear, investigation, and play develop during specific sensitive periods. Because there is variation in development between and within breeds, each individual puppy will develop at his own pace. As a puppy has new experiences, his brain's dendrites—specialized brain nerve-cell structures—reach out to make contact with other nerve cells. By the time he is eight weeks old, a puppy's brain mass is nearly 50 percent developed. By the time he is four months old, it has reached 80 percent of its growth. You can see, then, why this is such an important time in a puppy's education.

Puppy Development

Puppies go through distinct stages of development:

The **neonatal phase** is also known as the "newborn period." During this time, a puppy does little more than eat and sleep. It might seem as if not much is going on in the brain during this period, but well-published research shows that stimulating a puppy's neurological system in simple ways, such as holding him, turning him over, and exposing him to minor temperature changes, can benefit the puppy. Puppies who experience these minor changes to their environment are more trainable, can handle environmental changes more easily, have a greater tolerance for stress, and are neurochemically calmer.

At two weeks, puppies enter the **transitional period**. This is when the eyes open and learning ability starts to kick in. Even at this early age, puppies can learn to perform responses for food rewards. The eyes and ears open at about fourteen days, allowing the pups to explore with all five senses. Even at this young age, puppies can hear better than humans. They can stand and move around (although they are wobbly and need a little practice) to better explore their environment. At this young age, some pups will start to leave the nest to eliminate.

The transitional period ends at about twenty-one days, at which point the puppies enter the all-important **socialization period**, with all senses set to "go." They can taste, smell, touch, feel, see, and hear. They are suddenly active and busy. They begin playful biting and pawing behaviors and exhibiting the same body-language signals, such as play bows, that they will exhibit as adults. Suddenly, their environment is interesting, and they start seeking out odors and noises, venturing farther from mom and littermates to explore on their own. During this period, less exposure to the environment is likely to hurt the puppies because dogs will default to the fearful response if they are not positively exposed during this time.

During the **first fear period**, from eight to ten weeks, many puppies will be in their new homes, no longer with their mothers and littermates. It's especially important to make sure that all of your pup's experiences are as positive as you can make them. In addition to making

SOCIALIZATION BENEFITS

In our practices, we've seen what can happen when a dog isn't given proper socialization as a puppy. The results can be significant—in a bad way. They include aggression toward other dogs and humans, extreme shyness, the inability to be handled, or complete disconnection from people. Socialization is one of the few times in your pup's life when a lack of action will have a profoundly negative result.

Properly socializing a puppy can help create a more confident, relaxed, and well-adjusted dog. Even dogs who are naturally timid can make significant strides with the benefit of socialization. With your veterinarian's advice, you can socialize your puppy both at home and in protected environments in your community to help him become a well-adjusted adult dog.

ACQUIRING YOUR PUPPY

Before we go further, let's talk about where puppies come from. And no, we don't mean "the birds and the bees."

Puppies aren't all alike. Whether they are purebreds, crossbreeds (sometimes referred to as "hybrids" or "designer dogs") or Heinz 57

the trip to his new home during this time, he will make his first visit to the veterinarian in your company. This is a scary time for him, so it's important to make sure that these new experiences are positive.

This is a good time to try to identify fearful behavior. Although a puppy may not continue to be fearful of the same experiences, people, or objects over time, it's always a good idea to identify fears or note an inability to recover. While it's impossible to predict future behavior based on an eight-week-old puppy's responses, puppies who show strong fear responses when young may be more likely to develop fear-related behavior problems as adults. These puppies can be labeled as "at risk" and need specific plans for their socialization.

The **juvenile period** is between fourteen weeks to about eighteen months. This is when puppies start to become sexually mature. If not neutered, they may start to show interest in the other sex and show sexual behaviors, such as marking. Have a conversation with your veterinarian about the best time to spay or neuter your puppy. Some breeds, especially large or giant dogs, can benefit from a longer period to mature before they are altered.

A **second fear period** occurs between six and eight months. Growing puppies can develop fears of certain situations during this time. The age at which these fears occur varies, with smaller dogs typically experiencing them earlier. Be patient and kind and give your puppy opportunities, such as training classes and dog sports (e.g., rally and nosework) to build self-confidence.

A puppy may look mature by the time he is nine months to a year old, but he continues to develop both physically and emotionally. A puppy's brain continues to change and grow during adolescence and into maturity, starting to display adult behavior between twelve and thirty-six months of age. This time period, called **social maturity**, can be challenging. By this time, many of us have slacked off with our daily training and regularly exposing our dogs to the people, places, and animals in their environment. Many owners become frustrated during this phase, and thus dogs end up in shelters for behavior that is normal and preventable but often annoying and destructive. It takes plenty of patience, instruction, training, and consistency for you and your dog to make it successfully through this stage.

mixes, their personalities are shaped not only by genetics but also by the care and nutrition the mother receives during pregnancy as well as the environment in which they're raised during those first crucial weeks of life.

You may already have a puppy, or you may still be in the "thinking about it" stage. Here's what you should know about the options for acquiring a puppy and how each may affect your puppy-raising experience.

Hobby breeders raise dogs with the goal of improving the breed's looks (conformation), health, or working ability.

In the best possible scenarios, they're succeeding in all three areas. They exhibit their dogs at shows not only to be judged by experts but also because it's a fun activity—hence the term "hobby breeder."

People in the hobby breeder category usually have only one or two breeds. They may breed litters only once every year or couple of years and only when they have a waiting list for puppies.

Hobby breeders test breeding dogs for heritable diseases that may be found in their breeds, such as hip dysplasia or eye or heart

disorders. Their health certifications, granted by veterinary specialists in such fields as orthopedics, ophthalmology, and cardiology, are up to date and ideally can be found on an open health registry such as the Orthopedic Foundation for Animals (OFA) or the Canine Health Information Center (CHIC).

A hobby breeder puts a lot of effort into turning out nice puppies. Puppy prices usually vary according to locale, a breed's rarity or popularity, and whether a pup is considered "show quality" (meaning he doesn't have any obvious conformation flaws) or "pet quality"(maybe his eyes aren't dark enough or his spots are too big). A puppy purchased from a hobby breeder usually comes with a guarantee of good genetic health until the puppy is at least two years old. By that time, most hereditary conditions that are going to appear have already done so.

Not every hobby breeder is perfect, and finding and purchasing from such a breeder

Get it in **Writing**

A reputable breeder will require you to sign a sales contract. A good contract typically includes the following information:

- The sale price
- The puppy's birthdate
- The sire's and dam's names
- Who will register the dog and with which organization
- The breeder's health guarantees, return policies, and breeding restrictions or spay/neuter requirements
- A clause stating that the breeder will take the dog back at any time in the dog's life and that the breeder has right of first refusal in any situation in which the buyer cannot keep the dog

can entail some effort and a waiting period, but if you find a good hobby breeder, he or she can be a great resource for you throughout your dog's life. There are no guarantees in life, but buying a puppy from a reputable hobby breeder can help increase the likelihood that your puppy will be physically and emotionally healthy.

Casual breeders, sometimes referred to as "backyard breeders," might be your next-door neighbor whose dog had an "oops" litter or someone in town who decided to breed his or her dog to recoup the purchase price. Generally, casual breeders aren't concerned about pedigrees, haven't had their dogs checked for possible hereditary diseases, and haven't put working or conformation titles on their dogs. The puppies they produce may be attractive or friendly, but they don't usually come with a guarantee of good health that's backed by valid health certifications.

Commercial breeders, also known as "puppy mills," are large-scale producers of puppies of many different breeds. They often describe themselves as USDA approved, but USDA minimum standards are just that— minimal. The agency's standard for cage size— the primary enclosure in which breeding dogs live—is that it must be only 6 inches taller, wider, and longer than the dog inside. If the dog lives in a cage with twice the floor space required by this guideline, the USDA doesn't require the breeder to give the dog any outside exercise.

Puppies produced by commercial breeders are usually those found for sale in pet stores. According to a study published in the May 15, 2013, issue of the *Journal of the American Veterinary Medical Association (JAVMA)*, puppies purchased from pet stores—as opposed to those purchased from breeders—were found

Breeder **Red Flags**

- The puppies are kept in dirty kennels or living areas.
- One or more puppies look dirty or unhealthy.
- One or more puppies shy away from people.
- The breeder has no proof of health clearances or copies of the sire's and dam's American Kennel Club or United Kennel Club registration papers and pedigrees.
- The breeder makes excuses as to why you can't meet the dam (and the sire, if he is also on the premises), especially if the reason is that she isn't friendly toward strangers or is sick.
- The breeder has puppies available year-round or puppies of several different breeds.
- The breeder offers no health guarantees.
- The breeder requires you to buy a particular dog food or nutritional supplements from him or her and voids the health guarantee if you choose not to use those products.

to have greater aggression toward human family members, unfamiliar people and other dogs; greater fear of other dogs; more risk of developing separation anxiety; and more problems with housetraining.

Online sellers may be individuals, commercial breeders, or companies, such as NextDayPets.com or PuppyDogWeb.com. It's easy to be captivated by the pictures of cute puppies who can be purchased with a quick click of a mouse, but it's difficult to know how and in what conditions the puppies have been raised or what their temperaments are like.

Meet the **Parents!**

Getting an idea of the parents' personalities is just as important as evaluating the puppies. When you look at a breeder's adult dogs, what you see is very likely what you'll get in a puppy.

The breeder should have at least the mother on the premises when you come to see the pups. If the father is local, you should have an opportunity to meet him as well, but often he is in another city or state.

Other adult dogs on the premises, even if they aren't related to the puppies, can also clue you in as to the temperaments the pups are likely to have. Look for friendly, outgoing dogs with stable temperaments. They should be happy, easygoing, and easy to live with. A puppy who sees these traits in the adult dogs around him will be influenced by their behavior as he grows.

Pet stores sell puppies. Generally, these puppies come from commercial breeders, although some pet stores work with shelters or rescue groups to place puppies or adult dogs. The drawback to a pet store, as with an online seller, is that you have no way of knowing how or in what conditions the puppies were raised.

Animal shelters can be sources of puppies. The puppies may have been found as strays or brought in by casual breeders who were unable to find homes for them. Puppies in shelters have sometimes been raised in foster homes, where they receive good early training and socialization. The downside is that shelters don't always have puppies available and, when they do, they may not know the puppies' backgrounds, so you may be taking a leap of faith when it comes to predicting a pup's personality or size at maturity.

No matter where you acquire your puppy, it's important to understand that no federal or state laws mandate how puppies are raised. No regulations address socialization or require that breeders obtain health certifications on their breeding stock. Registration papers from the American Kennel Club, United Kennel Club, or other registries mean only that both parents were of the same breed. "Papers" aren't evidence that the parents have excellent health

or temperaments. And just because a kennel is inspected by the USDA or some other authority doesn't necessarily mean that inspection standards are high.

WHAT TO LOOK FOR IN A BREEDER

How do you recognize a great breeder? Here are six "tell-tail" signs.

- The breeder asks lots of questions, including why you want this particular breed, whether you've had dogs before, whether the dog will live indoors or outdoors, whether you have children and how old they are, and how you plan to train the pup.

- The puppies are raised in the home or in a clean, heated, well-lit kennel with plenty of time spent in the house with people.
- The breeder willingly and thoroughly answers your questions about the breed's temperament, care, and health. Good information to obtain from the breeder includes the strong and weak points of the parents' health and temperaments, which health screenings were performed and why, with what organization the health certifications are registered, the details of the health guarantee on the pups, whether the breeder provides a written sales agreement, and at what age the breeder recommends spaying or neutering and why.
- The breeder belongs to the national ("parent") breed club as well as to local or regional clubs. Club membership is not a guarantee of good breeding practices, but it's a clue that a breeder has a genuine interest in the breed and is recognized by others in the breed.
- The breeder has a good relationship with one or more local veterinarians and can provide you with the puppy's vaccination and deworming records when you take the puppy home.

Stress Test

A little adversity can be a good thing. Moderate amounts of stress during the socialization period can prepare a puppy to meet new experiences with confidence. The key word is moderate. Minor stressful situations in which the puppy can control the outcome and thus relieve the stress can enhance his resistance to stress, but extended or traumatic experiences can have the opposite effect. If your puppy doesn't recover from a stressful experience quickly, the results can be lifelong.

- The breeder keeps the puppies with their mother and littermates until they are at least seven weeks old to ensure that they learn proper canine social behavior from their mother and littermates. The optimal time to take a puppy home varies by breed. For instance, breeds such as Labrador and Golden Retrievers may be ready at seven or eight weeks of age, but breeders of toy dogs such as Chihuahuas and Pugs prefer to keep puppies until they are ten to twelve weeks old.

Is all of this worth it for a dog who will simply be a beloved companion, not a show or working dog? Yes! Not only are you more likely to acquire a puppy who is healthy in body and mind, but you will also have a valuable resource in the breeder, who can offer help and support if you have questions or concerns. Finding a good breeder takes planning and footwork, but it's worth the effort.

WHAT TO LOOK FOR IN A PUPPY

Once you've found a reputable source for your puppy, it's time for the fun part! Looking at

puppies is a delight. It's hard not to choose the first cute one who jumps into your lap, but there's a lot more to consider.

Within a typical litter, you can expect to find a range of personalities. One puppy might be independent, one bossy, and one more laidback. Sometimes these traits will be obvious, but it's always a good idea to ask the breeder to describe each puppy's personality. The breeder has been watching the puppies for weeks and will have a pretty good idea of how each puppy will turn out and which one is right for you, based on your personality and lifestyle.

Even if not every puppy in a litter is available to you—and, more often than not, you won't have your choice of all of them—the breeder's opinion is still helpful as far as helping you learn to evaluate what you're seeing from each puppy. It's all too easy to choose a puppy because you like his color or he was the first one to run to you, but more important is how you plan to spend your time with him. If you want a dog to jog with or who will accompany you on camping trips, one with an upbeat but easygoing personality is a good choice. A dog who will compete in dog sports needs a certain amount of independence and drive, and that dog is not necessarily the best choice for a family with young children or for a sedentary person.

Making the best decision for yourself and your family involves handling, playing with, and watching puppies interact both with each other and with people. Here are some tips:

Pick up a puppy and see how he reacts. A typical puppy may struggle a bit at first but then settle down and nestle into your arms. Hold him close to your heart so he can hear your heartbeat. If a puppy doesn't settle down, even after you rock him a bit, he's likely a puppy who's going to have excess energy or will require a large investment of training time and effort.

Does a puppy seem overly aggressive or frenzied? He may have temperament issues.

Does a puppy shiver or seem distant or frightened when you pick him up? You might feel sorry for him, but he's not a good choice. Puppies who freeze or who fight being held in your arms, tummy to the sky, have been poorly socialized. It's probably smart to avoid any puppy from that litter.

Clap your hands. It's all right if a puppy startles and then looks interested, but avoid puppies who shy away from the sound without recovering or who flat-out run away.

After you've looked at the puppies together, eliminate the ones you don't want before making your final decision. For instance, if you want a girl, ask the breeder to take away the boys. If you want a puppy of only a certain color or pattern, eliminate the puppies that don't have that look. It will then be easier to make a choice from among the remaining puppies.

Serious puppy buyers look at a litter more than once. Come back on another day and look at the puppies all over again. You may find that the best puppy for you was sleepy during your first visit and didn't make a good impression, or maybe he had just gotten up from a nap and was acting wilder than usual.

Puff Daddy's **Story**

The Great Pyrenees puppy lived outside with his parents until he was seven months old. At that time, the dogs' owner gave them up to a shelter. In his short lifetime, Puff Daddy, as he was later named, had encountered only some outdoor cats, his parents, and, briefly, his littermates. He had never even ridden in a car until he was taken to the shelter.

Shelter employees reported that Puff Daddy's parents were fearful. Their behavior, combined with the pup's lack of socialization during the socialization period, could have set him back fatally. Large, shy, fearful dogs aren't typically an adopter's first choice, but the family who chose him looked beyond his fear and saw potential in his sweetness. Nonetheless, a challenging road lay ahead of them.

His new owners struggled to help Puff adapt to his surroundings. He was terrified of the entire family and of being indoors. In the house, he would hunker down in one of two rooms, constantly on alert. The slightest noise or movement startled him.

Puff Daddy felt safe only outside. But even there, even slight changes, such as the appearance of a doghouse to protect him from the elements, caused him to react fearfully. He wouldn't eat if his meals were placed within a few feet of the doghouse.

For most dogs, the process of becoming accustomed to a new situation takes a short time. For Puff, it took months. When his people took him to training class, he shook the entire time and refused to take treats.

They then brought him to my class for fearful dogs. We have barriers behind which dogs can feel safe and a trainer-to-dog ratio of 1:2, with no more than five dogs in class. We work on skills to help dogs overcome shyness or fear and gain confidence.

For Puff, one of the skills we built on was his willingness to touch people with a paw. He would reach out and put his paw on a family member, and he liked having it held gently. It was the one behavior he would perform with high reliability that was not a fearful reaction (such as looking around anxiously or alerting to sounds). I had his owners "capture" the paw moment by marking it with a word or click and then rewarding him with a treat.

His willingness to take treats for this behavior was a big deal because he previously had been too stressed to accept them. It helped to encourage calmer behavior. He became relaxed enough that he could learn other behaviors and be rewarded for things such as making eye contact, focusing on people, or relaxing his body. Though it was slow going, it was major progress for him!

We also worked on his fear of going for walks. He would cower and move away fearfully from approaching humans or animals. One day in class, we worked on approaches out in a field. At first, he was comfortable only when people were some distance away—approximately 80 feet—but gradually he learned to move closer because he was allowed to control the distance and was rewarded for confident, more relaxed behavior with treats and the chance to have a fun jog with his girl, which he loved. This helped him build a better association with the approach of people and other animals.

—*Mikkel Becker*

The Who, What, and Where
of Socialization

Here is a sampling of people, animals, sounds and situations that your puppy should experience during his socialization period. Many of these things can be practiced from day one of your puppy's life with you.

People
- Men, women, babies, toddlers, children, teens, adults, seniors
- People of different heights and weights
- People of different ethnicities
- People with short hair, long hair, mohawks, brightly colored hair, shaved heads, and facial hair
- People with tattoos and piercings
- People wearing accessories such as hats, hoods, jackets, boots, high heels, and sunglasses
- People in uniform
- People using aids such as canes, crutches, walkers, and wheelchairs
- People holding umbrellas
- People on bicycles, skateboards, and scooters
- Veterinarians and vet techs

Animals
Dogs and puppies of both sexes and a variety of breeds, sizes, and play styles. Be certain the other dog is vaccinated and friendly toward other dogs. Avoid high-traffic areas, such as dog parks, until your puppy has had all of his vaccinations.
- Cats
- Pet birds
- Small mammals such as guinea pigs, hamsters, gerbils, and bunnies
- Horses and other livestock

Surfaces
- Grass
- Gravel
- Concrete
- Asphalt
- Carpet
- Tile/slick flooring

Environmental Noise
- Thunder
- Fireworks
- Dishwasher or washing machine
- Electronic sounds
- Animal sounds
- Construction noise
- Gunshots
- Household appliances (kitchen mixer, blender, blow dryer)
- Lawn equipment
- Music of all types
- Sirens
- Snow blowers
- Traffic noise

The best choice for most people is the middle-of-the-road puppy. He plays happily with his siblings and enjoys contact with humans, but he isn't the puppy who's on top of the heap or who grabs every toy whenever another pup has it. This type of puppy will usually require more work than the average person wants to deal with. Leave him for the owners who want to compete in dog sports or who are experienced trainers and already knowledgeable about the breed.

SOCIALIZATION: FROM BREEDER TO OWNER

In a perfect world, a good breeder or puppy-raiser has the socialization process well under way by the time your puppy is ready to come home with you. He or she has brought up the

Introduce new sounds at a muted level in a controlled manner while your puppy is doing something fun. For example, play the sounds of thunder or fireworks at a low volume while your puppy eats a meal. Gradually increase the volume as your puppy's comfort with the noise increases.

Handling
- Having all body parts touched and examined, including sensitive areas such as paws, nails, ears, tail, tummy, eyes, and mouth while you are feeding him yummy treats
- Being bathed
- Wearing various accessories, such as a collar, harness, head halter, or raincoat
- Being held or restrained in a variety of ways, including while standing or sitting
- Being groomed, including brushing, trimming, or nail clipping
- Making eye contact
- Being petted in different ways, such as being hugged by a young child

Places
Many businesses welcome well-behaved, well-supervised dogs. Always be sure to make a potty stop first so you're not embarrassed by any accidents. Here are some "field trip" suggestions:
- Banks and credit unions
- Outdoor malls
- Pet supply stores
- Restaurants with outdoor seating
- Dry cleaners
- Home-improvement stores

Situations
- Being crated
- Being left alone for short amounts of time in a puppy-safe area or crate

- Being handled by strangers ("pass the puppy")
- Being photographed
- Going for rides in the car
- City situations, such as automatic doors, escalators, and airports
- Training class or play group
- Different weather conditions, including wind, rain, and snow (for housetraining purposes, you don't want a dog who thinks he will melt if he gets wet!)
- Going to the groomer
- Going to rural areas, such as the mountains or a field
- Seeing passing joggers and bicyclists
- Playing with a variety of toys
- Seeing shopping carts, strollers, and other objects that move
- Visiting the veterinarian's office
- Having visitors to the home
- Walking around the neighborhood and on busy streets

Vehicles
- Bicycles
- Cars
- Scooters
- Skateboards
- Delivery trucks
- Garbage trucks
- Motorcycles
- Snowplows
- Trucks with trailers

puppy in a home environment with plenty of human interaction and common household sights and sounds. The age at which puppies are ready to make the transition to a new family varies by breed and circumstances, though.

There may be psychological and behavioral lessons that puppies can learn by staying with the litter a little longer; these include bite inhibition—learning not to bite down too hard with those sharp teeth—as well as other perceptual, motor, and social skills. Knowing how to interact with other dogs is crucial. When breeders do a good job of socializing litters by taking them to different places and exposing them to different sights, sounds, people, and animals in a controlled way, it is probably better for puppies to stay with them a little longer.

Not every breeder or puppy-raiser is able or willing to provide top-notch socialization. Even a good breeder may have a difficult time taking a litter of puppies to different locations often for socialization. Ask the breeder if he or she is taking the puppies to new places and how often. In cases where the breeders are not doing this type of socialization, it can be better for the puppies to go to a new home at an earlier age, where they can benefit from enriched home environments and opportunities to meet many different people.

SOCIALIZATION AT HOME

Far too often, dogs are not exposed in a positive way to a wide variety of situations while they are puppies. As a result, their natural response to new situations is to react with fear or aggression or to shut down. The more new experiences you can introduce your puppy to under calm, controlled, and positive conditions, the more likely he will be to accept new situations with a confident attitude.

The secrets to expert socialization are to make sure that your pup has only positive experiences and to reward calm, confident, and friendly behavior. Even a country dog who will see little beyond farm life needs to meet people and dogs outside the farm because at some point in his life, whether for a veterinary visit or an unexpected move, he may find himself in an unfamiliar situation.

MEET THE WORLD

It's important for socialization to continue and even increase after the puppy goes to his new home. Puppies need positive exposure to many new people, other dogs, other pets, bicycles, household sounds (blenders, vacuum cleaners, and the like)—anything that they might encounter on a regular basis throughout their

lives. If your puppy may live with a cat at some time in the future or will be visiting Grandma's farm on a regular basis, he needs exposure to cats and livestock.

It might seem as if your puppy is getting lots of exposure to people, but he might not be meeting enough different people. Puppies need novelty. Meeting the same eight people or other dogs over and over doesn't provide them with enough exposure to the many types of people and animals they may encounter throughout their lives.

"Novelty" means that a puppy meets brand-new people and other animals and has brand-new experiences every week, multiple times a week. It's been said that a puppy should meet a hundred different people by the time he is twelve weeks old. This gives the puppy a broad exposure pattern and broad experience to draw on later in life. A puppy who has met only middle-aged people or only his owner's friends is less able to cope when he meets people who aren't like those he's used to: young people, people wearing uniforms, people in wheelchairs, people of other ethnicities, and so forth.

With all of this exposure, keep your dog's experiences positive. If he is exposed to a person while he is fearful, he is more likely to be fearful in the future. So, remember, it isn't about practice. It is about perfect practice.

"The day the puppy meets a person who smells completely different…or is wearing weird clothes, he can look at that person and think, 'Well, this is not too far outside my realm of previous experiences, so I'm going to assume it's probably okay,'" says board-certified veterinary behaviorist Lore Haug, who practices in Texas. Puppies who have a narrower variety of experiences may be less able to cope in new situations. "Socialization is really about inoculation against bad experiences in the future," Dr. Haug says.

GO SLOWLY AND REWARD GENEROUSLY

As you introduce your puppy to a new object, sound, sight, smell or environment, do so in a way that helps him to remain calm and unafraid. Pair new situations with lots of rewards, such as tasty treats or a favorite toy. The goal is for the puppy to have a rewarding experience with many different stimuli.

Never thrust a puppy into an unfamiliar situation (the old "sink-or-swim" method). As previously mentioned, this is called "flooding." Instead, encourage him to interact with the new stimulus at his own pace. This will help to increase his confidence.

Treat trails are a great way to encourage your puppy to approach new objects or people. Simply drop treats in a line from the puppy to the person or object. Be sure the treats aren't too far apart. Think of ants transporting food from your kitchen to the anthill. Those ants are close together, and your treats should be, too. End the trail before it gets too close to the

Be Your Dog's **Advocate**

If you have a cute puppy—or any dog for that matter—people are going to want to pet him. If you know that your dog is fearful of being touched, whether it's by men, children, clowns, or women wearing big hats, there is nothing wrong with saying, "Please don't pet my dog." In fact, it's your job as your dog's owner and friend. You don't have to make an excuse or give a reason or be apologetic or be mean. It's not impolite. No one is entitled to pet, pick up, or otherwise interact with your dog unless you allow it. Simply state your request and move on.

person or object so your pup can still feel as if he's at a safe distance.

When you're introducing a dog to something new using a treat trail, keep everything consistent. For example, if the person is sitting down, he or she shouldn't stand up during the process. Also, have the person ignore the dog as he's making his way along the trail; the pup may get nervous if he's being watched. To entice him further, though, the person can drop or toss treats in his direction while continuing to avoid looking at him.

The pup's body language can give you a clue as to how he's feeling about the situation. If his tail is down, he is typically signaling that he is stressed, unsure, or fearful. His tail tucked beneath his stomach is a sure sign that he's very frightened. Holding his ears back is another sign that he is feeling fearful. A happy dog tends to wag his tail in a wide, sweeping motion, holding it more or less even with his back. He may hold his tail slightly higher if he is interested in something.

If your dog seems uncomfortable or frightened, stop. Go back to a point where he was confident. Don't be discouraged if your dog gives up before getting to the end of the trail. Start over by placing a treat in front of him to remind him what he's doing. Sometimes, it takes many sessions before the dog becomes comfortable. When he becomes comfortable with the person, object, or situation, you can move forward with other new experiences to build his confidence.

WAYS TO INTRODUCE NEW EXPERIENCES

Sometimes socialization occurs in a casual way, but many times it's best if you set it up in advance. You will need treats or toys on hand to give as rewards, and you may need the help of other people. Enlist dog-loving friends or neighbors as your assistants. They can be especially useful when introducing your puppy to children or teaching him to accept being touched in different ways or by unfamiliar people.

MEETING KIDS

If you want your dog to feel comfortable around young children, enlist the help of a trusted child (supervised by a responsible adult) and have him or her toss tasty treats on the ground. Don't worry about whether your puppy is sitting or standing or performing a trick. The most important thing is that you can tell by the puppy's body language and demeanor that he is relaxed.

Distance and intensity are two factors that influence how comfortable a puppy is likely to feel in a situation. Have the child start by standing away from the dog to toss the treats. This teaches your dog to associate the presence of the child with good things (treats) without expecting him to get too close to the child. The greater the initial distance from the situation, the more comfortable a puppy will likely feel. Gradually decrease the distance as your puppy gets comfortable until he can take treats directly from the child while remaining calm and confident.

If the puppy is afraid of the child (or if the child is afraid of the puppy), don't force the situation. Speak to your veterinarian about a referral to a qualified professional, such as a positive-reinforcement trainer. If your pup is profoundly fearful, your veterinarian may refer you to a board-certified veterinary behaviorist.

TOUCH

Maybe your puppy doesn't enjoy being handled. He may squirm or struggle when you try to touch him. Helping him get comfortable with petting and other handling is important at this age. Problems can arise with dogs who don't learn to relax for grooming, nail trims, veterinary exams, or examination at dog shows. Teaching your puppy to tolerate touching will also make him less likely to react if an accident occurs, such as someone tripping and falling over him.

Many dogs have specific areas where they are uncomfortable being touched, such as their paws and ears. Your goal is to get your puppy comfortable with being held, touched, and moved in a variety of ways, while paying special attention to more sensitive areas. Rather than forcing him to stay still while being handled, which doesn't eliminate the fear or discomfort that causes a panicked reaction, teach him that good things happen when you're touching him. Take an uncomfortable experience and turn it into something that he not only tolerates but also enjoys.

Choose a time when your dog is relaxed and comfortable. Put a couple of treats in your hand. As your puppy is eating, touch his ears or his paws. Then, pull your hand away and let him finish eating. Repeat this until you can pet him all over while he is eating and he barely lifts his head.

If your pup still shows signs of fearful body language when you are touching him, you will need to use counterconditioning to change how he feels about being touched. To start, decrease the amount of touching. For example, if your dog is uncomfortable with his paws being handled, start petting him on his shoulder. Always offer the food first, before you start petting, and pull your hand away before he is done eating.

Once he is excited about the reward and stays relaxed when you touch him, you are ready to change it up a bit by touching your puppy first and then feeding him. Start again with a couple of treats in your hand. Touch your dog lightly and then immediately (within one second) reward him. Continue like this with longer and longer bouts of touching each time, followed by a reward.

Move in small increments that are barely noticeable to your dog, and continue only as long as he stays relaxed. If he starts to show signs of stress, such as yawning or tensing his muscles, or if he tries to get away, move your hand back to an area where he is comfortable being touched. It will take some time for your puppy to get used to having sensitive areas touched, so be patient.

Over several sessions, your puppy should begin to relax enough to let you get closer to touching his paws. Work up to holding your dog's paws for three to four seconds. If your puppy stays relaxed, work up to handling the paws for longer periods of time and touching them in different ways, such as feeling the toenails or between the paw pads.

Repeat the process for ear handling. Start petting a different part of his body and, if he stays relaxed, slowly move closer to the ear. Once he is comfortable with having you touch an ear, add different types of touch, from briefly touching the ear to holding it for longer periods to being able to move the ear around and look inside. As you progress to more detailed touching, delay the reward—in other

words, make your puppy wait until you have looked inside his ear before you give the treat.

Gradually, you can replace frequent treats with other rewards, such as a play session after being handled. If your dog is fearful of or sensitive to touch, you may always need to reward him for accepting those interactions. That is perfectly fine. Think of something that you are afraid of and how you feel when you see or hear or touch it. Wouldn't it help you to get a tasty treat or something that would calm you? Can you imagine a time when you wouldn't need that extra help? Don't deny your dog that help!

Try offering one highly palatable treat after a longer period of handling—examining his ears, for instance—rather than a series of smaller treats. If your dog continues to be uncomfortable with being touched, even with training, or if he shows aggression at any time during the training, contact your veterinarian immediately for further advice or a possible referral to a board-certified veterinary behaviorist.

PUPPY KINDERGARTEN

It used to be that puppies didn't start training class until they were four months old and had all of their vaccinations. Based on many scientific studies, the veterinary community now knows that recommendation to be inadvisable. As you know, by the time your pup is four months old, the socialization period is over. Lack of exposure is the quickest way to create profoundly fearful and even aggressive puppies. Puppy kindergarten—reward-based training in a casual, nonthreatening setting—is a wonderful way to enhance socialization and learning. It's a controlled environment where puppies can meet other puppies and people and start learning how to learn.

Puppy kindergarten has other benefits as well. According to a study of 3,897 dog owners by the School of Veterinary Science at Britain's University of Bristol, attending puppy classes on at least two occasions before the dog was twelve weeks old was associated with a reduced risk of aggression toward unfamiliar people entering the home and a reduced risk of aggression to unfamiliar people outside the home.

WHEN TO BEGIN

Many pet owners and some veterinarians are concerned about taking puppies out in public before they've completed their vaccinations. But if they've had their first set of inoculations and deworming at least seven days prior to the beginning of class, puppies can thrive in the early-learning environment. Studies show that puppies who are well vaccinated and attend class at a clean facility are no more likely to get certain infectious diseases, such as parvovirus, as those who don't.

Depending on their vaccination status and how long they've been in the home, some puppies can begin attending puppy kindergarten as early as seven weeks of age. That's the position of the American Veterinary Society for Animal Behavior, which argues that more dogs die because of behavior problems than from disease.

WHAT PUPPIES LEARN

Pups who attend puppy kindergarten classes do more than just roll and tumble with each other. Playing with other puppies helps them improve their canine interaction skills by learning to use body language and play signals effectively and controlling the power of their bite.

Puppies meet new people as well as new dogs. The location of the class can also play a role. If it takes place at a veterinary clinic, it offers positive associations with the clinic that can help counteract any frightening or painful events, such as vaccinations, that take place there.

During class, owners learn how to teach simple behaviors such as "Sit," "Down," "Stay," and "Go to Your Place" (mat or crate). Trainers can recognize small problems early on and address how to prevent them from becoming big problems.

Early classes are essential for helping puppies grow into well-adjusted adult dogs, but it is also important to socialize beyond puppy class. One hour a week for four to six weeks isn't enough exposure for your puppy to make full use of the socialization window.

BUILD CONFIDENCE FOR LIFE

Even though the socialization period ends at fourteen weeks, that doesn't mean your pup's exposure to the outside world should end. Would you send your child to school only through kindergarten? No! Your pup needs to get out in the world and keep experiencing new things until the end of the social maturity period, which is three years. The learning that socialization involves is a skill, and, like most skills, it's a use-it-or-lose-it proposition.

The experiences a puppy has during the early weeks and months of life are the most influential, but it's important to continue to challenge dogs throughout their lives. Exposing them to varied experiences, places, animals, and people—always with a positive spin—and teaching them to do different things can help to keep them mentally flexible for life.

BASIC TRAINING, LIFELONG SKILLS

Why do we train our dogs? Of course we want them to have nice manners in the home and in public. We want them to come when we call—for safety's sake, if nothing else—we want them to let us groom them, and we want them not to destroy our stuff. If your dog is fearful, teaching basic behaviors (Sit, Down, Come, Stay) as well as tricks, such as rolling over and shaking hands, can have a higher purpose. Even simple skills such as these can help your dog cope with stressful situations and be less fearful.

TRAINING FOR LIFE

Positive-reinforcement training can change your dog's emotional state from a negative one to a positive one. In addition, if he knows that he can stay safe by performing a certain behavior, he will be easier to handle in potentially stressful situations. A relaxed pup is almost always more willing and likely to do what you need him to do in a given situation.

Veterinary visits are a good example because they can be frightening— vaccinations, restraints, syringes, and thermometers! When dogs feel uncomfortable or scared, they may freeze and then progress to struggling, fleeing, or fighting to get away. Even laid-back dogs may pose unique challenges if they are being examined in sensitive areas or are afraid of certain procedures, such as nail trims. Or they

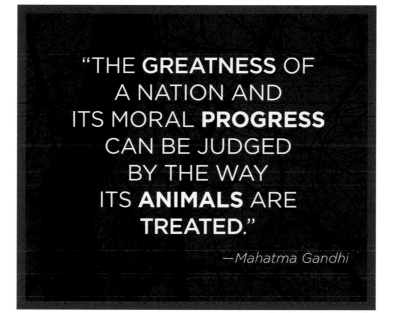

> "THE **GREATNESS** OF A NATION AND ITS MORAL **PROGRESS** CAN BE JUDGED BY THE WAY ITS **ANIMALS** ARE TREATED."
>
> —*Mahatma Gandhi*

may need guidance in tasks such as remaining calmly in place on the scale or during an exam.

When your dog panics, it increases his own risk of injury as well that of yourself and the veterinary staff. It can also lead to fear of future veterinary visits. That's no fun for anyone.

When dogs willingly participate in their care, they are more relaxed and easier to handle. Often, training your dog gives you the ability to help him to cope with handling or procedures, and this makes both you and your dog less stressed. The calmer you are at times when your dog is stressed, the more likely it is that you will be able to help him. When the veterinary team sees that you are able to help your dog, they will be able to do a better job, too.

Take tricks, for example. They aren't just for show. They can be fabulously functional. The ability to focus on performing a particular behavior or trick can help your dog calm down in exciting or stressful situations because he is focused on the trick and not whatever he is scared of.

Training is one of the building blocks of a strong human-dog relationship. A training class is where you learn how to teach your dog, and your dog learns how to learn. In class, you and your dog learn to interact with other dogs and people in different situations. Even better, training is a way to communicate with your dog. It will become for him a familiar language that may give him comfort in certain situations.

Finally, training is one of the most important factors in whether a dog stays in his home for life. In a study conducted by the National Council on Pet Population and Policy, researchers found that 96 percent of dogs given up to shelters had not

received any training. People and dogs who train together stay together.

In other words, if you want your dog to be your BFF (best *furriend* forever)—and we know you do!—training is the first step toward that goal.

CHOOSING A TRAINER

First, a note about dog trainers: there is no licensing for dog trainers, and anyone can call him- or herself a dog trainer. To find a trainer, first ask your veterinarian who he or she recommends. Your veterinarian is the best source for advice on qualified trainers. You can also ask friends whose dogs are well behaved.

It might seem as if sending your dog off to training boot camp and having him return as a canine superstar would be the logical way to go, but that leaves out an important part of the equation: you. Rather than expecting a trainer to do the work for you, look for a class where you will practice the concepts yourself, learn how to solve problems, and discover how to apply what you learn to many different real-life situations.

The trainer's answers to the following questions can help you evaluate his or her skills:

- What is your educational background in dog training and behavior?
- Do you have any certifications or other credentials?
- What training methods do you use?
- Have you taken any recent continuing-education classes? If so, what did you learn, and how has it helped you improve your skills?
- What equipment do you use and why?
- Do you belong to any professional organizations? Why or why not?
- Can I contact current or former students for references?
- What types of classes do you offer (puppy training, household manners, competitive dog sports, therapy-dog classes, and so forth)?

The best trainers not only understand dog behavior, they are also good at teaching and motivating people using positive-reinforcement methods. They don't rely on a single style of positive-reinforcement training but have a whole bag of tricks to draw on to teach dogs with different reward-based styles. If your dog is fearful, take care to find a trainer who understands how to bring dogs like yours along slowly and carefully so as to build his confidence.

Whatever his or her background, a dog trainer's most important characteristics are excellent communication skills and a thorough understanding of learning theory, training techniques, general dog behavior, breed characteristics, and, yes, human nature. If a trainer does not belong to an organization that requires members to have continuing education to maintain their certifications, do not work with this trainer. Training is always evolving, so it's important to learn from someone who keeps up with the latest concepts.

When you find a trainer who you feel is suitable for you and your dog, ask to observe a class or two before signing up. The trainer should be patient and creative in working with students, and the participants should appear to be having a good time. Do not choose a trainer who uses shock, choke, or pinch collars. There is no place for pain in dog training. Talk to people in the class and ask how they like it.

FINDING THE RIGHT CLASS

Training classes can help ensure that your dog has basic good manners in public and the basic coping skills that he needs to overcome his fears. Many training centers have provisions for fearful dogs, such as barriers to reduce reactivity. Then, over the course of the class, the

What to Look for **in a Class**

If you are observing a training class, here are some things you want to see. Does the trainer:

- Explain and demonstrate each behavior clearly before teaching it?
- Explain and demonstrate how to teach the behavior?
- Provide written instructions to give owners backup material at home?
- Allow time during class to practice each behavior?
- Spend time individually with students to work on problem areas?
- Treat people and dogs courteously?

trainer will ease your dog into the group when your dog is ready. Be sure to ask the training director how he or she works with fearful dogs in a class situation.

For a fearful dog, slow, positive training in a quiet environment can help build confidence. Once your dog has the basic coping skills, the type of class that you take isn't nearly as important as continued consistent and positive exposure to people and places as well as the relationship building between you and your dog. To have fun with your dog and continue to strengthen the bond between you, look for the following types of classes. As always, it's a good idea to check with your veterinarian before beginning any new activities with your dog, especially if they involve vigorous exercise.

AKC Canine Good Citizen: a class like this cements your dog's good manners and tests him on what he needs to know to go out in public safely and comfortably. City dogs can take an Urban Canine Good Citizen class prepares them to negotiate the crowds and distractions of city life. The CGC or Urban CGC is often a dog's first title.

Canine sports: A basic canine sports class gives you the foundation to get your dog started in activities such as agility, flyball, herding, nosework, rally and tracking.

Tricks and games: Focus on fun skills, such as teaching your dog to roll over, sit pretty, shake, ring a bell, or jump through a hoop.

Fitness: Gym for your dog? Why not? It's a great way to learn how to keep your dog in shape and have fun together. Some classes offer a combined workout for humans and dogs.

Therapy-dog class: Prepare yourself and your dog to make visits to nursing homes, hospitals, schools, and other facilities.

Baby training: Welcoming a new member of the family? A training class can help your dog adjust to this exciting event and teach you the best ways for the two to interact.

Small-dog training: Learn how to handle and train your small dog at his level.

One-off or drop-in classes: Focus on a single behavior with which you and your dog might be having problems, such as Come, Stay, No Jump, or Walk Nice.

It is important to note that some dogs are too fearful to participate in classes. If that is the case, contact your veterinarian or a veterinary behaviorist. Continued exposure to situations that scare your dog without proper conditioning will make him more fearful, not more confident.

BASIC TRAINING

Every dog, no matter his size, breed, or mix, should understand and be able to perform five behaviors on the owner's cue: Come, Sit, Down, Stay, and how to walk on a loose leash. These cues are the foundation of good behavior. If your dog knows these behaviors, then you have

Time **Limits**

A little training goes a long way. Keep all training sessions short and sweet. Repeat the lesson no more than three to five times, or limit it to five minutes. End on a high note, when your dog has been successful. Repeat your lessons several times a day, but wait at least an hour between training sessions. Remember the old show-biz adage: always leave 'em wanting more.

laid the foundation for counterconditioning, one of the most effective treatments for fears and phobias.

These skills will also make it easier for both you and your dog when you must take him to the veterinarian, groomer, or other places where he will meet and be handled by people and perhaps undergo some unpleasant experiences, such as injections, exams, a bath, or blow drying. A dog with basic skills can remain calmer in the lobby of the veterinary clinic or in the exam room because he has something else to focus on other than his fears. A dog who knows how to "shake paw" can present a paw for examination or nail trimming. And a dog who knows the Stay cue can sit or stand still while he's being combed, brushed, or dried. Teaching these basic skills is as simple as click, treat, repeat.

SIT

While Sit is helpful in everyday life to keep your dog from jumping on you, to have him wait politely while you finish a phone call, or to stop mauling you as you prepare his dinner, it can also be helpful for the fearful dog. This simple exercise can help to add structure to your dog's life so that he knows what is coming next. It can also be a tool for calming behavior as you build the Sit-Relax behavior or the Sit-Watch behavior. As you use the Sit cue more and more, your dog will begin to regard it as a safe behavior to perform that helps him in stressful environments.

You can learn how to teach Sit from your positive-reinforcement dog trainer or from reward-based training books. Teaching a fearful dog isn't as easy as teaching a relaxed dog. Even an experienced trainer may not be sure how to proceed when training doesn't go as planned.

For example, if you think that your dog is stressed, take a break. Walk away for a couple of minutes and then come back to the behavior. Often, standing over a dog (something we do when we lure dogs to sit), is very intimidating. Your dog may not respond to this method

Fear and **Listening**

How do you know that your dog really knows a behavior? And how do you know that he is really going to listen? When your dog is fearful, sometimes he won't listen. Fear, anxiety, and stress always trump cognition or the appetitive response, so as an owner of a fearful dog, you have to be willing to back up and help him. Leave your ego at the door!

and may need to be shaped, or you may need to capture the behavior. Be flexible and try different methods.

One of the foundations of building a very reliable response is *generalization*. This concept means that, in general, your dog will respond to the Sit cue regardless of where he is or what is going on. To achieve generalization, your dog needs to practice in every type of condition. For an easygoing dog, this is no problem, but for a stressed or fearful dog, it can feel like climbing Mount Everest. As you start the generalization process, work slowly and always keep your dog's emotional state in mind. Know when to call it quits.

DOWN

Down can be especially challenging for the fearful, stressed, or anxious dog because the Down position is a vulnerable position. Many training techniques start with making direct eye contact or by leaning over the dog. Some

When Your Dog **Doesn't Obey**

There's going to come a time when you ask your dog to do something that you know your dog knows—you've proofed it in all kinds of different situations—and he is going to look at you as if he has no clue what you're talking about. It might be during adolescence—in fact, it probably will be—or he might have just gotten up on the wrong side of the dog bed. Or he could be in a situation that has made him afraid. Keep in mind that a dog is not a robot. Do you perform your job or play your sport with the same prowess and accuracy every single time? Likewise, your dog will not always respond in the same way. There are a limited number of reasons your dog may refuse to do what you are asking, but whatever the cause, how you respond is important.

1. He is distracted. Maybe a squirrel, bunny, or lizard crossed his path just as you said "Sit." When your dog is distracted and doesn't listen, help him by repeating the cue. Make a note in your training journal that you haven't taught your dog to respond adequately in that particular situation.
2. He is afraid. In this case, back up to a point where he isn't afraid and help him by repeating the cue and showing him the reward. Make sure that the reward is stellar so that the desire to eat overcomes the fear. Make a note that your dog is afraid in that situation so that you can work on it later.
3. Your dog isn't motivated. This is extremely common. If you are offering dog food as a reward, and there is a squirrel running on the fence in front of your dog, he most likely won't listen. In many dog brains, running after a squirrel trumps dog food. But if you had steak—well, that may be a different story. In this case, keep multiple types of food in your training pouch in different snack bags so that your dog never knows what he will get. It will keep him motivated.
4. Your dog is confused. At home, you may use an upturned hand and verbal cue to get him to sit, but at the vet's office, when you were holding your car keys and your leash, you used only the verbal cue. Well, it isn't the same signal to your dog, so he didn't respond. In this case, you will have to work on training your dog in more situations and keeping your cues consistent so that your dog knows what you are asking and how to respond.

dogs will walk away from their owners because they are so intimidated. Often, owners raise their voices or repeat the word "Down" several times, getting louder and louder each time. This only serves to scare the dog more, so the dog refuses to comply. The poor dog may be labeled as "stubborn," but he in fact is fearful.

With the right training method, however, you can teach your fearful dog almost any cue. Remember that orangutans and elephants in zoos are taught to stand still for blood draws and medical care. You can teach your fearful dog to lie down. We can guarantee you that yelling isn't going to do the trick, though.

COME

This may be the most important behavior your dog will ever learn. For him, it's important because you use it to let him know that dinner's ready or that it's time for a walk or a car ride. For you, it's important because this cue could save his life if you need to call him away from a dangerous situation. It's not difficult to teach your dog to come when you call; the real trick is making sure he responds instantly instead of on his own schedule. As is the case when teaching any fearful dog, keep in mind that fear, anxiety, and stress trump intellect. If your dog is running from a loud garbage truck that scares the life out of him and he hears you say "Come," he may not return to you. This is not disobedience. It is fight or flight. Never punish your dog when you finally get to him, even if he has been running away for hours. Just be thankful that you got him back and take precautions so that the situation doesn't occur again.

The Value of **the Recall**

Fearful Callie bolted at unusual sounds or the sight of new people or dogs. One day, after becoming startled, she jumped out of her owner's arms and ran toward the street. Her owner called her, using "Come." They had practiced this so often in class. Callie immediately returned to her, eagerly awaiting her reward. The word "Come" was so conditioned in her that she forgot her fear and responded almost without thinking.

Mikkel Becker

WALKING ON A LOOSE LEASH

When it comes to your dog, few things are as aggravating as being dragged along when he is following an interesting scent or wants to meet the person walking toward you. It can also be dangerous if your dog pulls you off balance and causes you to fall. Many fearful, anxious, or stressed dogs will pull toward home when they get scared. They may pull into the street to get away from a stimulus.

The First Commandment

We hope that everyone already knows this, but we'd like to reiterate it just in case: never call your dog to you and then scold him for whatever he was doing (digging up your garden, eating a fast food wrapper, enjoying an interesting scent). Tell him what an absolutely fabulous dog he is every time he comes to your call. And last but not least, don't call him so you can do something he dislikes, such as trim his nails or give him a bath. Go get him instead.

STAY OR WAIT

Usually combined with Sit or Down, the Stay and Wait behaviors come in handy many times, whether you want him to remain in place on his mat while visitors enter the house, wait at a street corner as a bicyclist goes by, or not dash out an open door.

When teaching Sit or Down to your fearful pet, remember that a hand coming toward your dog's face (often the signal for Stay) can be intimidating and can make him get up to move away from you. While hand signals can be helpful, your voice is powerful, too. If your dog is afraid of hands coming toward him, don't use hand signals.

ADVANCED TRAINING

As we've mentioned, tricks are more than just fun and games. Teaching your dog some simple behaviors that are usually thought of as tricks can help you successfully manage some real-life, stressful situations. For example, you can distract a dog who barks at or chases people on bicycles or other animals by asking him to

Others are reactive and will pull toward dogs, people, bicycles, and other animals while barking and lunging. As previously mentioned be sure to choose a trainer who doesn't use leash corrections because that will scare your dog even more. Focus on the positive, rewarding him for his good behavior each time the leash is slack.

Accepting **Petting**

If your dog is fearful of being touched by a particular person, such as another family member or a frequent visitor to your home, try to identify triggers that may be causing him to be anxious or upset. For instance, is the person wearing a hat? Have him or her remove the hat in your dog's presence.

Another option is to teach your dog to associate the presence of the hat with a reward. Have the person place the hat on the floor. Reward your dog for staying calm around the hat or for moving toward it or sniffing it. As your dog gets used to the hat, have the person hold the hat in his or her hand and eventually place it on his or her head. Continue to reward your dog as long as he stays calm.

Be patient. It can take time for dogs to get over their fear, even with consistent positive reinforcement.

—*Mikkel Becker*

and stay there when the doorbell rings will keep him from rushing the door. You can use this behavior as well to prevent begging at mealtimes or to keep your dog out from under your feet while you're unloading groceries or preparing meals—including his. When it's time for him to eat, ask him to go to his mat and wait until you bring his food.

At the veterinary clinic or someone else's home, a mat can act as a kind of security blanket for your dog; it's a safe, familiar place where he can relax with a chew toy, food puzzle, or dropped treats while you wait for the veterinarian. In the exam room, a mat with a nonskid bottom can give your dog's paws

perform a series of active tricks such as Sit, Roll Over, and Spin. This can keep him occupied until the "chasee" is no longer in sight. Here's how you can use tricks to help your dog relax in stressful situations or cooperate without fear during veterinary exams, grooming, or other situations that require handling or management.

GO TO YOUR PLACE

Teaching your dog to go to a specific place, such as his bed, crate, or mat, is helpful in many different situations. If your dog barks at the doorbell or greets people a little too enthusiastically, teaching him to go to his mat

Tricks Save the Day

Val, an 11-year-old Greyhound, had been diagnosed with a type of kidney disease. Every three months, her owner took her to Michigan State University Veterinary Medical Center for a physical exam, blood draw, urinalysis, and blood pressure check. That was a big problem for Val.

"From the day I adopted her, she has been terrified of going to the vet," says her owner, Christie Keith. "She shakes and drools and her eyes roll back in her head. I have never had a dog who was afraid at this level."

Checking Val's blood pressure, which is essential to monitoring the progress of her disease, was next to impossible because her fear sent it skyrocketing. Fortunately for Christie, she's a member of Dr. Marty Becker's team, and she discussed the problem with him. "Have you tried distracting her by having her do tricks?" he asked.

Prompted by the sight of the large jar of treats in the waiting room at check-in, Christie remembered Dr. Becker's suggestion the next time she had to take Val in. She grabbed a handful of treats and asked Val to sit. The Greyhound was so surprised by the unexpected request that she sat promptly and was rewarded with a treat. Christie then asked her to shake. They went through her repertoire of behaviors.

"She doesn't know a lot of tricks, but we kept doing them over and over," Christie says. "She calmed down so much that it was the first time they were able to get a normal blood pressure reading from her."

traction and stability on potentially slippery surfaces, such as the floor, scale, or exam table. A dog who is trained to go to his mat is more willing to step onto these spots at the vet's office.

PLAY DEAD

This is a simple and entertaining way to calm an anxious dog. If your dog is upset, excited, or just needs a break, ask him to play dead. The trick also comes in handy if you want to check your dog for fleas or ticks or your veterinarian needs to examine him. The Play Dead position offers better access to areas that are normally difficult to examine, such as the belly or the undersides of the legs. Most dogs don't like being turned on their sides, but this position will be less stressful for them if it's a behavior for which they've been highly rewarded in the past.

HAND TARGETING

Teaching your dog to follow your hand or other target has many uses. A dog who jumps on people in greeting can learn instead to touch his nose to a visitor's hand. It's also a simple way to move your dog off a piece of furniture or onto a scale at the veterinary clinic or to direct his focus away from food or objects he's not allowed to have. Following and touching a target can help reduce a dog's fear of a stethoscope, nail clippers, and similar objects.

PET OR TOUCH

With this simple word, your dog can learn to accept petting or handling from other family members, from veterinary or grooming professionals, or from strangers, whether they are small children or dog-show judges. It can also be a useful cue with dogs who are visually impaired and might be startled when someone touches them or picks them up.

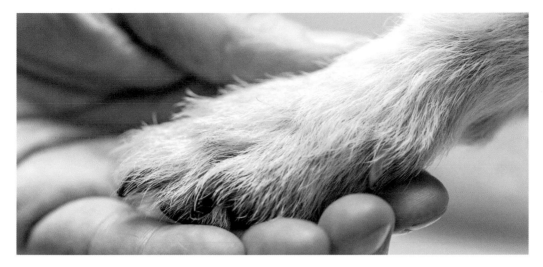

Start by saying the word "Pet" or "Touch." Touch the dog gently and then click and treat. Repeat. Always stroke in neutral areas such as the chest or side; you don't want your dog to feel vulnerable.

Depending on the dog, his startle reflex should diminish quickly. Practice with different people in different areas. If you are doing this exercise beause your dog is fearful of strangers or of a certain person in your household, start with people he knows and likes before moving on to people with whom he's less familiar, doesn't know at all, or doesn't like. Have the person stroke your dog only once or twice at first, followed by a reward. As your dog relaxes and becomes more accepting, the person can increase the time spent petting him.

SHAKE

This trick is a fun way to help boost a dog's confidence. It can help your dog accept nail trims and examinations by the veterinarian. As with any behavior, there are aspects of Shake that can frighten fearful dogs and decrease their ability to learn from this behavior. When teaching Shake, people often stand up and lean over their dogs. Remember, leaning over a dog

is often regarded as a direct threat. Fearful dogs may refuse to interact or may show signs of fear, anxiety, and stress, such as averting their gaze, looking down at the floor, licking their lips, or turning away.

Action **Jackson**

Jackson, a young male Papillon, was nervous and aggressive toward new people. He was too fearful to approach them or to accept petting.

I advised his owners to have him meet people in a large space, such as a lawn or driveway, so he wouldn't feel cornered. Afterward, everyone would go into the house together.

This helped soften Jackson's behavior, and he began to warm up to meeting people, but what really helped was teaching him the Touch command. Learning to do Touch helped Jackson have a predictable way to meet someone new, and he quickly gained confidence with the exercise.

—Mikkel Becker

SEPARATION **ANXIETY**

Pete followed his new owner everywhere she went. When she took a shower, he was there. If she walked outside to get something out of her car, he was there. If she turned around too quickly, she ran the risk of tripping over him. While it might seem as if Pete really loved his owner, his behavior was actually the first sign of separation anxiety.

Think about it. If your spouse followed you everywhere, even to the point of waiting for you outside the bathroom door, would you think that was love? Of course not! It's not normal behavior for dogs, either.

If your dog pees or poops in the house or chews destructively, especially at doors and windows, when he's left alone, or if the neighbors report that he barks or howls in distress when you're gone, he's not necessarily being bad. He may well have separation anxiety, a common canine behavior problem that causes fear, anxiety, and stress.

Dogs with separation anxiety are unable to cope with being alone. Often, these are dogs who were poorly socialized, have endured the trauma of abandonment, or simply have never learned how to be comfortable when alone. Besides being noisy or destructive, dogs with separation anxiety may drool excessively, pace, lick themselves incessantly, or refuse to eat or drink. When their people are home, they may be clingy, insisting on always being as close to them as possible. The good news is that behavior modification and medication, if necessary, can help.

THE SCIENCE BEHIND SEPARATION ANXIETY

Fear, anxiety, and stress related to being left alone is one of the most common behavior problems we see in dogs. It's thought to affect some 20 percent of dogs in the United States.

Separation anxiety is a disorder of hyperattachment. Dogs with separation anxiety experience a physiologic panic response when their owners leave them. Dogs become attached to the person with whom they are most comfortable or spend the most time. They also have a keen ability to read their environments. They learn to pair the stimuli, or cues, that precede their person's departure with that person's absence.

Cues such as picking up keys or putting on shoes become associated with the physiologic panic response. This is called classical conditioning and is outside the dog's control. What may result is barking, crying, urination, defecation, destruction, and other signs of distress when the owner leaves. Some dogs can even be aggressive, attempting to block the owner as he or she tries to leave the house.

Any dog can develop separation anxiety. We don't have scientific evidence that certain breeds or mixes may be more prone to it than others, although one study found that the Weimaraner, a sporting breed nicknamed the "Gray Ghost" for both his color and his predilection for hunting close to his owner, may be prone to the condition.

We see separation anxiety most commonly in single-owner households. It occurs with the same frequency in households with male or female owners, multiple dogs or only dogs, and in families that spoil their dogs and ones that do not. Dogs who have been through an animal shelter are more likely to have this disorder. While it hasn't been studied specifically, we

suspect that it is not the shelter itself that causes the disorder, but instead the fact that the dog has been rehomed.

Dogs are individuals, and every situation is different. It's not surprising, then, that separation anxiety can take several forms:

- Some dogs become anxious any time they are alone, whether it's for only a few minutes or all day.
- Others get upset if a certain person is gone, even if other people are in the home, while others are fine as long as another family member or a pet sitter, for instance, is present.

The Human-Canine **Bond**

Separation anxiety is related to the dog's social nature and affinity for humans. Dogs bond closely to us; it's one of the reasons we love them so much. But the traditional canine-human lifestyle has undergone a radical transformation in modern times. For at least 10,000 years, dogs have spent most of their time with us, actively aiding our survival as hunters and guardians. Two or more generations of people usually lived together. Now, cultural changes, such as dual-income families and separate family lives, mean that many dogs may spend long hours by themselves. For a social animal like the dog, this way of living can cause fear, anxiety, and stress if he isn't prepared for it.

- A dog may not show separation anxiety for years but develop it after experiencing a frightening event, such as a powerful storm, while home alone.
- Dogs may develop separation anxiety when a family member's schedule changes after months or years of remaining the same.
- Separation anxiety can occur in senior dogs undergoing cognitive changes.
- Some dogs simply never learn how to be comfortable alone.

SIGNS OF SEPARATION ANXIETY

You may not realize at first that your dog is suffering separation anxiety. It's not unusual for people to believe that their dogs are being spiteful in response to being left home alone. Luckily for us, dogs don't think that way. Unluckily for us, destructive or nuisance behavior is the only way dogs have of letting us know that they are fearful, anxious, or stressed. That's the message your dog may be sending when he expresses one or more of the following behaviors:

- Housetraining accidents
- Destructive chewing, especially at doorways or windows
- Loud and continuous whining, barking, or howling
- Drooling
- Panting
- Pacing
- Refusal to eat or drink
- Moving the owner's things around the house

You may also notice that your dog expresses his fear, anxiety, or stress while you are still at home. That's because he recognizes the signals that you are preparing to leave, such as getting dressed, styling your hair, packing your lunch or picking up your keys. Behaviors he may exhibit in your presence include pacing, whining, refusing to eat or drink, following you, and seemingly desperately seeking your attention. If he isn't destructive after you leave, however, you may not associate these behaviors with separation anxiety.

Early signs of separation anxiety in a puppy, such as following you everywhere, should cause you spring into action. Because a physiologic response is at the root of the disorder, prevention focuses on keeping the pup from having that emotional response and pairing it with your departure cues. While obedience training is helpful in many aspects of your dog's life, separation anxiety is not a problem of obedience and does not respond to obedience training. And if it goes untreated, it can worsen throughout a dog's life.

DIAGNOSING THE PROBLEM

A veterinary visit is important to rule out medical causes of the behavior. In addition to a physical exam, the vet may do lab work, such as a complete blood count, a chemistry profile, a thyroid profile, a urinalysis, and a fecal exam. Possible health problems that could cause some of these signs include dental disease, gastrointestinal distress, an ear infection, arthritis, urinary tract infection, diabetes, and Cushing's disease, to name just a few.

If your vet gives your dog the all-clear, it's time to consult a board-certified veterinary behaviorist. It can be useful to have a trained, expert set of eyes evaluate your dog's behavior. And how you proceed may depend on whether your dog is a puppy or an adult.

Other Possibilities

Separation anxiety is not always the cause of destructive behaviors. Some of the reasons include the following:

- Destructive chewing can be normal puppy behavior, an attempt at exploration, or a search for food
- Inappropriate elimination, a.k.a house-soiling or breaking housetraining, may be the result of failure to properly housetrain the dog, loss of housetraining for medical or cognitive reasons, or marking behavior.
- Vocalizations can be play or watchdog behavior or a means of seeking attention.

During a consultation, you may be asked some of the following questions:

- What does the dog do?
- How old is the dog, and how old was he when the behavior began?
- Have there been any changes in his environment or a family member's schedule or presence (child going to school for the first time or leaving for college, for instance)?
- When does the behavior begin (while you are still at home or after your departure)?
- Does the behavior occur only in certain locations?
- Which members of the family are present when the behavior occurs?
- Does the behavior occur only when the dog is alone?
- Who is primarily responsible for taking care of the dog?
- Have you tried anything to manage the problem? What was the result?

If the behaviorist suspects separation anxiety, he or she may ask you to record your dog's behavior while you're away from home. These days, dog owners can do this easily with the use of smart phones, laptops, tablet computers, or home security camera systems.

TREATING SEPARATION ANXIETY

If your dog is diagnosed with separation anxiety, your goal will be to reduce his dependence on your presence and to help him be comfortable with his own company when necessary. This is accomplished by behavior modification.

In many cases, the use of antianxiety medication or an antianxiety supplement can help reduce the dog's level of fear, anxiety, and stress. When this happens, he can then respond better to behavior-modification techniques. Medication also can slow or stop the progression of the disorder.

Thoughts on **Medication**

Among my clients, just as with any other group of people, opinions about medication vary. Some owners are ready to medicate their pets at the first visit, and others will not medicate unless it's a last resort. Still others will give their pets only something "natural."

I don't view medication or supplements as a last resort in treating emotional disorders in pets. I view it as kind and loving. I feel this way because after many years of seeing only pets with emotional disorders, I can see the animals' suffering. I wonder if someone who had a panic attack every single time his or her spouse left the house, causing physical illness and exhaustion by the time the spouse returned, would be told to take medication only as a last resort. On the contrary, this person's doctor would prescribe a medication to decrease or stop the suffering while he or she worked through whatever emotional trauma was causing the panic attacks.

My clients frequently asked me if their pet will be a "zombie" on the medication I prescribe. While the pet could become sedated, creating a "zombie" is not one of our goals. If the pet is too sedated or "out of it" on the medication, we will simply discontinue the medication, and their pet will be back to normal within a couple of days. There are so many options in veterinary behavioral medicine right now that there's no need for your pet to feel sick in order to feel better.

Clients also ask how long their pet will be on medication. Sometimes I tell them that their pet will be on the medication or supplements for the rest of his life. Sometimes it is only for six months. Generally, the earlier in the pet's life we get started with treatment, the sooner we can discontinue the medication or supplement. As a board-certified veterinary behaviorist, I am not concerned about keeping a pet on the medications or supplements that we commonly prescribe because they are extremely well tolerated, and I have many patients on these medications for virtually their entire lives. Of course, it's important to give drugs as prescribed. Never give your dog your own medication.

I want to make one last comment about medications and supplements. Clients often ask me about a "natural" product. I am a true believer in the value of good diet and natural products to improve health and well-being, including the emotional well-being of our pets. With that said, I prescribe only supplements or additives that have been tested and proven safe for use with animals and are made by a veterinary company. I would not give myself, my child, or my dog a supplement or medication if I could not be sure that its manufacturer could ensure quality. I do no less for my patients.

Medications and supplements that alter mood can increase the quality of life of our pets. They deserve it!

—Dr. Lisa Radosta

Further Considerations

Separation anxiety can be a frustrating problem for any dog owner, but it's especially concerning for those living in apartments, condos, or townhomes, who don't want to bother their neighbors or have neighbors complain to management. I have dealt with many clients who are desperate and need to take immediate measures or run the risk of getting evicted from their residence.

Some people have the luxury of taking their dogs to daycare or having dog walkers come in several times throughout the day to limit the number of hours the dog is left alone. Others work for organizations that allow them to take their dogs to work. Sounds great, right? But it is not an ideal situation when you need to use the restroom or go to a meeting and your dog cannot stay alone in your office or at your workstation without being disruptive toward your coworkers.

Often, owners resort to desperate measures such as shock or citronella collars to prevent their dogs from barking. While this sometimes helps stop the barking or howling temporarily, it does not help with the dog's anxiety. The dog may even exhibit more anxiety and fear when the owner leaves because he cannot express his distress.

Other measures involve locking the dog in a kennel or one room of the house. I have treated dogs who tore the skin off their nose, ripped off toenails, or fractured teeth and jaws trying to get out of their kennels or rooms. Several clients came to me after their dogs jumped out of windows several stories high. One canine patient set the house on fire with his frantic behavior, knocking everything over on the kitchen counter and somehow turning on the burner. Luckily, he and his canine housemate were rescued.

Many owners of dogs with separation anxiety are virtual prisoners in their own homes. They hire pet sitters to come over, or they take their dogs with them whenever they leave the house, even to go grocery shopping or to a doctor's appointment. They take great pains to find places in which their dogs are also welcome.

Depending on the city and what the owners like to do, this severely limits their choices. I know owners who have not gone to dinner or a movie—no date nights or fun excursions at all—for months and sometimes for years. Not only does the dog have a poor quality of life, the owners have a poor quality of life.

Owners can't always afford to take their dogs to daycare, however, or their dogs do not get along with other dogs or people, making a pet sitter or daycare unworkable. These dogs with severe separation anxiety require medication to manage their daily anxiety and panic. Not all dogs need medication, but there are many cases in which medication helps to reduce distress in dogs. Once the dogs are less stressed, the owners are less stressed.

It is so important to seek professional help right away if you notice that your dog exhibits anxious behavior in your absence. The sooner you address the issue and work on the problem, the better the prognosis.

—*Dr. Wailani Sung*

MEDICATIONS AND SIDE EFFECTS

Medications and supplements used to treat separation anxiety fall into two general categories: the kind that you give only before you leave the house and the kind that you give every day whether or not you are leaving. Your veterinarian or board-certified veterinary behaviorist will counsel you on which specific medications are right for your dog.

In general, if you are able to give your dog a medication one to two hours before you depart, and your dog doesn't have any concurrent behavioral diagnoses, such as generalized anxiety or fear-related aggression, your pet's doctor will likely suggest a supplement or a medication for use only prior to departures. If your schedule is erratic, where you come in and out all day, or if your dog has multiple behavioral disorders, your pet's doctor will most likely prescribe a daily medication or supplement. Often, patients go home with both a daily medication/supplement and an as-needed one. This is based on a couple of factors including severity of the disorder.

Medications and supplements can have potential side effects. In general, the medications and supplements that are used to treat emotional disorders such as separation anxiety can have the following side effects: sedation, decreased or increased appetite, constipation, vomiting, diarrhea, and agitation. Most patients never see any side effects, but it's still important to be aware of what can happen. If you're using a medication or supplement to alter your pet's mood, and your pet shows any of these signs or starts doing something that you haven't seen before, contact your veterinarian or your board-certified veterinary behaviorist.

Tick, Tick, Tick

Veterinary behaviorist Nicholas Dodman recalls the client who trained a dog with a metronome. While it was on, the owners played tug with the dog or gave him a chew treat. He always had a wonderful time while the metronome was ticking. Once it was turned off, that was the end of the good times. Whenever the people left the house, they started the metronome. It became a transitional sound, or a *bridging cue*, as professionals call it, helping the dog overcome separation anxiety.

As with so many things in life, there is no quick fix for separation anxiety. Medication alone is not a solution; it won't solve the problem without accompanying behavior modification. The use of medication along with behavior modification provides the best prognosis for resolution of this behavior issue.

The most difficult part of treating separation anxiety can be changing your own behavior when it comes to interacting with your dog. You will need to avoid rewarding attention-seeking behavior, change your routine when you leave the house or return home, set up ways to keep your dog occupied during your absence, change your dog's response to the signals that you are preparing to leave, and help him develop a calm, relaxed demeanor when you are gone. We know it sounds like a major undertaking, but it can really help if you are thorough and consistent. Most important, never punish your dog physically or verbally for separation anxiety-related behavior. Punishment, especially if given hours afterward, will do nothing but increase his fear, anxiety, and stress.

Homemade **Treat Toys**

Puzzle toys are a great way to stimulate your dog's brain and keep him occupied while you're away from home. If you simply toss a treat on the floor, he scarfs it up in a second, but if he has to work for it, his brain is busy figuring out how to get at it.

Treat-filled containers that will challenge your dog's scent skills and perseverance can be fun to make at home. The simplest is to take a small paper bag, fill it with some nice, stinky treats and tape it closed. Make a few of them and hide them around the house. You can also do this with a cardboard box, such as an empty oatmeal or cereal box or paper towel tube. Poke holes in the side so the treats will fall out as your dog shakes it.

Some hard rubber toys have a hole at the bottom and a hollow interior. Fill them with squeeze cheese or peanut butter and mix in kibble, small treats, and pieces of high-value foods such as low-fat cheese and white-meat chicken. Your dog will spend hours trying to remove all the goodies. It can be a good idea to start by stuffing the toy loosely so the dog is instantly successful at getting treats out of it. As he becomes more proficient—and more determined—you can stuff it more tightly. Freeze it the night beforehand to make it last longer. Keep several such stuffed toys in the freezer so you always have one on hand.

It's important to note that you must be cautious about leaving your dog alone with any type of toy because pieces of any toy, homemade or otherwise, could become a foreign object in the dog's body if swallowed. Inspect your dog's toys carefully and ensure that the toys are of the proper size and durability for your dog's size and strength. Don't leave your dog with any toy that is worn or that has pieces that could break off.

Whether you make your own or purchase a treat-release toy, choose one that is suited to your dog's abilities and personality. Like some people, some dogs are willing to put in only a certain amount of effort. If you leave your dog with a food puzzle that's too difficult—or too easy, for that matter—he will give up or get bored with it. You'll need to walk a fine line between what your dog will work for and what is too easy. You want him to spend some time to get at the contents but not become so frustrated that he gives up.

While your dog is seeking the treasure you've left for him, he is performing a natural behavior—foraging for food. He's not being anxious, distressed, or concerned about your absence.

FIRST STEPS

Your veterinary behaviorist will likely recommend that you ignore your dog's attempts at gaining your attention in inappropriate ways. This means not looking at, talking to, or touching your dog when he jumps up, paws at you, barks, or whines. You may need to walk away from him or leave the room altogether. Instead, teach him a calm way to interact with you, such as asking him to sit before he gets petted.

At first, your dog may double down on his efforts to get your attention. This is expected. This is called an *extinction burst*. It's important not to become frustrated or to feel sorry for him. Rewarding anxious, attention-seeking behavior will set back your efforts. Don't worry; you can still give your dog just as much love as before you started treating him. Now, the love will come after the Sit behavior. Dr. Radosta tells her clients that they are giving the same quantity of love, but it is just preceded by Sit.

You'll need to change your arrival and departure routines as well. This may involve giving your dog no attention for a set time, such as five to ten minutes before you leave, and waiting until he is calm after you return. He doesn't have to be perfectly calm to get attention. He just has to not be frantic. Departures and returns should be non-events.

PROVIDE DISTRACTIONS

When you leave, give your dog something that takes his attention away from your departure, such as a puzzle toy filled with goodies or a favorite chew toy that comes out only when you leave. Give the object about ten minutes before you leave.

Set up cues that will help your dog feel comfortable in your absence. Most dogs find comfort in chewing or eating. Others may appreciate a T-shirt with your scent that he can snuggle with or music playing in the

I Love When
My Owner Leaves!

Increase the value of your absence by matter-of-factly giving your dog a treat ten minutes before you leave. If you do this consistently, your dog will be happy to see the signs that you're preparing to leave. If you have taught him to go to his crate, his mat, or the sofa when you leave, he will rush to get into place so he can get his treat.

background. You can even put his dog toys in your dirty clothes so that they smell like you. Ask him to go to his mat or another area of your choice, calmly give him a food-stuffed toy, and then leave. When you prepare him in this way and treat your departure as a normal event, your dog learns to view it that way as well.

The board-certified veterinary behaviorist will work with you to teach your dog calm, relaxed behaviors that he can draw on when you leave. This may also involve developing bridging cues that signal him to figuratively wrap himself in a cloak of security upon your departure.

RETURN CALMLY

When you return home, instead of giving your dog an excited, emotional greeting—"Oh, Max, I missed you so much! Have you been a good,

mental stimulation when you are at home helps him feel comfortable when he must stay by himself.

Recommended activities include training practice, which provides structure and self-confidence. Practice obedience exercises daily, even if it's only for a few minutes. Training, walking, or playing with your dog on a consistent schedule can help reduce his focus on your departure, especially if you follow it up with a puzzle toy to draw his attention instead. And when you work with a young puppy on basic training cues and crate training, you help to teach him some self-control and patience—things every dog should learn.

SHORT-CIRCUITING SEPARATION ANXIETY

If you start with a puppy from day one, you have an excellent opportunity to ward off separation anxiety altogether in his life. The following techniques will help him learn to be self-reliant in your absence.

HOME ALONE

One of the most important things you can do in your dog's life is give him chances to be alone. Whether he is a puppy or adult, condition him in nontraumatic ways to being left for short periods.

good dog today?"—walk in matter-of-factly, set down your belongings, pour a glass of water, and check your voicemail or email. Then, if your dog is calm, greet him pleasantly, give him a pat, and take him out to play fetch or tug or go for a walk.

PROVIDE CONSISTENT ACTIVITY

Another element of reducing your dog's separation-related fear, anxiety, or stress is exercise. Providing him with physical and

Getting Territorial

When you take your dog with you as you're running errands, pay attention to his behavior while he's left alone. Ideally, he's hanging out, looking with quiet interest at passersby. Territorial signaling—aggressively barking or lunging at people walking by—is something you'll need to work on. It doesn't help to get him used to being alone in the car if he is going to develop territorial behaviors to go along with it. If you notice these behaviors, you seek the advice of a board-certified veterinary behaviorist who can help you to modify his behavior.

Start at home. If he is crate-trained or you're in the process of crate-training him, put him in the crate while you're doing housework or otherwise going in and out of the room. Seeing you go out and come back in every few minutes reassures him that you'll always come back.

DOWN TIME

For an older puppy or dog with some obedience training, practice Down-Stays by sending him to a mat, asking him to lie down, and telling him to stay. Reward him with a treat. Then, walk one step away. Return to him and reward him with a treat. Come back quickly, before he has a chance to get up. Repeat this until you feel very confident that he will stay. At that point, you can add two steps, and then three, and then four, rewarding randomly.

Eventually, you should be able to leave the room, always returning to reward him for staying on his mat. If he doesn't stay on his mat, just go back to the mat and put a treat on it. Ignore your dog entirely if he gets up to follow you. Walk past him and put a treat on the mat. Continue to walk away from him, staying within the distance at which you feel reasonably confident he will be successful, and then return to the mat and put a treat down. Over the course of a couple of sessions, you should see that he stays on his mat because he only gets attention from you or treats if he goes there.

LET ME ENTERTAIN YOU

For people and dogs alike, an essential element of staying alone is being able to occupy oneself in an interesting way. Whether your dog stays in a crate, in an exercise pen or dog run, or behind a baby gate, or is well-trained enough to stay out on his own, your dog needs toys or activities that will stimulate his mind without encouraging destructive behavior.

We've already mentioned treat-release toys, or food puzzles. These toys all work by extending the time it takes a dog to get a treat or kibble. Favorite chew or squeaky toys can work as well. Find your dog's bliss. Whatever you choose should be safe, sturdy, and attractive enough that your dog or puppy spends his time and attention playing with it, barely noticing that you've left him on his own. You can also hide some of his daily ration of kibble around the house or in the yard. Having him search for it bit by bit will give him a rewarding job.

Other relaxing distractions include turning on a radio to a classical or easy-listening station or turning on the television to a nature show. The noise also helps to block out sounds from outdoors that may otherwise cause your dog to bark from fear, anxiety, or stress.

TAKE THIS SHOW ON THE ROAD

There are other ways to teach your dog to accept being alone, even if you're with him. Take him in the car for brief errands. This not only gives him good experiences with car rides, it also conditions him to being left alone for a few minutes while you pump gas, drop off your child's lunch at school, or pick up your dry cleaning. Your dog learns, "Hey, I just hang out here for a minute or two, and then she's back. No big deal."

The caveat, of course, is that your schedule and the weather must fit your dog's needs. Don't try this on a hot day or when you're running errands that don't involve a quick in-and-out stop. An hour and a half in Target while your dog is in the car? No way. Getting out of the car to go to the ATM? Sure.

COMING AND GOING

If you are just starting out with a puppy, one of the most important things you can teach him is that your arrivals and departures are no big deal. Here's what to do

- Do not pay attention to your pup when he follows you.
- Ask your puppy to sit before interacting with him. If he doesn't know sit yet, lure him with a treat. This sets up a predictable, structured relationship between you and your puppy and helps him learn how to get attention from you.
- Spread the responsibilities for your dog's care among different family members. This helps him not to become excessively attached to a specific person.
- Teach your pup to lie down and stay as you do things around the house. Practicing these behaviors will help him focus on

Boredom Versus
Separation Anxiety

You come home from work, and your dog has destroyed most of your house. Is he just young and rambunctious, or does he have separation anxiety? Dr. Katherine Houpt says that in some cases you can tell the difference by what he does and where he does it.

A playful adolescent dog who is looking for some action while you're away from home typically wreaks havoc in a variety of places and ways. He tears up the sofa cushions, pulls your shoes out of the closet, and gets into the trash.

A dog with separation anxiety directs his destructive talents at exit points in the home: doors and windows. He's trying to escape so he can come find you—or anybody—to relieve his anxiety about being alone. However, he may still also tear up the couch and engage in other destructive behaviors.

The best way to determine if your dog is frightened, anxious, or stressed versus simply being bored or playful is to record what he does while you're gone. That way, you can tell if he is displaying stress signals such as frantic behavior, whining, crying, pacing, panting, and destruction aimed at any item.

something other than your absence and to feel more secure during it. It also allows you to reward him for being independent instead of clingy and to realize that even if you disappear, you'll come back.

- Avoid letting your pup see you get ready to leave so he doesn't learn to associate cues such as putting on shoes or picking up keys with your departure.
- Crate your dog at least once during the day for ten to fifteen minutes (unless you have a dog with confinement anxiety) when you're at home. He should view crate time as normal and even fun, rather than associating it with your departure.
- Whether you're leaving or returning, be matter-of-fact. Ignore your dog until he is calm and has all four paws on the floor. No emotional farewells or hellos!
- This means that he should not be following you to the door when you leave. Leave him with something fun to eat.

- Associate your departure with a rare and wonderful treat that he gets only at that time of day. Your dog learns that being left alone is not a big deal, is not stressful, and can even be desirable.

Practicing neutral departures and arrivals helps your dog learn that it's not a big deal for you to leave or to return. He should view it no differently than if you just walked out, got the mail, and came back in.

If you start early, you can teach your puppy that being home alone does not need to involve eating the sofa, howling, or licking himself raw. With patient conditioning, older dogs can learn this lesson as well. A dash of dog psychology, some tantalizing treat-release toys, plenty of training and exercise, and a puppy-proofed home can all help your pup feel safe and secure and stay out of trouble while you're away.

NOISE AND THUNDERSTORM PHOBIAS

The black-and-tan Cavalier King Charles Spaniel was normally a calm dog. Her owners never noticed any unusual fear of loud noises. That all changed one year when they took her to a friend's home for his annual Independence Day party. Everything was fine until the fireworks shows began. Although no one was setting off fireworks at the party, the house sat on top of a hill that overlooked the Los Angeles basin with a view of numerous fireworks displays for miles around. The dog began trembling fearfully and couldn't stop.

This dog's fear of fireworks is a common one among dogs. Every year, animal shelters take in large numbers of dogs who escaped from homes or yards during Fourth of July festivities.

Fireworks and thunder are the most common causes of noise phobias. Other loud or unexpected sounds that can spark fear, anxiety, and stress in dogs include gunshots, backfiring cars, or even normal household noises, such as the beep of a clothes dryer or the rustle of a trash bag. Sharp or echoing sounds may also serve as triggers. But anything unusual can initiate a dog's fear. Board-certified veterinary behaviorist Terry Curtis at the University of Florida's Department of Small Animal Clinical

Sciences recalls one client whose dog was afraid of the sound of the toilet paper roll.

Up to 20 percent of dogs of all ages and breeds suffer from noise phobias so severe that their owners seek professional help for them. When they hear fireworks or when a thunderstorm rolls in, they can go into full-blown panic mode. It's not unusual for these dogs to jump through windows, run through glass doors, dig through carpets at doorways, or dig beneath gates to escape their yards.

Fear, anxiety, or stress related to noises or storms has a detrimental effect on a dog's quality of life, putting him at risk of injury or worse if he panics and runs away. And the fear isn't traumatic solely for the dog in question. It's stressful as well to the owner, who feels helpless to calm his or her pet.

WHAT CAUSES NOISE AND THUNDERSTORM PHOBIAS?

Sensitivity to sound is instinctive to all dogs. In some, however, the reaction is extreme. Fears of loud or unexpected noises are triggered by what's called the *orienting response*. It's the brain's mechanism for awareness. When dogs (or humans) hear certain sounds, the brain instantly processes the noise to determine if it signals danger. In a more perilous past, that's what allowed them to stay alive. But now, in a world where most dogs have little to fear from predators or other dangers, oversensitivity to sound can overwhelm a dog and cause fear, anxiety, and stress.

This type of fear or phobia is suspected to result from alterations in levels of neurotransmitters,

Thunderstorm **Phobia**

Thunderstorm phobia is complex. It encompasses not only sound but also changes in barometric pressure and ozone levels, darkening skies, flashing light, the buildup of static electricity, and the presence of wind and rain, making it one of the most difficult noise phobias to manage. If your dog is fearful, anxious, or stressed during thunderstorms, ask your veterinarian for a treatment plan or a referral to a veterinary behaviorist who will work with you on a treatment plan.

such as serotonin. It's possible that this affects the limbic system and other areas of the brain related to emotions.

Dogs with a predisposition to fear, anxiety, and stress are more likely to develop noise phobias. Statistically, approximately 70 percent of dogs who react to disparate sounds develop storm phobias as well. Some 90 percent of dogs with storm phobias react fearfully to other sounds.

It's as if all of their fears become entwined. For instance, it's common for dogs with noise and storm phobias to also suffer from

How Dogs **Hear**

Although their hearing is more sensitive than ours, dogs process sound the same way humans do. Sound waves enter the ear and stimulate the auditory nerve. Those impulses are then transmitted through the brainstem into the higher brain center, which processes and identifies the sound.

separation anxiety. At one clinic, approximately 88 percent of dogs with noise or storm phobias also experienced separation anxiety. Fear, anxiety, and stress may increase exponentially if the dog is alone when he experiences the frightening sound.

For any dog owner, it's important to know that dogs with one type of fear are at risk for other fears. Having that awareness may help owners prevent or at least prepare for potential problems.

WHEN FEAR OF SOUNDS BEGINS

Noise and thunderstorm fear, anxiety, or stress can occur at any age, including in young puppies, and in any breed. Sometimes fear of certain sounds can be linked to a specific event: an unusually severe thunderstorm, a smoke detector going off unexpectedly, or, as in the Cavalier's case, a fireworks display.

In other dogs, the fear builds over time. It's not unusual for people to notice that their dogs are a little nervous during storms when they are young, only to have the condition become full-blown later in life. Dogs who live in the Midwest or Southeast, where thunderstorms are common, may become more and more fearful with each storm season. People who themselves are frightened of or startled by storms may unwittingly contribute to their dogs' fear as well.

This type of fear may also have a genetic component. Research has found that herding breeds are most likely to be predisposed to thunderstorm phobias. Selected over time for alert natures and quick reactions, they may have also developed a lower tolerance for loud noises or storms. Certain family lines of other types of dogs also show predispositions to these types of fears. It may be that genetics influence predisposition to noise or storm phobias in the way that a dog detects and

Garbage Truck **Fear**

Asumi, a shepherd/Chow mix, was terrified on garbage day. She knew exactly which day it was every week and would fearfully anticipate the arrival of the garbage truck, hearing its progress down the street well before her owners did. If the owners weren't at home on trash day, they would take Asumi to a family member's home so she wouldn't be exposed to the trigger while she was alone. The husband began to work with her outdoors before the truck arrived, practicing the Sit and Touch cues to help her relax as the truck approached.

—Mikkel Becker

interprets information about potential threats, how he recalls past experiences, or by altering the metabolism of neurotransmitters.

SIGNS OF NOISE OR THUNDERSTORM PHOBIA

When dogs who are fearful, anxious, or stressed by certain sounds encounter the frightening noise, the body reacts automatically. Physiologic signs include increased heart and respiratory rate, dilated pupils, and higher levels of cortisol—the stress hormone.

Behavioral signs are also common. They may be subtle at first and then grow increasingly severe. Here's what to look for:

- Unusual watchfulness
- Pacing
- Panting
- Trembling
- Increased vocalizations, such as whining, barking or howling
- Drooling
- Hiding
- Seeking attention

- Reacting aggressively when handled
- Inappropriately urinating or defecating
- Engaging in destructive behavior
- Attempting to escape
- Panicking

You may notice that these signs intensify each time the dog experiences the frightening sound or storm. And once his response to a sound or storm is set, it doesn't change.

DIAGNOSING THE PROBLEM

As with any fearful, anxious, or stressed behavior, it's important to start out with a veterinary exam. On the behavior side, it can help rule out (or confirm) separation anxiety, cognitive dysfunction, territorial aggression, and housesoiling. Medical issues may also cause some of these signs. They include ear or skin problems, seizure disorders, intestinal issues and hypothyroidism.

Once the vet crosses other potential causes off the list, he or she can make a diagnosis based on a history of the behavior. The veterinarian may ask when the dog starts to show signs in relation to the sound or storm, how he acts during the event, and how long it takes him to recover.

MANAGING SOUND AND THUNDERSTORM FEARS

The first thing to know is that your dog won't grow out of his fear. That's a common misconception, and it can cause owners to wait until the fear is well established before seeking help.

Don't wait if you notice that your dog reacts fearfully to certain sounds. Whether he is afraid of fireworks, thunderstorms, or other noises, you can take steps to help him stay calm. He may never completely overcome his fear, but he can be more comfortable in his own skin.

In all but the mildest cases, a multimodal approach—making use of many different techniques—is best. Generally, a fear of a few specific, easy-to-identify noises, such as the

Siren **Call**

One of my canine clients became anxious when he heard certain sounds, including sirens. He would howl for minutes when he heard one, which was usually at least a couple of times a day. Using an audio recording and rewarding calm, quiet behavior, we conditioned him to relax when he heard the sound of a siren.

—Mikkel Becker

vacuum cleaner or passing cars, is easier to address than a severe fear of a wide range of noises.

AVOIDANCE

With some noises, the simplest solution is to ensure that your dog never encounters them. Don't take your dog to see fireworks or to places where guns are being shot.

Of course, it's not always possible to avoid scary household sounds, such as vacuum cleaners or blenders. And most people can't pack up and move to an area that doesn't have thunderstorms. In those cases, behavior modification, desensitization, counterconditioning, pressure wraps, pheromones, music, and medication may be called into play. Other ways to manage the environment are sound- and vibration-proofing if feasible.

BEHAVIOR MODIFICATION, COUNTERCONDITIONING, AND DESENSITIZATION

Start by helping your dog relax. Find a reward that he likes—a special treat, a favorite toy, play, or attention—and use it to encourage him to destress in presence of the noise. Choose a reward that will come out only when the dog will encounter the scary noise (pay attention to those weather reports!). Start doing this well before he is exposed to the frightening sound. Don't plan on starting it on July 3 and hoping it works in one day.

Fireworks **Facts**

We all know when fireworks are likely to pop, pop, pop through the sky. Independence Day and New Year's Eve are the most common national holidays for fireworks. Or maybe you live near Disneyland or Disney World, with their nightly fireworks displays. The point is that it's usually easy to plan to protect a dog during these times. Here's how to keep him safe:

- Bring your dog indoors before night falls, making sure he has a chance to potty first. Make sure that gates are securely latched in case he gets out anyway.
- Close doors and windows to help muffle the sound. It's a good excuse to turn on the air conditioner if the weather is hot.
- Even if he's indoors, be sure he is wearing identification. Some dogs will make every effort to escape when they hear a frightening sound, and many of them succeed.
- Prepare a food puzzle or stuff a hard rubber toy with goodies to keep him occupied or have him practice catching popcorn that you throw to him.
- Give him a comfortable place where he can retreat if he's scared.
- It's OK to pet or massage him on the side and say, "Hey, buddy, everything's all right. I'm here with you."
- Consider taking a vacation or short trip with your pet during peak times, such as July 4 or the first day of hunting season.
- Ask your veterinarian about natural solutions, such as compression garments, pheromones, or what we call "chill pills" (can contain a green tea extract, milk product, tryptophan, or all three).
- If the more natural products won't work, ask your veterinarian if he or she recommends any prescription products that can reduce anxiety and fear and/or sedate your dog.

When your dog is in a relaxed state, say "Relax," "Settle," or "Calm." As long as he stays relaxed, reward him every few seconds. Practice this daily. Gradually start to wait for longer periods before rewarding calm behavior. Eventually, you should be able to give the verbal cue and have your dog respond in a relaxed manner.

Next, you can gradually expose him to the frightening sound. If he doesn't like the sound of the vacuum or the blender, have him relax in one room while a helper turns on the appliance several rooms away with the door closed.

For dogs who are fearful of fireworks or thunderstorms, try using CDs or MP3s with those sounds. Start with the sound set very low, so it is almost inaudible. Trust us; your dog will hear it. Gradually increase the sound until your dog is indifferent to it. The drawback to this technique for storm-phobic dogs is that it doesn't simulate the true experience of a storm.

You can spend too much time trying to make this work instead of seeking more effective help for a severely affected dog.

Reward relaxed behavior in the presence of the sound. You want your dog to start to have good associations with the sound that scares him. For instance, for a play-focused dog who enjoys retrieving or tug, start a game as soon as a storm hits and continue until it's over. Play these games indoors so you and your dog are sheltered from the elements and the full power of the sound.

A fearful dog can sometimes be redirected before he panics, especially if you do it in the early stages of the response. When noises occur that scare your dog, downplay your own anxiety, which dogs perceive and react to, and ask him to perform a behavior that he knows well or that he enjoys doing or that requires some brainwork. Practice his favorite tricks or obedience commands, asking him to do them in rapid sequence. Give lots of high-value rewards to help distract him. A challenging puzzle toy may also keep his mind off the frightening sound.

Prompt a behavior that's instinctive to dogs. Throw something for him to chase, dangle a fishing pole toy and encourage him to run after it, run down the hall and reward him for following, or start a group howl. The chase or howl may break the cycle of fear, even if just for a moment, because it engages a different area of the brain, which helps you switch your dog's focus from the sound or storm to an activity he enjoys.

For food-oriented dogs, associate delicious treats with the storm. Hand out a bite of boiled chicken or turkey hot dog every time thunder booms.

PUT ON THE PRESSURE

Gentle pressure seems to have a calming effect on some dogs. By increasing the flow of feel-good endorphins, snug-fitting T-shirts or compression garments can help decrease fear, anxiety, or stress in many dogs, especially if they are applied before the frightening sound or storm occurs or as soon as it starts.

Dogs who are panicked from a frightening sound or storm may be unable to focus on treats, tricks, or play. Wearing a compression garment can help them to regain their equilibrium and become more receptive to relaxation techniques and rewards that allow them to build a positive association with the scary sound or storm.

MAD MAX? INSIDE THUNDERDOME

Your dog may seem most comfortable in a particular room during a storm or when fireworks are going off. Practice the relaxation

Shock
Avoidance

Static electricity can build up in a dog's coat during a storm. Unexpectedly receiving a static shock during a storm may be what tips some dogs over the edge from mild fear to frantic panic.

To prevent a shocking situation, keep your dog in an area with hard floors instead of carpet. You can also lightly rub an unscented dryer sheet over his fur to reduce static electricity or spray his brush with Static Guard and then run it through his fur. For some dogs, including my own, this is all they need to help them relax.

Some people are concerned about using dryer sheets on the fur. Occasional use isn't harmful, especially if it works, but if your dog licks himself frequently, it's probably best to use another technique so he doesn't ingest substances from the dryer sheet.

A cape with a special lining, such as Storm Defender, is an alternative. The lining helps prevent static buildup.

—Dr. Marty Becker

techniques there. Access to a "safe room" will enhance his ability to relax.

A storm room has a denlike ambience—a canine den, that is. It may be a small, cozy, dark interior room, such as a basement, closet, or bathroom that is insulated from outside noise and light. Some dogs choose to go under the bed or into a bathtub or shower stall.

The area should have the atmosphere of a hideaway, giving the dog a feeling of escape and safety. If it has windows, keep the blinds and curtains closed. Flashes of lightning or bursts of fireworks can add to a dog's fear. Eye shades may help these dogs cope. A crate, with the door left open, can give the dog an added sense of security. Stock the room with a comforting toy and food and water. Make sure the dog always has access to it, even if you're not at home.

If a dog has been crate-trained from an early age, he may find respite in his crate. The purpose of a crate, after all, is to give a dog a denlike retreat, but not every dog is comfortable being confined to a crate. Shutting a fearful dog in a crate can make the situation worse. The same is true for a dog in an outdoor kennel. If this sounds like your dog, you'll need to find a better option so he doesn't hurt himself or increase his level of fear.

THE SOUND OF MUSIC

For some dogs with noise or storm phobias, music has a calming effect. It may affect behavior because sound consists of waves, and when sound waves travel through the auditory nerve to the cerebral cortex, they influence brain waves, says Susan Wagner, DVM, a board-certified veterinary neurologist.

Dr. Wagner has studied the calming effects of music on dogs with noise phobias. She says that music "entrains" brain waves, speeding them up or slowing them down. In the same way, it influences heart rate and breathing. "When brain waves, heart rate, and breathing slow, we become calmer," she says. "I believe that's what's happening with dogs as well when they listen to psychoacoustically produced calming music."

Whether it is music specifically created to calm dogs—yes, it exists—or soft classical or jazz sounds, music can help dogs relax as well as dampen scary sounds. For best results, especially in the case of a thunderstorm or fireworks in the surrounding area, play music with a strong beat. It should be loud enough

to drown out whizzes, cracks, and booms. A different option is to use a white-noise machine or an electric fan to mask the scary sounds.

You can also get a set of compact discs that combines music and sound effects to gradually accustom dogs to certain noises in a positive way. You start by playing a music-only CD while the dog performs obedience skills or tricks that he knows. Praise him or give him food rewards as he accomplishes his tasks. He learns to associate the background music with good things.

The next CD intersperses the occasional distant sounds of thunder, sirens, or fireworks with the music. The dog continues to receive rewards and/or praise while practicing his training skills. Gradually, the noises become louder as the music plays in the background, serving as a bridge between the dog's pleasant experience of being rewarded by his owner and the less pleasant experience of hearing the frightening sounds, which are now easier for the dog to handle because of the desensitization and counterconditioning.

You can also record your own sound clips of noises to which your dog reacts, such as the sound of trucks or a construction site. Play the noises quietly in the background while you practice various behaviors, such as Sit and Stay with your dog. Be sure to reward with treats and praise. You can increase the intensity of the noise over time as your dog remains relaxed.

The thing to remember about desensitization in general, and storm or noise CDs in particular, is that they're not a quick fix. It can take consistent use in all areas of the home over a long period of time for them to be effective. And, in the case of dogs with severe storm phobias, they may not help at all. Without the environmental changes that accompany storms, such as the sounds of wind and rain, dogs know very well that they're not experiencing the real thing.

EXERCISE

Daily activity boosts a dog's mood-regulating serotonin levels and releases endorphins that fight stress and help build a dog's resiliency. Exercise is also a productive outlet for pent-up energy, allowing dogs to relax more afterward. If you know a storm is coming, exercise your dog preemptively. If he's tired, he won't have as much energy to focus on his fears.

PHEROMONES

Synthetic pheromones mimic substances naturally produced by canine mothers to soothe their pups. In some cases, they may alleviate stress or help dogs to relax.

Known as DAP, or dog appeasing pheromone, the product is available as a spray or a diffuser. You won't smell it, but your dog will. You can put a diffuser in your dog's safe room (or even place several throughout the house) or spray his crate with the formulation.

MEDICATION

While the above techniques are useful and some are even highly successful, often antianxiety medication is the necessary foundation that supports successful management of noise and thunderstorm phobias. Drugs alone can't solve the problem, but they can be an important part of the solution when tailored to a specific dog's needs. Medication takes the edge off the dog's fear, allowing the other therapies to perform more effectively. Expect a wait time of two to four weeks before you see a response.

Medication is used in two ways. It may be given on a regular basis, whether or not the dog will be experiencing the frightening sound or storm. This is known as chronic dosing. Your veterinarian may prescribe an additional drug that you will give your dog only when a frightening event will occur, such as when a storm is predicted or a holiday celebration will involve fireworks. There's no reason for your dog to be traumatized by the rockets' red glare and bombs bursting in air when alprazolam (generic Xanax) is simple, safe, and effective.

Among the most commonly used medications for these types of fears are alprazolam, fluoxetine, and clomipramine. An antidepressant called trazodone can benefit any pet who routinely experiences emotional distress. Gabapentin, prescribed to treat seizures or chronic pain in pets, can also provide some sedation and relief of anxiety.

Alprazolam can cause drowsiness or sedation or, rarely, a paradoxical reaction of overexcitement. Possible side effects of fluoxetine include sedation, lack of appetite, liver abnormalities, or increased anxious behavior. Potential side effects of clomipramine are urine retention and higher eye pressures, as well as a lower threshold for seizures, especially in dogs who have a history of seizures. Trazodone's possible side effects include lethargy, vomiting, diarrhea, and panting. Gabapentin can cause drowsiness, vomiting, or diarrhea. In all cases, your veterinarian can adjust the dose based on your dog's response.

Only give drugs prescribed specifically for your dog. Never give your dog your own medication or the medication that was prescribed for your neighbor's dog who had the same problem. Doses vary by size, and your dog may be taking some other medication or have a medical problem that would be exacerbated by certain drugs.

Calming
Concoctions

For pets with relatively mild fear, anxiety, or stress, several products are available that can help them feel calm and relaxed in the face of what is normally a disturbing situation for them. Among them are chewable "chill pills," such as Anxitane; calming supplements, such as Composure Pro; and antinausea medication, such as Cerenia. Zylkene, a hydrolyzed milk protein, also helps to reduce a pet's anxiety. It's an ingredient in certain calming dog foods, but is also sold separately.

WHAT YOU SHOULD KNOW

Most important, never punish or become angry with a dog who has sound or storm phobias because punishment will simply increase his distress. Instead, set up a predictable routine and safe space for him that will help him cope. Seek professional help sooner rather than later.

Can noise or thunderstorm phobias be prevented? Early exposure, before fourteen weeks of age—and especially between the ages of seven and eleven weeks—can help inoculate a puppy against fears of storms or loud or unusual sounds. In puppy class, the

Quest to Calm **Quixote**

One of our family dogs is a mixed breed named Quixote. He is fearful of thunderstorms (which are common in Idaho), the beeps made by appliances, and even rumble strips on roads. Fortunately, we've found several solutions that have worked well for us and for him.

When we first discovered that Quixote was afraid during thunderstorms, I had never heard the myth that it was wrong to comfort a fearful dog. A storm hit, and Quixote came into my room, shaking, panting, and pacing. I picked him up and set him on the bed with me. I drew the blinds so he wouldn't see any lightning flashes, turned up the music I was playing, and started to act happy and playful with him. By acting happy myself and buffering the sound and light with the music and drawn blinds, I had a dog who was back to normal in just a few minutes.

When we're driving, Quixote tenses up if the car passes over a rumble strip, and he reacts in much the same way as he does during a thunderstorm. If we accidentally go over a rumble strip—we do our best to avoid them when Quixote's in the car—everyone in the car immediately begins to howl. In seconds, Quixote joins in and quickly forgets what he was afraid of. His instinct to join in the family howl overrides his fear of the bumpiness and the noise. The same tactic helps decrease his fear at the beginning of a thunderstorm until we can put on some music to dampen the sound of the storm.

Finally, Quixote is also fearful of beeping noises, such as the battery alert in the fire alarm, because he associates them with the power going off during a thunderstorm. Fortunately, he's been conditioned to these beeps over time. For instance, Quixote used to tremble every time my brother Lex used a new appliance to prepare food, associating the sound it made with a storm. But after a few meals, Quixote's fear disappeared because no thunder followed—only tasty food!

—*Mikkel Becker*

trainer may have you practice what to do if your pup alerts to certain noises, such as the heater or air conditioner coming on, a lawnmower, or other dogs barking. Pair the sound with something your dog enjoys—receiving a treat or playing with a favorite toy, for instance—until he is calm and focused again.

Take the initiative. When puppies and young dogs show concern, don't soothe or punish them. Distract them. Give them something positive to do, such as practicing cues and tricks with lots of treats or playing a favorite game. In other words, ignore the storm, distract the dog, and set the tone by acting unconcerned.

Teach a dog early on that storms are fun. Throw "storm parties" for puppies. This gives them a chance to associate storms with playing with special toys, eating delicious treats, and wearing a compression garment. With this use of classical conditioning, puppies can learn that storms are special.

The aforementioned strategies are the best defenses against noise and storm phobias. The next best step is recognizing the signs before they become serious and seeking the advice of a veterinary behaviorist who can initiate behavior modification and prescribe appropriate medication.

FEAR OF THE NEW AND **STRANGE**

Fearful dogs can be afraid of anything they haven't encountered previously, no matter how harmless it may seem to you. We've seen dogs frightened by garbage bags or bags filled with grass clippings, inflatable holiday decorations, metal grates on city streets, fire hydrants at dusk, people on bicycles or skateboards whizzing by, children's toys, house flies (true story), and spray bottles.

At veterinary clinics, the sight of something unusual, combined with the stink of fear left behind by other animals, can cause dogs to cower. Frightening things might include double doors swinging open, a scale, a stethoscope, or a receptionist leaning over the desk and

peering down at him. The presence of other dogs and cats—especially ones who are fearful themselves—can also be frightening.

Dogs can be fearful, anxious, or stressed in the presence of strangers as well. The approach of a person or animal they don't know, whether in public or in the home, sends some dogs into a spiral of fear. They try to hide behind their humans, duck under the bed, or run for any other safe space they can think of. Sometimes, these dogs drop down and freeze, refusing to move at all.

For these dogs, daily life can be miserable because anything new they come across makes them fearful. As with other types of fears, signs

Negative Associations

Early negative associations give birth to fears as well. A Pug who had been rescued from a hoarding situation was terrified of baby gates. She would tremble and cower whenever they were used in her foster home.

Though it seems like a strange fear, it was a legitimate one. In the hoarding household from which she had come, baby gates were used to enclose dozens upon dozens of dogs in horrendous conditions. Other Pugs from the same situation were fearful of anything new, including cars, leashes, and collars. Because they had experienced so little, nearly everything was new to them.

Katie, an Irish Setter, was afraid of house flies. She reacted to them the same way some dogs react to thunder. As puppies, she and her siblings had been found in a dumpster, so buzzing flies may have recalled bad memories.

Fears like this can become generalized. For example, if buzzing flies are the primary fear, the dog can then become afraid of buzzing power toys. In people and most likely in dogs, truly traumatic events are never erased. They remain stored in the amygdala for life.

can include the following behaviors, as well as many others:

- Avoiding eye contact
- Barking or growling
- Clinging to owner
- Lowered or flattened ears
- Cowering
- Hair standing on end (piloerection, in scientific terms)
- Dilated pupils
- Extreme vigilance (constantly tense and on guard)
- Freezing
- Hiding
- Furrowed brows
- Licking lips
- Sudden heavy shedding
- Submissive urination
- Lifting a paw
- Panting
- Tightly closed or pulled-back mouth
- Whites of eyes showing
- Startling
- Rigid forward stance
- Running away
- Tucked tail
- Yawning

NOVELTY KNOW-HOW

Fear, anxiety, or stress in the presence of the unknown isn't unusual. Many of us may be somewhat apprehensive the first time we must do something different, go someplace new, or meet a stranger. Once we experience it, we usually find that our concerns were unfounded. But dogs who are fearful of novel items, experiences, places, or people can't simply shake off their feelings.

These dogs are usually extremely fearful of people, sudden or rapid movements, unfamiliar objects, and loud noises. Dogs with these behaviors may have come from puppy mills, where they received little handling or attention; may have been abandoned to shelters early in life; or simply grew up in a backyard with no opportunity for socialization.

Some of these dogs may be genetically predisposed to fear, anxiety, or stress. Their behavior isn't something that can be fixed with socialization. The "fear" genes they inherited may be triggered at certain developmental stages. This can occur even in dogs from reputable breeders and puppies who have been socialized properly.

As we've mentioned previously, the critical period for exposing pups to a varied environment is from three to fourteen weeks of age. By the time they are four months old, their best chance to become confident canines is over. It's not impossible for them to develop coping skills after this time, but it is more difficult.

SOUND ASSOCIATIONS

Items that move and make noise are common objects of fear to dogs. Think vacuum cleaners, blow dryers, leaf blowers, skateboards, and bicycles. A dog may try to attack the vacuum cleaner or run like heck to escape it. One dog we know of ran right through a screen door to get away from a vacuum. Now, when his owners need to clean the carpet, they must restrain Wilson, who whines all the time.

Beeping noises, such as the sounds made by refrigerator doors left open, microwaves, and fire alarms, can also cause fear, anxiety, and stress in dogs. In some cases, that fear may have developed in connection with fear from another situation, such as a storm. Maybe the power went off and the dog associates the beeping with that event.

Sandie was afraid of the toaster oven, moving away in alarm when it beeped. Then she began barking at it, prompting family members to yell at her to be quiet. This only worsened the situation and caused her to begin barking before the appliance beeped. The owners resolved the situation by helping their dog develop more positive associations with the sound of the beep and teaching her

Toy Trauma

Even something as simple as a child's toy can light up a dog's fear circuitry. When QT came to stay with us while my parents were away on a trip, he was terrified of a Barbie horse that neighed and made other noises. We had to condition him with target training to help him develop a positive association with the toy horse and learn not to be upset by it. We did similar training with other objects, such as the vacuum cleaner.

Dogs like QT develop fears of objects with visual and auditory components. For instance, he was afraid of water bowls, especially if they produced unusual reflections. If his dog tag happened to touch it at the same time, he'd really jump. Any combination like that was enough to scare the living daylights out of him.

—Mikkel Becker

an alternative behavior (Go to Mat) when she heard it.

HOLIDAY HORRORS

We tend to associate holidays with good times, but for fearful, anxious,or stressed dogs, they can be filled with terrors: people in costume, gigantic inflatable jack-o-lanterns or spiders billowing in the breeze, eight reindeer pulling a sleigh holding jolly old Saint Nick, snowmen, 6-foot bunnies holding baskets of eggs. You get the idea.

Our colleague Dr. Nicholas Dodman treated a Silken Windhound who responded to neighborhood Christmas decorations as if she were running a fiery gauntlet. Light-up reindeer and moving Santas were enough to send her into an all-out panic and cause her to attempt a mad dash for home.

THE VETERINARY CLINIC

What aren't dogs frightened of at the doctor's office? A dog's fear begins to build even before he walks through the front door as he passes posts, walls, or doors where hundreds, if not thousands, of other dogs have posted "pee-mails," indicating their own fears. They've also deposited poop piles scented with anal gland secretions that emit warnings as well: "Abandon hope all ye who enter here."

Then he goes inside, only to be greeted by the smell and sight of other dogs and cats, not to mention strange humans. A receptionist behind the counter stares down at him. The harsh odor of cleaners and disinfectants shuts down his olfactory neurons—for as long as a week! Coming from the back room are the sounds of frightened animals barking, crying, meowing, squealing, or howling.

Double doors swing open and the dog is led, lifted, or pushed onto a scale. He enters an exam room and is placed on a cold, slick, elevated metal surface. His rear end is violated with a thermometer, and a stethoscope stinking of fear

Fear Aggression

Does your dog bark and growl fiercely when he encounters something he's afraid of? An agonistic response to unknown humans or other animals, to sudden movements, or to an unexpected experience is what's known as fear aggression.

Although it appears as though the dog is going on the offense, he's really behaving in a defensive manner. His goal is to put distance between himself and whatever or whoever has scared him. If he can't run away because he's restrained by a leash or otherwise unable to escape, he'll use his bark, his teeth, or whatever he's got to protect himself from what seems like a dangerous situation. Going to a place that the dog associates with an unpleasant experience, such as a veterinary clinic or grooming shop, may also elicit an aggressive display.

Dogs who haven't been properly socialized or who have a genetic tendency toward fear aggression usually begin to exhibit aggressive responses to fear when they are six months to two years old. Males and females of any breed or mix can become fear aggressive. This behavior can begin at eight weeks in affected pups. It's something to watch for so that treatment can begin before behaviors become ingrained.

Early signs of fear, anxiety, and stress are lip-licking and showing the whites of the eyes. With some dogs, these may be the only warning signs you get before they move on to aggressive behavior.

Any time you see fearful body language or an attempt to escape a person or circumstance, remove the dog from the situation before his fearful behavior escalates to growling, barking, lunging, or biting. Watch carefully to see what objects, people, or situations make him afraid. Pay attention to how close a person or other animal can get before your dog displays signs of fear. That's the kind of information that can help you and a behavior professional identify his triggers and develop a plan for behavior modification—before the problem becomes worse.

Finally, never punish a dog for fear aggression. It just confirms his belief that he was right to be scared. Teaching him that seeing a woman carrying a large red handbag, the trash collector, or a police officer in uniform means he's going to get a great treat is by far the better way to go.

from other animals is placed on his chest by a stranger looming over him and restraining him so he can't move. Emanating from the dog's owner is a distinct sense of fear and discomfort as the veterinarian pulls out a syringe and prepares to inject a vaccine or draw blood.

Heck, it's no wonder that dogs don't like going to the veterinarian. The visit is full of surprises—which dogs don't like—and not especially pleasant ones at that. Even the most laid-back dog—let alone a fearful, anxious, or stressed one—can become uncomfortable or downright scared in this situation, especially if he is in pain or being handled in a sensitive area.

Dogs can become accepting of veterinary visits when they are taught what is expected of them and ways to remain calm. They can learn to sit quietly in place on a scale or exam table. The veterinary staff can help by hiding the presence of the scale or providing a nonskid surface on the exam table. We'll talk more about ways to help your dog relax at the veterinary clinic in chapter 10. The bottom line is that when dogs willingly participate in their care, they are easier to handle.

TREATING NOVEL FEARS

Dogs with extreme fears need professional help. If you have a fearful dog who wasn't socialized, or you don't know your dog's socialization history, don't flood him with new experiences in an attempt to make up for the lack of socialization. The likely result is that his fear will increase exponentially. The techniques we discuss in this chapter may help, but if they are not working, seek guidance from a veterinary behaviorist.

For adult dogs with these types of fears, gradual and patient desensitization and counterconditioning can help to overcome fear: pairing the scary thing in small doses with something the dog likes. You can do this by carefully exposing your dog to a particular frightening object, person, or situation and using food rewards to replace the fearful response with a calm and relaxed emotional response. Our colleague Dr. Wayne Hunthausen of Animal Behavior Consultations in Westwood, Kansas, says: "The secret is controlling the volume, the size, or the distance of exposure to the thing a pet's afraid of and gradually increasing the exposure."

OBJECT FEARS

Take a dog who is frightened of trash bags. Start by picking up a small piece of a bag, say, 3 inches square. When your dog notices it, give him a treat and set down the scrap. As your dog becomes comfortable with that, you can gradually increase the size of the piece, continuing to reward him when he sees it and remains unafraid. Eventually, he'll associate the sight of the bag with a treat, not trepidation.

Another option is to teach the dog to touch his nose to an object in exchange for a treat or other reinforcement. This method is called targeting. It could be useful for a dog who is fearful of inanimate objects, such as spray bottles or stethoscopes. More detailed explanations of these exercises can be found in the Appendix.

FEAR OF OTHER ANIMALS

You may have a dog who is fearful of other dogs, or cats, or squirrels. Maybe he barks, lunges, or begins huffing indignantly when he sees them. Counterconditioning can work for this type of fear as well.

Always have treats easily accessible when you walk your dog. If you see another dog in the distance, stop and ask your dog to sit and watch you. This takes his focus away from the approaching dog. While the other dog is still at a distance, reward your dog with a treat or attention for remaining calm.

Teach him to perform an alternative behavior to barking, growling, or huffing when he sees other animals. This could be looking at you, sitting, offering a paw, or turning around. With practice, your dog will learn to look to you when he sees another animal instead of reacting fearfully.

PEOPLE PANIC

A similar technique can be used with dogs who are fearful of people. Let's say your dog was startled when your new beau, who the dog hadn't yet met, walked into the house carrying a large bouquet of flowers. Your dog barked and growled and now won't go near him.

To bring about what should be a congenial threesome, use special treats and mealtimes to associate the new person with good things. While the person is in the room, give the dog cubes of cheese, steak, or hot dogs. Give these treats only in the presence of the feared person.

If your dog won't take the treats, the person is too close; have the person move away to a

Nosing **Around**

Building a dog's confidence is a super way to decrease fears of novel objects and environments. One way to do this is through the sport of nosework. Any dog of any age, breed, mix, or ability can play. It's also perfect for dogs who are reactive to other dogs because only one dog searches at a time. The others wait their turn while crated in a separate area.

The dogs learn to identify specific scents—anise, birch, and clove—and search different types of spaces and containers, including vehicles, rooms, and boxes. Working at their own pace, they gradually become comfortable with many different types of objects, flooring, interiors, and more. As they learn, the boost to their ego is almost tangible.

No obedience commands—and no corrections—are necessary. What dogs do get is plenty of food or toy rewards and praise when they find the hidden odors. It's not unusual for dogs low in confidence to rapidly gain self-assurance as they participate.

point where the dog is comfortable. Gradually, your dog will become more comfortable in the person's presence, at which point your significant other can begin to toss treats to the dog while looking away from him.

Eventually, you can have the new person in your life give the dog his meals. That usually seals the deal, especially for food-motivated dogs. For dogs who are not food-motivated, the person can offer toys, praise, attention, and play instead.

Maybe your dog is afraid when guests enter your home. There's no need to stop having friends over for weekend barbecues. Again, you can gradually expose your dog to visitors from what he considers a safe distance and reward him with treats when they are in sight. Have your guests toss him treats without looking at him. If you do this every time you have guests, your dog will come to associate them with his favorite turkey hot dogs or cheddar squares. He may learn to love seeing visitors walk into the house.

Dogs who are afraid of guests don't need to be exposed to them for the entire visit. That can be extremely stressful for you, your guests, and your dog. If you aren't prepared for or desirous of working with your dog during a particular visit, other options are available. For instance, the dog can stay in a sanctuary room, one where he is comfortable and has his needs met: a resting place, water, a long-lasting treat-filled toy, and other toys for entertainment. Take the dog to the sanctuary room ten minutes before guests arrive and bring him out after they leave.

It's OK for the dog to come out of his room and join the party for a short period and then go back to his room for some peace and quiet. An alternative to a sanctuary room is to use an exercise pen to set up an area where he can retreat (or be taken) if he seems overwhelmed. This allows the dog to keep his owner in sight without directly interacting with guests.

For dogs who are fearful of strangers approaching during a walk, use a similar technique of rewarding him while they are still at a distance and then moving away before the person gets too close. As you see improvements, let the person get closer. If you can set it up the scenario in advance, have the person toss a treat to the dog from a comfortable distance, without looking at or speaking to the dog, and then walk away. End each session while your dog is still comfortable in the situation.

In any of the aforementioned situations, or any fearful situations, dogs who show aggression should be seen by a board-certified veterinary behaviorist. Owners should avoid trying to treat them on their own with these techniques.

Your dog will gradually become more comfortable as strangers approach because he associates them with tasty rewards. When he is finally comfortable in their presence, you can have people offer him a treat by hand, being careful to hold it beneath the dog's mouth.

In any such situation, always go slowly and go back to a previous comfortable distance if the dog begins to show fear. Be sure he has an escape route or otherwise feels protected from the person's approach so he doesn't feel the need to bite or show other aggressive behaviors. If you are patient and kind, there's a good chance that your dog can become less fearful of or even welcoming to others.

FADE THE FEAR

Whatever your dog's fear, it's important to stay calm. Never expose your dog to a frightening item or person beyond his comfort level. If he shows signs of anxiety, such as drooling, licking his lips, putting his ears back, yawning, or scanning the room for an escape route, back off. You're moving too quickly. It's important to remember that it can take time to build on your successes.

In some cases, medication may help a dog make the transition to a fear free life. A pharmaceutical solution in tandem with a

Same Person, **Different Look**

Sometimes it's necessary to desensitize dogs to the same person in different positions or areas. Your dog might be comfortable with a person who's sitting down but anxious if the person stands or is carrying a briefcase or puts on a hat. And some dogs are fearful of people in uniforms—even people they know and love—but are fine once that person changes into street clothes. You can use the same techniques to accustom the dog to these changes in posture or appearance.

behavior modification plan can benefit fearful dogs both in the short term and for a lifetime.

Remember that punishment will never help a dog to lose his fear, but patience, compassion, and, if necessary, professional guidance from a behavior professional can help your dog cope with or overcome his issues.

PART III

PUTTING YOUR DOG'S SKILLS INTO PRACTICE

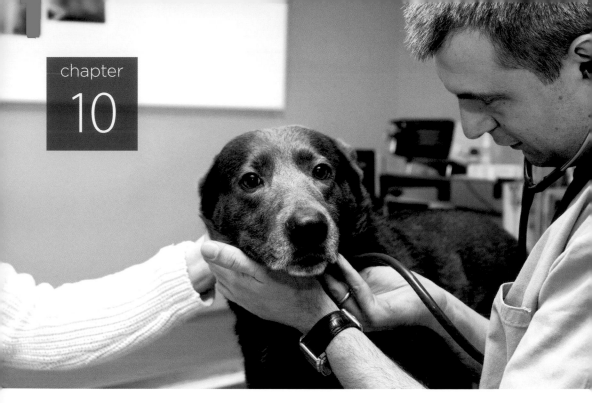

VISITING **THE VETERINARIAN**

Keeper walks into the veterinary clinic willingly, but as soon as the vet places him on an exam table, he turns into a brown-and-white twister, trying every move possible to escape. He was found as a stray and brought to a shelter, so his owners don't know his background, but they do know that he had to be treated for heartworms and that the intramuscular injections were painful. That may be the reason that Keeper fights with all he's got to stay off that exam table.

He's not alone. Many pets have had frightening or painful procedures at the veterinary clinic. Although we now have better ways to reduce pain, we can't always prevent it,

but we can take steps to prevent or reduce the fear factor.

Keeping pets calm during vet visits helps to ensure that they are easier to handle during exams or other procedures. When stress doesn't mask or change vital signs such as temperature, pulse, respiration, and blood pressure, a more accurate diagnosis is possible. Blood work is more accurate, too, and it's easier to identify signs of sensitivity, pain, or illness.

Reducing a pet's fear, anxiety, or stress is better for everyone involved. Dogs are less likely to panic and become aggressive, and that makes the dogs, veterinarians, technicians, and owners safer as well. Discuss the following

Prepare Your **Pup for Veterinary Handling**

- Perform mock veterinary exams at home, running your hands over your dog's entire body, including sensitive areas, such as paws or the groin area, as well as the following exercises:
- Practice giving him a restraining hug—without getting in his face.
- Get him used to being held in your arms. It can help to give rewards and add a verbal cue, such as "Still."
- Play "pass the puppy" at training class to help him become accustomed to being held and handled by many different people. Reward him with treats and praise when he remains calm while being handled.
- Ask if your veterinarian offers a class that provides puppies with a positive play and training experience at the clinic, as well as experience with the environment, such as standing on the scale or associating the smell of alcohol with training and play.

These techniques are appropriate for dogs who are not fearful or aggressive. Consult a board-certified veterinary behaviorist for help if you are dealing with a dog who is aggressive.

ideas with your veterinarian to help create better visits for your pet. If you're seeking a veterinarian, look for one who is Fear Free certified. Your pet will love you for it.

START AT HOME

That's right: your pet's relaxing and fun veterinary visit begins at home, well before he needs to go to the veterinarian. He needs to become accustomed to staying comfortably in his carrier and to riding in the car. Getting him used to and even enjoying those two things is half the battle.

THE CARRIER

You may use your dog's regular crate as his carrier, or maybe you have a different carrier that you use only in the car. Either way, it should be your dog's "happy place." The ideal carrier has an easily removable top so you don't have to wrestle your pet in or out of it because that just adds to the potential for fear, anxiety or stress.

Start by leaving the carrier out in a conspicuous area in your home so your dog can investigate it at his own pace. Spray the interior with a canine pheromone product, which mimics the calming pheromones that mother dogs produce after giving birth. It's a chemical communication processed by the vomeronasal

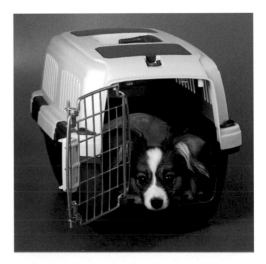

Slick **Trick**

One of the things dogs can object to about a veterinary visit is the slick floor. Slip-sliding away isn't their idea of a good time. A slippery floor can cause a dog to feel unsteady on his feet, leading to panic, or it can make it challenging for him to stand, move, or stop, especially if he has a health problem that affects his mobility. For instance, dogs with arthritis are often hesitant on slick floors because it's painful for them to struggle to stay upright or they may have weak leg muscles from disuse.

If you have a puppy, now is the time to teach him to traverse slick floors with confidence. A positive experience now will help him cope anywhere he finds slick floors, including the veterinary clinic.

While early socialization is important, it's not too late for older dogs who don't have arthritis and missed out on this training to gain confidence or reduce their fear. Training can help them relax on slippery floors and associate them with rewards.

Start with mealtime. If you have wood or tile floors, and your dog is fearful of walking on them, place his food bowl on a nonskid surface next to the flooring he's afraid of. At each meal, move the food slightly closer to the slippery floor and eventually onto it, placing it farther out each time. Change the position only by inches and only as far as the dog is comfortable enough to eat. This tactic helps him gradually become accustomed to the scary surface as well as to associate the pleasure of eating with being on the slick floor.

Alternatively, you could lay a treat trail across the slick floor for him to follow, or you could toss treats to encourage him to venture onto it, followed by more treats for staying on the floor. A related technique is to put peanut butter or squeeze cheese on a wooden spoon or a pretzel rod for the dog to lick as he follows you onto the floor.

You can also play a low-key game of tug or fetch with a soft toy, tossing it to get his attention and gradually moving the game farther onto the floor as he becomes comfortable. Always give him the option of moving onto the floor on his own; never drag or push him onto it because that can increase his fear, anxiety, or stress.

Practice training exercises on slick surfaces. If your dog knows a "Heel" or "Walk nice" command, walk back and forth across the floor, offering plenty of rewards to sweeten the deal. Techniques such as hand targeting can also encourage your dog to step out on a slippery floor (see appendix for techniques).

For dogs who are unsteady on their legs for physical reasons, give them a little traction with helpful accessories such as canine booties with nonskid bottoms and disposable paw grips and nail grips. To reduce slippage, it's also important to trim your dog's nails and the fur between his paw pads.

If your dog has arthritis, skip this training. Put down nonskid mats or rugs so he can walk safely and comfortably on your floors.

organ rather than by the olfactory pathway. Your dog may recognize and associate it with a feeling of security.

Randomly stash treats inside the carrier for your dog to find. If you notice him inside the carrier, praise him—"Good crate!"—and reward him with treats or a special toy that he gets only when he's inside the crate. You can also give him a nice neck massage when he's inside the carrier and even give his meals inside it. These practices will help your dog associate his carrier with good things.

THE CAR

If you have a puppy, he may not have had any bad experiences with car rides. Make his time fun and desirable by associating it with positive experiences. First, spray the interior of the car and the carrier with a pheromone product. Your nose won't notice it, but your dog's vomeronasal organ will.

Next, have your puppy hang out in the crate inside the car without starting the engine. Give him some treats or feed him a meal while he's there.

When he's comfortable with the carrier, it's time for some test drives. Take him on short errands that don't require you to get out of the car, such as driving around the block or a trip to a drive-up bank teller or drive through window at a restaurant. There's a good chance that the bank teller will have a treat for him, or you can

Carrier Tips

Ask your dog to enter the carrier on cue or lead him into it with a treat trail. If those techniques don't work, gently place him inside it. If you put him in the carrier inside your house and then take it to the car, carry it as if it were a large piece of your Grandma's best china, supporting it with your hands beneath the carrier.

Easing Motion Sickness

A dog of any age can experience motion sickness. Puppies can be prone to motion sickness because their inner ear structures, which control balance, aren't fully developed, but they may outgrow the problem. If you're dealing with a carsick dog, here are some tips to help:
- Limit your dog's food and water, starting a couple of hours before the car ride.
- Provide fresh air by rolling down the windows a few inches.
- Keep the car's interior cool.
- Make sure the crate or carrier sits on a level surface.
- Ask your veterinarian for a prescription antinausea medication.
- Adopt a smooth driving style. Stay at steady speeds and avoid sharp turns or rapid stops.

give him a small bite of burger or french fry to enhance the experience.

Gradually increase the distance you travel and the amount of time he's in the car. Make trips to fun places, such as a nearby park or a local hiking area. With gentle, consistent handling and experiences, he should be a pro in no time.

Some dogs are fearful of riding in the car because they've had previous experiences with motion sickness, accidents, or places they didn't want to go, such as the veterinary clinic or grooming salon. Fear of car rides can also be

associated with a previous injury or frightening experience, such as being thrown to the floor during a sudden stop or being hit with a flying object when his head was hanging out the window (which could have been avoided if he had been safe inside a carrier). Fortunately, there are a number of ways to help your dog leave his fears by the wayside.

As previously mentioned, treat the car and carrier with a pheromone product and give your dog some pleasant associations with treats or meals given in the carrier while it's in the car. Once you start driving him places, always make sure the ride ends on a happy note, with a fun experience, treats, or praise.

Some dogs are anxious in a carrier. And in some cases, your dog's crate or carrier might not fit in your car. In these cases, a good solution is to train your dog to "Go to Place." The place should be a mat or another portable safe place where your dog can retreat, such as his dog bed, a blanket, or a yoga mat, for instance.

When you train "Go to Place" at home, load the mat or bed with long-lasting tasty treats.

Once your dog knows this cue, you can use the mat or bed in the car to provide him with a familiar place that will help him stay calm during the ride and at the veterinary clinic, both in the lobby and the exam room. For additional relaxation, treat the mat with Adaptil or soothing essential oils, such as lavender.

It's also important to tell your veterinarian about your dog's fear of car rides. It's possible that an underlying health condition—for instance, motion sickness, vertigo, seizures or pain from arthritis, neuropathy or joint issues—

Car Safety

Part of making a car ride pleasant for your dog is to make sure he rides safely. You don't want him sliding around, sitting at a slant, or becoming injured or even thrown out of the car because he was riding loose. The following tips will help him stay secure and out of harm's way:

- If you have a small dog in a small carrier, place the carrier on the floor behind the front passenger seat. Studies show that it's the safest place for a dog to be in the event of an accident.
- Avoid buckling crates in with the seatbelt unless this is advised by the manufacturer as a tested and approved method. Buckling it in can increase the risk of damage to the crate and injury to your dog.
- Consider purchasing a vehicle crash-tested harness or carrier to transport your pet. He may seem safe in a crate or pet safety belt, but crates can buckle and crumple on impact, and some harnesses can cause injury if they haven't been tested properly or aren't made of durable materials. Information on vehicle safety-tested products is available at www.centerforpetsafety.org.

may be related to his behavior in the car. Your dog's behavior may change once the health issue is addressed.

PRACTICE RUN

If at all possible, it's best to make at least one or two "practice" visits to the vet before your dog experiences the real thing, especially if he is fearful. It is best to go slow and have multiple short, happy visits building up to the real deal. Your veterinarian's team should want to work with you to ensure that your dog is comfortable in the clinic. As much as you do, they also want your dog to think it's normal and fun, not scary and painful, to come to the clinic.

Set up "victory visits" that allow you and your dog to practice going to the hospital for different elements of the visit. For the first one, you might simply go in to say hello to the receptionist and have your dog receive some treats. Or he might go in and get on the scale and be rewarded by staff.

On another visit, let him explore the lobby and get a tour of an exam room—without getting put on an exam table. Ask him to

Relaxation by **Laser**

Another way to help your dog relax and enjoy his veterinary visit is for the veterinarian or a technician to give him a soothing low-level laser treatment. Laser therapy stimulates the parasympathetic nervous system and helps pets be less fearful. Your dog won't feel a thing except relaxed.

perform some tricks. Doing something he's good at will help him relax and give him another opportunity for a reward. Later, you can work on handling and practice mock procedures to prepare him for the full care he'll eventually receive.

Check with the staff beforehand to find out what days or times tend to be quiet. Some veterinary clinics have open hours for practice visits. Others set up specific appointments so a technician or trainer can work with you.

BRINGING IT ALL TOGETHER

So, it's time for your dog's visit to the veterinarian. We're going to discuss ways to proceed for dogs making a first visit or who haven't had any bad experiences at a veterinary hospital as well as for fearful, anxious, or stressed dogs.

GETTING READY

In the case of a fearful, anxious, or stressed dog, you may need to start planning for a veterinary visit a day or two in advance. This could involve acquiring medication or a compression garment, for instance, or limiting the amount of food your dog receives. Unless he has a medical condition that dictates otherwise, it can be a good idea to withhold food after 6 p.m. the night before the visit. This ensures that he's a little hungry when he gets to the clinic and will respond more eagerly to food rewards. On the other hand, if you know that your dog gets cranky or agitated when he misses a meal, go ahead and feed him as you would normally or simply give a little less food.

If it's not already out, place your dog's carrier near the door at least a day or two beforehand. Ideally, it is out in your home all the time so that it's a normal part of his environment. That way, the crate's appearance doesn't necessarily signal a trip to the veterinarian.

Using a diffuser or spray, release pheromones in the room where your dog spends most of his time. This will help put your dog in a relaxed state of mind. About an hour before you depart, to give the pheromones time to spread, line the bottom of the carrier with an absorbent pad and top it with a towel or other bedding treated with pheromone spray. It's also a good idea to place an item in the carrier that holds your scent, such as a T-shirt you've worn.

Don't forget to pack plenty of treats. Bring food your dog gets only on special occasions, such as deli turkey or cheese cubes. These can be a lifesaver in a potentially stressful environment. Feel free to hand them out liberally to help your dog associate the clinic with good things.

What if you already know that your pet is fearful, anxious, or stressed in the car or at the veterinary clinic? Let your veterinarian know beforehand so he or she can recommend a chewable "chill pill," calming supplement, or antinausea medication to help reduce your pet's anxiety. Be sure you get instructions on when to administer the medication. Depending on the type of medication, you may be able to give it with something your dog loves, such as whipped cream, yogurt, cottage cheese, or canned dog food.

Cover **Up**

Fearful, anxious, or stressed pets may also benefit from riding in a carrier with a cover, such as a towel, over it. A cover blocks visual stimuli during transportation and while the animal is in the waiting room. Limiting his vision can help him remain calm.

Still worried about trying to get your dog to take medication? He can wear calming items instead. Ask your veterinarian about a pheromone calming collar. Put it on your dog one to two days before the veterinary visit and leave it on for two to three days afterward.

Some veterinarians have a "lending library" of vision-restricting headgear or soothing compression garments. A compression garment

Double Up

Often pet owners will bring more than one dog in at a time for vaccinations or wellness checks simply for convenience. I encourage this because many times a dog is much calmer if he has a buddy with him for moral support. But if that doesn't work, we have other ways to help.

I remember one time when a pet owner brought in two dogs to see me at North Idaho Animal Hospital. One was an older black Lab named Lucy, and the other was a small terrier named Gruff, who had hair that stood up like Rod Stewart's. Both dogs had taken "chill pills" before coming in. They had worked great on the Lab, but Gruff was jumping around the room as if he'd swallowed a bowlful of jumping beans.

In the past, we might have just powered on through the exam without too much concern for Gruff's emotional well-being, but knowing that Gruff was fearful, anxious, and stressed, I stopped the exam to give the dog a little love. After handing his owner a jar of peanut butter and a couple of pretzel sticks to keep Gruff occupied, I put the "treat" into treatment by using a Class 2 laser along the dog's dorsal spine, from the base of the skull to the tip of the tail. This laser projects in two parallel beams (four frequencies), so you can actually see the red laser light along the whole body.

In less than thirty seconds, Gruff's head began to sag from relaxation; after a minute, he was so relaxed that he could hardly sit. The owner was delighted with our use of high-tech, high-touch tools to take her dog from wild to mild in just one minute.

—Dr. Marty Becker

Now that you know the signs of fear, anxiety, and stress, you can experiment to see what types of interactions or distractors work best with your dog while he's in the car; these could include talking (or not talking) to him or playing certain types of music. Know what your dog likes and use it. If you normally talk to your dog in the car, carry on, but if you hardly ever talk to him in the car and then suddenly switch to baby-talk during the drive, you may inadvertently send the message that something unusual or unpleasant is about to happen, which could make him fearful, anxious, or stressed. Instead, turn on the radio or carry on a normal conversation with anyone else who's in the car with you.

Don't forget the value of music or music designed specifically to calm pets. A study led by Deborah Wells at Queen's University in Belfast, Northern Ireland, demonstrated that classical music calmed dogs, making them rest more and stand up less. Depending on your tastes—and your dog's—try Vivaldi, Mozart, harp music, Harry Connick, Jr., or show tunes. Pet-inspired music includes *Songs to Make Dogs Happy, Calming Music for Pets,* and *Through a Dog's Ear.* Just don't choose anything that's so

fits snugly and may give your dog a feeling of security. It can help to spritz it with pheromones before putting it on your dog.

If you are making your first visit to a Fear Free veterinary practice, the veterinarian may ask you in advance to fill out a checklist of actions that cause your pet to become fearful, anxious, or stressed. These may include such things as being weighed; being lifted onto an exam table; being restricted; lying on his side; having ears, teeth, or other body parts examined; being pilled; having his temperature taken or his nails trimmed; or having the vet's face come in close for an exam. You may not have noticed some of these things previously, and your dog may not react to them, but they are common "fear factors" for dogs. It's always good to be aware of the possibility.

ON THE ROAD

If you are using a carrier, be sure to place it in a comfortable, untilted position. Lift him into the carrier if you can, or teach him to walk up into the car using a ramp. It's a good idea to first place the ramp flat and teach the dog to walk across it on the ground before transitioning to having him walk up it into the car.

Music Soothes

Veterinary neurologist Susan Wagner has studied the calming effects of music on dogs. In one study, she and psychoacoustic expert Joshua Leeds discovered that when classical music was simplified with less instrumentation, lower tones, and a dropped tempo, dogs relaxed. Their brain waves, heart rates, and respiration slowed, they became substantially calmer, and some even fell asleep.

Color **Code**

When you walk into your veterinarian's clinic, do you feel welcome and relaxed or anxious and irritable? Your subconscious reaction may be related to the color scheme—and it might affect your dog, too.

Studies have shown that color affects mood and perception. For instance, the color blue can evoke feelings of relaxation as well as suggest competence. Bold primary colors, such as red and yellow, can suggest energy and warmth. A mix of warm and cool colors can give a feeling of friendliness and comfort.

But what about dogs? Aren't they colorblind? Not exactly. They aren't able to distinguish as many colors as humans, but they can see better in low light than humans and can see the ultraviolet UVB spectrum. Therefore, white objects—like lab coats—can appear bright white to dogs. If you find certain bright colors, such as goldenrod, jarring to the eye, you can imagine how dogs might react negatively to shades of white. On the opposite end of the spectrum, dark colors in an enclosure such as a kennel or a small area such as an exam room can make it more difficult for dogs to see well, which could make them feel fearful, anxious, or stressed.

What are some color palettes you might notice the next time you visit the veterinary clinic? We bet you'll see combinations of neutrals, bold greens, blues with gray or purple tones, and small hints of bright colors, such as red or orange. You might also notice that colors are suited to particular areas. Yellow can lend a welcoming feeling to a waiting room, while green can seem soothing and natural in an exam room. Blue can help to induce a calm feeling in a surgery or other treatment room.

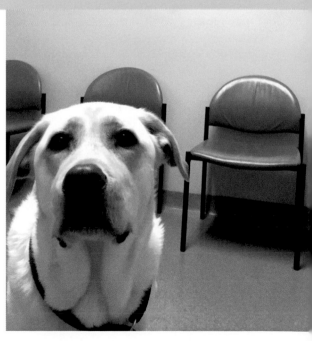

relaxing that it makes you feel sleepy while you're driving. And remember that dogs are as individual in their musical tastes as humans. If your dog relaxes to reggae instead of calming to classical, go for it.

ARRIVING AT THE CLINIC

Your dog can become fearful, anxious, or stressed before he even walks in the door of the veterinary clinic. Between the car and the front door, he's encountering all kinds of odors and sights that can put him off his stride. Here are just a few of the things that seem commonplace to you but threatening to your dog:

- The vertical surface outside the front door of the practice, with its warning "pee-mails" from hundreds or even thousands of previous pets who have passed through the door.

Embrace the Face: **The Benefits of Muzzle Training**

No one likes the idea of having a dog wear a muzzle, but trust us: sometimes it's the best thing for all involved, including the dog. It protects the humans involved from a nasty bite, and it reduces the potential emotional trauma for the dog because he won't face physical restraint by multiple people. And you may be surprised at how willingly your dog takes to wearing a muzzle if you train him correctly.

If your dog is aggressive or panics when handled or in new or frightening situations, it's smarter and easier to train him at home to wear a muzzle willingly instead of trying to shove one on his face when he's in panic mode at the veterinary clinic. If he's afraid, even the nicest dog can inadvertently snap and scare staff members.

Here's how to teach your dog to learn to love the muzzle, ideally before he ever needs one. If your dog is aggressive or if you are anxious about training him, seek the help of a veterinary behaviorist.

First, choose the right muzzle for your dog. We like basket muzzles for dogs with long noses and air muzzles for short-nosed breeds, such as Pugs and Bulldogs. A dog wearing a basket muzzle can still pant, take treats, and be examined easily.

Begin by letting your dog examine the muzzle while you hold it. If he shows interest by sniffing or moving toward the muzzle, mark it with a click or word ("Yes" or "Good") and give a treat. Remember to let him move toward it at his own pace rather than pushing it toward him. If he doesn't show interest, place it on the ground and scatter treats around it to make it more interesting.

Once he approaches it willingly, make the muzzle even more attractive by smearing the inside of it with peanut butter or squeeze cheese. Hold it in your hands with a treat in your fingers. He should be able to get the treat only by placing his nose in the muzzle. Reward him with a treat and praise when he does so.

Another way to do this is to smear baby food, peanut butter (xylitol-free), unsweetened applesauce, or yogurt at the bottom of the muzzle; set the muzzle in a cup or bowl; and allow the dog to drop his nose down into the muzzle to lick out the treats. To ensure that your dog doesn't "cheat" by trying to lick the treats from the outside of the muzzle, place some duct tape at the end of the muzzle and then place the treats inside it. He'll have to stick his nose inside the muzzle to get at the goodies. Remove the duct tape after he's trained.

Always be sure to allow the dog to act on his own. Don't pressure him to place his nose inside the muzzle. Never force the muzzle on or trick your dog by pushing it on just as he is starting to put his nose inside it. You want him to be excited about pushing his nose into the muzzle, eagerly anticipating the treats within.

Eventually, you will be able to put the muzzle on and fasten it. Reward him with praise and treats for wearing it and have him practice wearing it around the house just for fun. You will find throughout your dog's life that the ability to wear a muzzle can allow him to go more places, such as on public transportation in certain cities, and can help ensure safety for yourself and others when he is injured or scared.

- Doggy doo outside the clinic scented with anal-gland secretions that signal a warning.
- The sight of other dogs going in or coming out of the door.
- Double doors (if he hasn't seen them before).

Going inside the clinic can bring more unexpected or unpleasant experiences to your dog. Not every dog enjoys meeting people or other animals. If you have a shy guy instead of a social butterfly, own it. Get your dog a collar, bandana, T-shirt, or vest with wording such as "In Training," "Please Don't Pet," or "Shy Dog, Don't Approach." This will encourage people to think twice before approaching your dog, thus helping reduce his fear, anxiety, or stress.

In a best-case scenario, though, your dog isn't fearful, anxious, or stressed about visiting the veterinarian, and you can just walk him into the lobby to sign in. It's always a good idea to take a quick peek first just to see what other animals are there. You may want to wait outside or in the car if the lobby is crowded or noisy. Otherwise, bring your dog on in. The receptionist should greet you pleasantly and give your dog a treat.

Find a comfortable spot to sit. Ideally, choose a seat away from other pets who might set off your dog's alarms, such as hissing cats or barking dogs, especially if your dog is prone to fear, anxiety, or stress. If the carrier is small enough, set it either under the seat, so your legs are blocking his view, or on top of the seat with a towel or cover over it to block his view and dampen sounds.

Dogs walking in on their own should always be on leash. Keep the leash short so he doesn't make any unwanted approaches to other dogs, people, or cats. After all, you don't know if they're feeling sick or stressed, too. It's a commonsense way to avoid stressful or noisy

Calm Down

Stay calm yourself, even if you have reason to be concerned about your dog's condition. He'll pick up on your anxious attitude, which will affect his demeanor as well.

interactions. If others want to pet your dog or introduce their dogs to him and you know he doesn't like that, don't hesitate to politely ask them to give your dog some space.

To keep him occupied, ask your dog to perform any tricks he knows; good choices are Sit, Down, and Shake, but feel free to use any tricks that your dog knows well. A simple Stay command works, too. All of these behaviors will keep his focus on you, and it's a great opportunity to give him treats and praise, reinforcing that the veterinary clinic is a great place to be. It can also be a good idea for a veterinary team member to ask your dog for a Shake or Roll Over and then give him a treat to relay the message that the veterinarian and technicians are friends, not threats.

If your dog tends to be fearful, anxious, or stressed, consider staying in the car with him until he can go straight into the exam room. Roll down the windows and sit with him, listening to the radio or an audiobook, until you're called in. Give the receptionist your cell phone number for quick, easy contact.

IN THE EXAM ROOM

Some dogs do better when given a chance to relax for a few minutes in the exam room, with a chance to explore the room and get some treats and petting from the staff, before the exam starts. Others become more and more anxious the longer they wait. Discuss with the staff beforehand what you think is right for your dog.

To help your dog be comfortable, you can put down a non-skid towel or mat with the familiar scent of home. Squirt some pheromone spray into the air if your veterinarian hasn't already prepped the room with it, or use your phone to play some pet-friendly music. Lavender, geranium, and sage essential oils can have a calming effect if applied to a towel or blanket. And here's a weird trick: the scent of Calvin Klein Obsession and Calvin Klein Euphoria can be attractive to your pet, too. Some veterinary clinics have a spalike ambience, with a veterinary technician giving your dog a massage before the exam.

When pets are willing to approach the veterinarian or technician, they are less likely to hide, panic, or become aggressive. Once your dog has relaxed, and the technician or veterinarian has made friends with him by dropping treats on the floor while he or she talks to you, the exam can begin. You or the technician can make the exam table

Old Dog, New Approach

At North Idaho Animal Hospital, a woman brought her senior Pomeranian to see me. The Pom was a puppy-mill dog, purchased at a pet store and bounced from home to home because of behavioral issues. She was in a near-constant state of fear, anxiety, and stress. The woman brought the dog to me, hoping to fix the behavioral problems and give this sweet little female the calm, safe, loving, forever home she deserved.

We put the woman and dog in the exam room for ten minutes before anyone saw them. We explained in conversation and with a laminated briefing sheet left with the woman that we had done this purposefully to allow both of them to relax. While they waited, clinically proven calming music designed specifically for dogs filled the room. We also released the synthetic version of a naturally produced dog appeasing pheromone that was clinically proven to reduce anxiety and fear. On the floor were two heated pads, similar to hot water bottles, that were filled with warmed liquid paraffin and covered with a warm blanket. Dimmed LEDs instead of harsh fluorescents provided lighting.

After they were acclimated to the calming room, my wife, Teresa, came in and gave the dog a relaxing massage. After another ten minutes, I entered the room. From reading the briefing sheet, the woman knew that my voice and manner would be subdued, that I would avoid eye contact with the dog, and that I would try to get the dog to initiate physical contact with me.

As the woman sat on the floor next to the heated pads and blanket, I sat about 3 feet away on the floor, with my body turned sideways. We'd had the owner bring the dog in hungry, so in a slow motion I tossed some warm deli turkey to the dog. She ate. Success! Then I made a turkey trail leading from the owner to me.

The next thing we knew, the Pom, who had come in so frightened, started wagging her tail and wolfing down turkey. I could smell the turkey on her breath when she rose up on her back feet in my lap and began furiously licking my face. I could see the pet owner smiling. We put together a treatment plan that included nutraceuticals, pheromones, a Thundershirt, and training with an individual skilled in Fear Free principles.

—Dr. Marty Becker

more welcoming by placing a warm towel or nonskid mat on top of it. But dogs like Keeper, who you read about earlier, may be more comfortable being examined while he's sitting on a bench next to their owners or on the floor. A yoga mat in the exam room is great for this purpose. Some dogs do well if they are facing their owners and receiving treats as a distraction during their exams. Dogs who enjoy being petted can receive an exam from the veterinarian that seems very much like routine petting.

Other places to examine a dog that may be more comfortable for him include on his owner's lap, in the waiting room, or outside the clinic. Dr. Marty Becker is often seen examining dogs while he sits on the floor, on the dog's mat with him, or with the dog planted happily on his lap. It's all about doing what's best for the dog.

In extreme cases, it may be more comfortable for your dog if the exam is performed in your car. Discusss this option with your veterinarian beforehand to see if it is feasible.

During the exam, distraction techniques such as offering a treat-stuffed toy can help your dog focus on the good while a painful or sensitive area is examined or when he's on the receiving end of a procedure that causes fear, anxiety, or stress, such as having his nails trimmed or a wound checked, getting a vaccination, or having his ears examined or cleaned. Other distraction techniques include allowing the dog to lick some baby food off a spoon while receiving an injection or using hand targeting to change his focus while his paw is being examined. Having his temperature taken is uncomfortable, frightening, and invasive. Dab some squeeze cheese on the exam table to distract your dog while a rectal thermometer is inserted. Whatever the case, always reward calm focus on you with treats, praise, or petting.

Some dogs are leery about stepping on a scale. This is another instance where "go to mat" can come into play. Set the mat on the scale and then invite your dog to walk onto it. Voila! Some veterinarians are even sneakier and have scales built in beneath the floors so dogs don't even know that they are having their weight recorded as they pass from the waiting room to the exam room.

Maybe your dog is fearful of a particular instrument, such as an otoscope or stethoscope. You can work with him to target the area. If he sniffs or moves his nose toward the object, say "Yes!" and reward with a treat, toy, or petting. Gradually move the instrument closer to him and verbally mark when he stays in place, following with a reward. Continue to offer treats while the veterinarian is using the object.

Ideally, the veterinary staff is trained to perform stress-free blood draws, nail trims, and other procedures. Vaccinations can be less painful as well. Ask your veterinarian if he or she uses new needles with the smallest gauge possible. We like 25-gauge needles for less pain and 22-gauge needles for a quicker shot.

When examining a painful or sensitive area or doing anything else that causes an animal fear, anxiety, or stress—weighing him, examining his mouth, and taking his temperature—we often don't wait to see how the pet will react. We go straight to sedation with a drug such as Trazadone. This makes the experience happier for everyone.

Keep up the fun visits and training throughout your dog's life. They are deposits into his emotional bank account and will help balance out those times when visits aren't so fun.

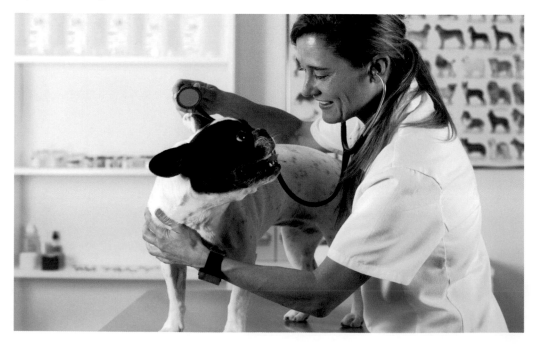

The Truth about
Muzzles

My long-time patient Josie, a brown pit bull with amber eyes, is sitting in the exam room on the floor, flanked by her mom, Susan, and myself. Josie has overcome many emotional troubles, such as storm phobia and aggression toward other dogs.

The partnership between Josie and Susan had taken them pretty far up to this point, but now we had a new challenge. Josie was an avid hunter of squirrels and lizards each day in the yard. One day, she cut her foot on the rocks around the fence while going after a lizard, and she needed to be seen by a veterinarian immediately. It was after hours, so Susan took her to an emergency clinic. Josie was scared, and she looked it. The veterinary team had to look at that foot, which was uncomfortable. The pain and the fear led to growling, which led to Josie being muzzled for the staff's safety. Susan had been appalled.

"Wait," I said. "Did you want the veterinarian to be bitten?" Of course, Susan hadn't wanted Josie to bite the veterinarian, but she felt ashamed that Josie had to be muzzled. Did that mean her dog was bad or that she was a bad mom? That was when I told her about Peanut, my own rescue Rottweiler, and the gift of muzzle training. Yes, the gift of muzzle training.

Peanut was sent to me because she was scheduled to be euthanized. By the age of seven months, she had been in three homes and had bitten several people. We kept her until she died of kidney failure at twelve and a half years old.

When she was young, I trained her to wear a well-fitting basket muzzle. As a result, when she needed to have her eyes examined, it could be done without sedation. When she needed surgery to remove part of her jaw due to cancer, she recovered in the hospital with the same high level of medical care that the nonaggressive dogs received. When she needed to have her urine tested during end-stage kidney failure, she was able to do so. When I needed to go away and the pet sitter had to give her intramuscular injections, she could get them.

Muzzle training was the loving gift of excellent medical care throughout her life. It was a selfless gift because I put my own feelings and biases aside and did what was right for her. Now, don't get me wrong. We did loads of work at my hospital, and she had all kinds of skills to make veterinary visits less scary. However, we never stopped using her muzzle, and she got the best I could give her until we had to let her go.

Susan got it. I am happy to say that Josie has a plan for the veterinarian now that includes her own basket muzzle and lots of squeeze cheese.

—Dr. Lisa Radosta

MEDICATING OR CARING FOR YOUR PET **AT HOME**

Sometimes, it isn't only dogs who are fearful, anxious, or stressed. Oftentimes, those emotions apply to owners—especially when it comes to giving pets a pill or injection, administering ointments or drops to eyes or ears, or applying topical parasite preventives.

Only about 20 percent of owners are successful in getting a pet's medication down the hatch as directed by their veterinarians. The reason is simple: it's hard to give medication to a dog who absolutely doesn't want it. Moreover, pet owners are embarrassed by their failure, assuming incorrectly that most other pet owners are successful in administering

medication. They don't want to call the veterinary clinic and admit defeat. That's why many medications end up in a cabinet instead of inside or on the pet.

However hard it is, your dog needs that medication in the correct dosage, at the prescribed intervals, and for the complete amount of time prescribed to live his best life and be as healthy as he can be. Fortunately, help is available. There are many ways of making medication more palatable for pets and easier for owners to administer. We're going to share that information with you here, as well as tips on giving medication successfully. We want to help you put the "treat" into "treatment" so

How to **Medicate Dogs Safely** and Kindly

- Many dogs are uncomfortable with restraint. This type of close contact can be very intimidating, increasing fear, anxiety, stress and aggression.
- Luckily, most nonaggressive dogs will respond to food restraint or distraction . I am able to examine all but the most aggressive patients with the use of food. Think about it: How does a keeper at a zoo medicate an elephant? He or she uses food and behaviors taught with positive reinforcement to get the animal to hold still.
- You will learn in this chapter how to teach your pet to hold still, but before you have these tools, food distraction can work wonders. If you need to apply a topical flea medication, for example, smear a small amount of something tasty, such as canned dog food or low-fat peanut butter, in a bowl. Put the bowl on the floor. Once your dog starts eating, massage the area where you are going to put the flea medication. Let him finish the bowl of food. Then, add more food, taking care to smear it so that he has to use his tongue. That technique will buy you some time. On the second try, squirt the topical flea medication on him while he is eating. Then, follow with a third repetition of food in the bowl so that he will be left with a positive association.
- If your dog is aggressive, fearful, anxious, or stressed when he must be treated or medicated, talk to your veterinarian about alternative options.

—Dr. Lisa Radosta

you can get the medicine out of the bottle and into your fearful, anxious, or stressed dog.

GETTING STARTED

Before he ever needs any kind of medication, you can teach your dog some techniques that will help him willingly accept a pill or the other handling involved in administering pills, ointments, drops, and injections. Ideally, you'll begin this training when your dog is a puppy—long before he needs medication, we hope—but it can also work with adult dogs.

We've discussed in earlier chapters the importance of accustoming a puppy to being handled all over his body, from letting you open his mouth to letting you lift up and look beneath his tail. That is going to pay off in spades when you need to give medication.

After all, medication isn't always pills. For instance, you may need to flush the anal area with medication if your dog has a ruptured or abscessed anal gland. Not pleasant for either of you, but a heck of a lot easier if your dog has learned to let you touch him all over.

For any part of the body, teach your pet the associated word and join that to the action of touching the specific area. Then, hand him a treat. Say "Ears" and then touch the ears and follow with a treat. You can do the same for paws, teeth, or tail. As he grows more comfortable, touch the inside of the ear or between the toes, for example.

Next, say the word and touch the area with a medication bottle. Don't just do this once or twice when he's a puppy. Practice throughout his life so he doesn't forget.

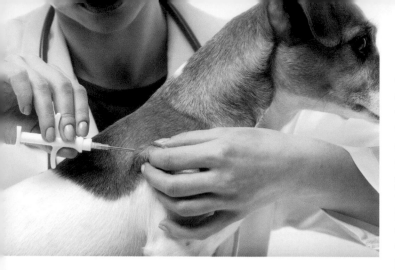

event. Give a cue such as "Shot" and touch your dog, following with a treat. When he's used to that, graduate to grabbing a small piece of skin and fur, followed by a treat. Eventually, you can poke him lightly with the empty syringe. A pet who learns this will be much more willing to undergo daily or weekly injections if necessary later in life.

If your dog runs away from you or shies away during this training, stop what you are doing. Take a break and then come back later, but this time hold your hand near his ear, for example, instead of touching it. Always reward every time that you touch your dog as you are practicing, even if your dog shies away a little bit. For these exercises, you are pairing the hand and the touch with the treat. Your dog doesn't have to do anything special.

A note here about aggression: If your dog is aggressive toward you, speak to your veterinarian or seek help from a board-certified veterinary behaviorist before attempting these exercises. If you do the exercise incorrectly, you can increase his aggression.

When you need to medicate those areas of the dog's body (and we're willing to bet that you will at some point), your dog will already be used to having them touched and will be prepared for that type of interaction. You can then administer the medication and follow it with a reward.

You never know how you might have to administer medication someday. It's possible that you may have to give injections if your dog develops diabetes or has allergies. It's easy enough to ask your veterinarian for an empty syringe case to help you practice for such an

BEFORE YOU LEAVE THE VETERINARIAN

You might think it's a victory if you get your dog to take half the pills prescribed for half the number of days they're prescribed. The trouble is, that's just not good enough. If you aren't able to give medications as prescribed, there's a good chance that your dog will be back at the veterinary clinic sooner rather than later. That's no fun for him or you.

Don't leave your veterinarian's office until you've gotten a demonstration of how to give the medication. If you don't ask for it, your veterinarian may assume that you know how to give it. Even if you think you know how to give it, asking for a demo is always a good idea.

Ask some other questions while you're at it. The answers can help you understand how the medication will work and what you should look for as far as results.

What's the purpose of the medication? Whether it's to manage vomiting or diarrhea or reduce pain or kill bacteria dead, knowing what the medication should do contributes to your overall knowledge of your dog's problem and how it fits into the treatment plan.

How do I give the medication and when? Have you ever gotten home from the veterinarian and realized you don't know if you should start the medication that day or whether you should give it with food or on an empty stomach? Get all of that info before you leave the veterinary clinic. Ask someone to put it in writing, or take your own notes. Be sure you that you understand the frequency. If you're to give a medication three times a day, does that mean morning, noon, and night or at precise eight-hour intervals?

What if I'm not home during the day? Your veterinarian will understand if you and your spouse are both working and can't give medication midday. He or she can often offer alternatives that work with your schedule. Some options include dropping him off at the clinic so he can be medicated at the appropriate time or having a pet sitter come in to administer the medication.

Is it okay to open a capsule and sprinkle it on my dog's food or to hide the pill in his wet food or something tasty like peanut butter? Often this isn't a problem, but, in some instances, your veterinarian may have reasons that it's not a good idea. Sometimes it's because the pill has a bitter taste if bitten into or because it's imperative that all of the medication get into the dog.

How soon will the medication work? This is good to know because if you don't see results within a certain period, you may need to report back to the veterinarian. And remember that just because your dog seems improved, it doesn't mean you should stop giving the medication and save the rest for "next time." It won't be effective if your dog doesn't get the full course of treatment.

What if my dog misses a dose or spits the pill out, but I don't find it until later? Should I give it a few hours late? If your dog doesn't get his medication at the normal time, contact your veterinarian. In most cases, you should never double up on the dose, but by asking your veterinarian beforehand, you'll know if that's appropriate for a particular medication.

What are the possible side effects? If you know that your dog will start peeing more frequently or have a greater volume of urine as a side effect of a drug, you can be prepared for it so he doesn't have accidents in the house. Knowing what might happen also helps you know when you should be concerned and whether you should report the issue to the veterinarian right away.

MEDICATION TIPS AND TRICKS

With the following tips and techniques, you'll be a pro in no time. First, some overall advice:

- Relax. If you're cool, your dog will be more likely to be cool.
- Don't rush. You'll do a better, more accurate job if you don't try to rush through it.
- Give medication in a quiet place without other pets or kids hanging around. Use pheromone sprays or diffusers or calming essential oils such as lavender in the area beforehand to help your dog relax.

- Read the directions and get everything ready before medicating your dog.
- Don't call your dog to come for medication. Go and get him or take it to him.
- If possible, have an assistant distract your dog with a treat or toy.
- Praise your dog and give him a treat after he takes his medicine.
- Smear food on a plate to distract him , as previously mentioned. This is the best technique for medications that you must apply topically.

PILL POPPERS

Remember watching *Mary Poppins* when you were a kid? She was on the right track when she sang "A spoonful of sugar helps the medicine go down, in the most delightful way." Sugar isn't the treat of choice for dogs, but a piece of hot dog or some peanut butter, squeeze cheese, or cream cheese can be a perfect alternative. Here are some ways to use them to get your dog to swallow that pill:

Become a magician with the three-pill trick. It's a variation on the old "shell game" that you might see on a city street or in a casino. To pull it off, start by giving your dog a piece of cheese or a soft treat—the promise. The second treat contains the pill—the deed. Finally, give another treat (no pill)—the chaser.

Use sleight of hand. Hold a ball of soft food in one hand. Drop the medication into the food with the fingers of the other hand or use tweezers or a spoon to put it in place. Using the fingers of the hand that did not touch the medication, close up the food meatball. Use that hand to offer the food meatball. Remember that dogs have forty times the scent receptors that humans have, so you don't want your dog to smell the medication on the outside of the food ball.

Compounded **Medication**

- If your dog has a negative association with taking pills or liquid medications, or if he must take medication on an ongoing basis, you may want to consider having his medication compounded into edible treats in pet-friendly flavors. If you can find a form and flavor your dog loves, medication time will be easier on both of you.

- Compounding involves combining, mixing, or changing a drug's ingredients to change its flavor or form, allowing it to better meet a pet's needs. Examples might include making a chewable beef-flavored medication or offering a chicken-flavored liquid instead of a tablet. This pharmaceutical alchemy is performed by a licensed pharmacist or veterinarian or by someone under the supervision of a licensed pharmacist. The law permits compounding from FDA-approved drugs if a veterinarian believes it is necessary to alter a drug to meet the needs of animals with diagnosed medical conditions.

- Besides making a medication more palatable to a pet, compounding has other benefits. It can be useful if a dog needs a lower dose than is normally available from a pharmacy. It may also be necessary if a particular drug isn't commercially available because of shortages or discontinuation. And it can combine two active ingredients into a single form.

- While it has advantages, compounding isn't always the right choice. One drawback is that the FDA does not verify the safety or effectiveness of compounded drugs. There's no guarantee that a compounded medication will be safe or effective for your dog's condition.

- Drugs and compounds may act differently in animals than in humans. Compounding can complicate the situation because formulation into a different delivery system may affect how the drug works in the body. If drug concentrations are above or below the therapeutic range, it can lead to increased or unexpected side effects or cause the drug to be less effective.

- For these reasons, it's important that a medication be compounded by a skilled and careful pharmacist. Before you have a medication compounded, ask if the pharmacist has specialized training or credentials in veterinary compounding. Another good question to ask is whether documentation supports the effectiveness and stability of the compounded formulation.

Other things to look for:
- The pharmacy should be accredited by the Pharmacy Compounding Accreditation Board to ensure high quality and practice standards.

- The pharmacy should follow United States Pharmacopeia (USP) guidelines for good compounding practices, as well as drug strength, purity, quality and stability.

- The pharmacy should be licensed in your state, even if you're purchasing online.

- The pharmacy should use FDA-approved drugs in a compounded medication.

- The pharmacy should be certified by the USP.

Make the pill smaller. Sometimes it's easier to get a pill down a pet if it's just not so darn big. If your pet isn't willing or able to swallow a pill whole, ask your veterinarian if you can use a pill splitter to break it into halves or quarters (some medications can be compromised if they are crushed or split or may give off a bitter flavor). Your veterinarian may even do this for you. You can then insert the pieces into a meatball or hide them inside a glob of peanut butter, for instance.

The lineup. Using squeeze cheese, make a line of cheese dabs on a plate or other surface. Place the pill inside one of them.

Bait and switch. Practice the pilling motion (more info follows) first with treats. This associates the motion with good things.

If your veterinarian gives the okay, use a pill crusher to pulverize a tablet. Then you can thoroughly mix it into your dog's food. Do this only if the medication won't have a bitter taste that will cause your dog to back away from his dish in disgust.

LIQUID MEDICATION

For liquid medication, be sure your veterinarian sends you home with some large, needleless syringes designed for administering liquid medication. They are marked on the sides to make measuring easy, and they make it easier to deliver liquid medicine in the right place (an eyedropper can also work).

To accustom your dog to the syringe and associate it with good times, put something yummy on the end and let him lick it off. You can teach him to hold his head up to make the administration easier. You can also distract him with a food-filled toy by having an assistant hold the toy above him at nose level or using food on the counter to focus him so that you can put the liquid in.

EYE DROPS OR OINTMENT

Just as you would for pills or liquids, get an assistant to hold a treat or a food toy just above the dog's nose level or place a bowl of food on the counter. You can also feed him something soft, like canned food or peanut butter, from a dosing syrings or squeeze bottle. Hold the bottle of eye drops in your dominant hand and deliver the prescribed amount while he is looking up.

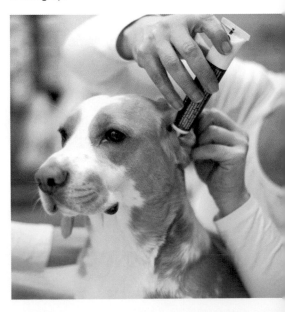

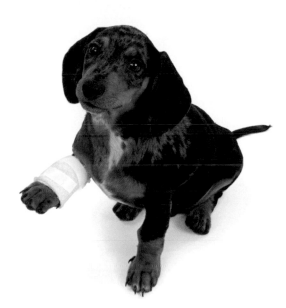

For ointment, feed him soft food through a syringe or squeeze bottle it the entire time to keep his head up. Hold his head still and use a finger to draw down the lower eyelid. With the tube in your dominant hand, squeeze a small amount of ointment onto the eyelid. Release the lower eyelid and gently rub the upper eyelid to distribute the ointment over the eyeball. In both cases, try not to let the applicator tip touch the eye.

EAR MEDICATION

Putting drops into a dog's ear requires skill and timing because if he shakes his head before you're finished, most of the medication gets splattered all over you instead of going into the ear, where it belongs. It may help if the tube or bottle has a long, narrow applicator to help ensure that the drops go deep into the ear.

Relax your pet first with strokes and soothing words or wait until he's lying calmly at your side.

Distract him with food as previously described. Place the applicator inside the ear and dispense the prescribed amount. Gently hold the ear closed and give a nice massage, using a circular motion. This helps work the medication farther into the ear so that less of it is lost when your dog inevitably shakes his head.

Begin feeding him before you start giving the medication and then continue to feed him for five or ten seconds after the process is finished. This is a good rule regardless of what you are

Mind Games

Sometimes, no matter what you do, getting medication into a dog can seem like wrestling an alligator. Even the sweetest, most biddable dogs suddenly turn into crazed, squirming furballs. That's when a little psychology can help, especially if you have more than one pet in the house.

Start by grabbing some really good treats. Call the dog who's not getting medication, and they hopefully will both come running, especially if they heard the rustle of the treat bag.

Give some treats to the dog who doesn't need treatment. Fondle his ears (or whatever part of the other dog needs to be medicated). Give more praise and treats. Release that dog.

By this time, the dog who needs medication should be eager for your attention. Repeat the scenario, giving lots of treats and praise before, during, and after administering the medication.

doing to the pet because it is much nicer and less stressful than trying to holding the pet in place.

TOPICAL MEDICATION

The word "topical" simply means that a medication is applied to the skin. It can be in the form of a liquid, gel, lotion, ointment, or patch. Shampoo can also be considered a topical medication. Topical products are used to repel parasites, treat skin conditions, or provide pain relief, among other things.

Some of the most common topical treatments are for flea or tick control and are sometimes referred to as spot-ons. Medicated shampoos may be prescribed for skin conditions and patches for pain relief. Each type of topical has special requirements when it comes to applying it.

Spot-Ons

Flea or tick preventives are examples of this type of product. They are liquids applied to the area between the shoulder blades. Read the directions before applying and make sure you're using a product made specifically for your type of pet. It's not safe, for instance, to dose a small

dog with a product made for a large dog, even if you use less of the medication.

Try to apply a spot-on when your dog is relaxed but aware of what you are doing. This way, you can help him make a positive association and won't scare him by sneaking up on him when he's sleepy.

As always, start with treats and the promise of another treat; for example, by placing his favorite toy on the counter. Apply the medication and then immediately toss the toy as a reward. You can also have an assistant give him treats while he's getting, er, treated.

Apply only the amount directed. More is not better. Pay attention to his reaction. If he cries, seems agitated, or acts as if he's in pain, do not apply any more of the product. Talk to your veterinarian about the reaction. Your dog may have an allergy or skin problem that is causing a reaction. A different type of product may be a better choice.

Creams, Lotions, and Ointments

These types of products are applied to skin, usually to treat wounds, hot spots, or other skin problems. They can be messy, especially if you have a furry dog, but some are made to absorb rapidly, which not only helps prevent mess but also reduces the risk that the dog will lick them off the skin.

Use the previously described tips to distract your dog with treats or a favorite toy. Gently massage the product into the skin, rewarding your dog as you do so. If the area is painful, your dog may be reluctant to have you touch it, or he may be uncomfortable because the product stings. Continue to distract him with a toy or treats while you apply the product. Keep in mind that you can get most things done with the judicious use of food!

You will probably need to prevent your dog from licking the medicated area. One trick we like to recommend is to apply the medication and then immediately feed your dog his meal or take him for a walk. These activities distract him from his desire to lick until the product has

Pain-Relief **Benefits**

Treating pain is about more than just relieving discomfort. That's important, of course, but it also plays an important role in your dog's recovery.

Veterinarians used to think that pain was a good thing because it kept pets from moving around. We know better now. Treating pain improves respiration, shortens postsurgical hospitalization times, and improves mobility. Pain left untreated slows healing time, interferes with sleep, and depresses the immune system.

—Dr. Marty Becker

dried or been absorbed. If he doesn't fall for that, he may need to wear an Elizabethan collar so he can't get at the medication.

Patches and Transdermal Gels

These products are typically used to provide pain relief after surgery. Patches are applied to the skin while transdermal gels are usually applied to the inner ear, where they are easily absorbed into the skin. The drugs that these products dispense are powerful, so follow the recommendation to wear gloves when applying them and wash your hands thoroughly afterward.

Keep an eye on the patch to make sure it stays in place. You don't want another pet chewing on it or accidentally wearing it.

Injections

Your dog may need an insulin injection once or twice a day if he ever develops diabetes. If you're needle-phobic, as many people are, this might seem like a nightmare scenario, but

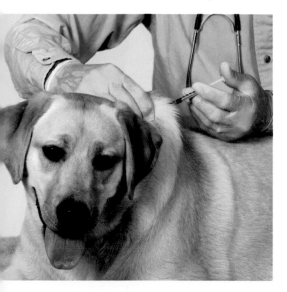

Insulin injections are subcutaneous, meaning under the skin, and are much less painful than intramuscular injections. Chances are, your dog will quickly become used to subcutaneous injections, but we have some tips to help you reach success quickly.

Start with—you guessed it—food, and have some toys ready, too. Make sure your dog is happy before progressing. Prepare the syringe and then grasp the loose skin at the back of the neck or between the shoulder blades, making a tent. Holding the syringe so it is almost parallel to the body, insert the needle, and then pull back slightly on the plunger to make sure you haven't hit a vein. If you see blood inside the syringe, discard the syringe and prepare a new one. Fortunately, this is an unlikely occurrence. Once the needle is in place, press the plunger to deliver the insulin.

The best way to make an injection a positive experience for your dog is to feed him immediately afterward. Give him a treat before the injection or even as you open the refrigerator to get the insulin.

we promise that your dog can learn to accept his injections and you can become a pro at delivering them with just a little practice.

Before you do anything, get a demo from your veterinarian and practice in the office under supervision. The veterinarian or technician can show you how to draw the medication into the syringe, make sure the syringe doesn't have any air bubbles, and then deliver the injection. Usually this involves practicing on an orange so you don't need to worry that you will hurt your dog while you're learning.

Safe Disposal

Have a "sharps box" for disposal of used syringes. Place the cover back on the needle afteuse and then place the entire syringe inside a box, jar, or other container with a secure lid. Ask your veterinarian about the best way to dispose of the container when it's full.

COLLECTING URINE SAMPLES

Your veterinarian may need a urine sample to check for a bladder infection, kidney disease, diabetes, or other conditions. Unfortunately, you can't just hand your dog a paper cup—you're going to have to be involved in the collection process, which can be a problem because dogs aren't always interested in cooperating. Your dog may walk away or stop urinating altogether if you get too close behind him. And it's hard to stick a collection cup beneath the rear of a tiny dog who's practically squatting on the ground.

Alternatives to the
"Cone of Shame"

Nobody likes it. The dreaded Elizabethan collar, e-collar, or "cone of shame," as it's often called, is hated by dogs everywhere, which usually means that owners hate it, too. It's a struggle to put It on, It causes your dog to suddenly becomes "paralyzed," and your dog keeps running into the wall or furniture because he can't see where he's going. An e-collar is the best way to keep your pet from licking or chewing at a wound, but if the unwieldy plastic lampshade look is just not an option for you and your dog, we have some possible alternatives.

- Several types of protective collars have a more streamlined shape or are made of softer material while still preventing your pet from licking or chewing wounds or stitches. Others are inflatable, making them more lightweight and comfortable. Firm paper collars aren't as durable as plastic e-collars, but they are softer and more lightweight. Consider them for dogs who aren't heavy-duty chewers.
- Cover the area to be protected by dressing your dog in a T-shirt, onesie, or pair of boxer shorts. You can use socks, booties, or bandages on paws. You may need to spray them with a bitter-tasting substance specially formulated to keep dogs from chewing.
- To keep your dog from scratching at wounds in the head or neck area, put a plastic e-collar around his waist so it looks like a skirt. He may accept this way of wearing it more readily than around his neck.

First, unless you have a tall dog, forget the cup idea. Use a small, flat, clean plastic container to collect the sample. A soup ladle can also work. For a dog who's low to the ground, it can help to attach a handle to the collection container so you don't have to bend down so far. Your veterinarian may be able to loan you a device with a telescopic handle that allows you to collect a sample from a distance.

Wait until your dog starts to urinate and then place the container beneath the stream. When he's done, put a lid on the container or transfer the urine to a clean container with a lid.

Now all you have to do is get the sample to your veterinarian, pronto. If you can't get it there right away, be sure to refrigerate it to prevent it from undergoing chemical changes that could affect the results. Deliver the sample within twelve hours of collecting it.

DON'T GIVE UP

You may know from past experience that your dog is fearful, anxious, or stressed when it comes to taking medication or receiving other treatments. Ask your veterinarian if options such as long-acting antibiotic injections, compounded medications, or new technologies, such as pain patches, are appropriate for your dog's needs. Having the veterinarian or technician perform the treatment at the office or make a house call is another possibility.

Taking your dog to the veterinarian but not following through with medication or other care is a waste of money for you. Worse, it can be harmful to your pet. Medication doesn't work if you don't give it. Noncompliance is upsetting for your veterinarian, too. We want your pet to get well as much as you do. So if you need help, ask! Your pet isn't able to administer his own medication, so he relies on you to know what to do.

GROOMING

Keeping a dog clean and tangle-free can be one of the most enjoyable experiences of his life. We all like to be clean and smell nice and look good. Dogs are no exception. They just feel better. And you can tell that they know when they look good. Don't tell us that a freshly groomed Poodle, Afghan Hound, Maltese, Schnoodle, Golden Retriever, or any dog doesn't strut his stuff when he's fresh from the grooming salon or has just been bathed and blow dried at home.

But grooming can also be one of the most uncomfortable and unpleasant experiences of a dog's life. Think painful quicked nails, shampoo stinging the eyes, or hair being pulled as a tangle is combed out. Nobody enjoys those things, dogs included. And just one bad experience can tarnish his appreciation for grooming for the rest of his life.

We want grooming to be a bonding experience for you and your dog, not one filled with fear, anxiety, and stress. That's because good grooming habits are important for more than just looks. For starters, grooming keeps your dog healthy and free of parasites. Even better, it gives you hands-on information about your dog's condition. When you comb your dog, brush his teeth, wipe the goop out of his eyes, and clean his ears, you're getting a close look at his entire body.

Grooming can give you an early heads-up if something's wrong. It's a chance to check for lumps, bumps, scabs, or other skin problems; to check teeth for tartar buildup; and to ensure that eyes and ears show no signs of irritation or infection. Many of these problems are easily treatable when caught early.

What we think is best about grooming, though, is that it's a great way to spend quality time with your dog. You know from having your hair styled, getting a manicure, or having a massage how pleasurable grooming can be when it's done right. By showing a young dog how good grooming can feel, you can reduce or eliminate any fear, anxiety, or stress associated with the processes. Our goal is for you and your dog to look forward to grooming time.

INTRODUCING GROOMING

Whether he is being petted, groomed, or examined by the veterinarian, your dog should welcome being touched by people. In a perfect world, your dog was introduced to gentle handling by his breeder, and his experience with appropriate handling continued during his socialization period with you. If you have a new puppy or dog, we're going to share some techniques for getting him accustomed to being groomed and examined by you and other people. We'll also address ways to help dogs who are already fearful, anxious, or stressed when handled or groomed.

Meet the **Groomer**

Look for a puppy socialization class that includes exposure to the sights, sounds, and touches involved with being at a grooming salon, maybe in the form of a field trip. This might include having him walk over surfaces such as rubber mats, stand in a sink or on a grooming table, experience being brushed or having his nails filed by someone new, and hear the sounds of a Dremel tool or hair dryer. You can also practice some of these things at home, always making sure that they are positive experiences for your dog.

—Mikkel Becker

From the first day you bring him home, show your dog how special touch and grooming can be. You don't have to make a big production of it. Just a couple of minutes at a time of brushing, combing, or massage can get him used to the idea that grooming is good. This is especially important if he will have a long coat or feathering as an adult. Even though puppies might have very little coat at all, now is the time to accustom them gradually to the amount of time it will take and the techniques used. You'll thank us when your little pup has grown into a big dog who stands still for grooming and even loves it.

Start by gently handling every part of his body. Rub his ears, lift up his lip to look at his teeth, rub that sweet spot between the eyes, sniff his ears, hold the paws and look at the nails and pads, stroke his soft belly, and lift his tail for a look-see at the hind end. You don't have to do everything at once, but try to look at every part of his body weekly. Pick a different area each day to check out.

and enjoy the attention and get used to the feel of the grooming tools. Be gentle if you come across a tangle or mat. Jerking the comb or brush through it is one of the quickest ways to turn your dog off grooming for good. During this time, give your dog a continuous stream of delicious treats to drive home the message that grooming is great.

End with praise and one more yummy treat—before he starts to squirm. Depending on the type of coat he will have, gradually extend the amount of time you spend grooming him.

Try to do this exam at a time when you're not rushed or distracted and both you and your dog are relaxed. Maybe he's sitting in your lap while you're watching television, or you've just had a fun playtime and he's a little tired and relaxed.

Next, add some brushing or combing. If your dog doesn't have much coat, it doesn't need to take more than a couple of minutes at first, but this early practice will help him learn to accept

BEST PAW FORWARD

Dogs don't love having their paws touched, and they like having their nails trimmed even less. Your dog may jerk his paw away when you try to touch it, or he may even start to cry before you even touch a nail with the clippers. He probably has been "quicked" in the past by a too-aggressive previous owner or groomer who cut too deeply into the nail and hit the sensitive bundle of blood vessels and nerves there. The quick is the dark line that runs down the middle of the nail, ending just where the nail starts to curve downward. It's easy to see if your dog has light-colored nails, but more like a game of Russian roulette if his nails are dark.

Whether you have an innocent puppy who doesn't yet know the pain of being quicked or a suspicious, fearful dog who wants nothing to do with a nail trim, the following techniques

High **Ground**

In the chapter on veterinary care, we talked about how some dogs are fearful of being placed on the exam table. A veterinary exam can be done on the floor for these dogs, but grooming is another matter altogether. Having a dog at eye level, whether he's on a grooming table in a salon, on a picnic table in your backyard, or on top of your washing machine, makes the process much more efficient—not to mention it's a heck of a lot easier on your back.

should help you give your dog a proper "pawdicure" without pain.

Start by handling or playing with the paws on a regular basis, as previously described. Sweet talk your dog as you hand him lots of special treats that he doesn't usually get: small cubes of cheese or bits of deli turkey, for instance.

Teach your dog to hold his paw out for examination. This is a fun trick that he can do for a reward, and it's also a sneaky way to teach him to give you his paw voluntarily for a nail trim.

When you start trimming his nails, do so slowly. Do just one nail a day, barely trimming the end so you don't run the risk of quicking him. If you trim off a little bit and then see a black dot in the center of the nail, don't trim any more. That's the quick, and your dog will quickly run away bleeding and screaming if you cut it. If possible, have a helper who can distract your dog with a wooden spoon full of peanut butter or squeeze cheese. The goal is to get the nail even with the paw pad and then keep it that way.

Most importantly, never force a nail trim. It can ruin your relationship with your dog. Take things slow so you don't jeopardize his trust in you.

BATH TIME

Baths keep a dog's skin and coat healthy, shiny, and clean. You may have heard that too much bathing can dry out a dog's coat, but that's an old wives' tale. Regular baths—weekly or even more often—are important for cleanliness,

Great Lengths

If your dog's nails are longer than they should be, and he puts up a big fuss about getting them trimmed, take advantage of any procedure that requires him to be anesthetized, such as spay/neuter surgery or a dental cleaning, and ask to have his nails trimmed while he's in la-la land. Then you can start fresh with trimming them yourself and keeping them at an appropriate length.

Another option is to work with a dog trainer to give your dog some alternatives to the clippers, such as scratching his nails on a homemade or commercial nail filing mat. For instance, if your dog likes to dig, the trainer could work with you to capture the digging motion and then transfer it to scratching on a filing mat.

especially if your dog shares your furniture and bed.

When dogs are introduced properly to baths, most can learn to tolerate them with good grace. Some even enjoy them, reclining in the tub or sink and relaxing into the shampooing as if they're at a high-end spa. Others seem to think they're at a water park, splashing until you're soaked. Whatever the case, here's how to make a bath more comfortable for your dog.

Before bathing your dog for the first time, teach him to enter the bathroom on cue, using treats to make his presence there a positive experience. Then, teach him to target the nonskid mat you've placed in the tub or shower stall. Increase the length of time the dog spends in the tub or stall by smearing peanut butter on the side of the tub or shower.

While he's in the tub or stall, you may also want to slowly run the water to get him used to the sound. Over subsequent sessions, start putting more water in the tub and begin slowly pouring water on his legs and hind end before getting the front half of the body wet.

When it's time for the real thing, plug in a pheromone diffuser or spray pheromones where you'll be giving the bath. The chemical calm will help your dog relax during his sudsing.

Premix the shampoo with water: 1 part shampoo to 10 parts water. Premixing is good for fearful dogs because they won't be startled by the sound the shampoo makes when it glugs out of the bottle. Instead, you can just pour the mixture over the dog without making a sound. Premixing also makes it easier to work the shampoo into the fur.

Get the water ready in advance. Remember how Goldilocks wanted her porridge not too cold, not too hot, but just right? That's how your dog's bath water should be. When you put your dog in the tub or sink, the water should be close to body temperature— approximately 100 degrees Fahrenheit. You can increase it from there. Just don't let it get too hot.

Put a nonskid mat in the sink or tub before your dog gets in. If he has secure footing, he'll be more comfortable with the process. Also, have your towels ready. Most dogs are going to shake more than once during a bath. Use one towel to protect yourself from flying water and shampoo and have a couple more towels for drying your dog. You'll need one to squeeze moisture out of your dog's coat and another one to give him a good rubdown and remove more moisture.

Use a rubber grooming brush to scrub your dog. It works the shampoo well into the fur and helps remove dead hair, but the best thing about it is the pleasurable massaging sensation that its nubby fingers give.

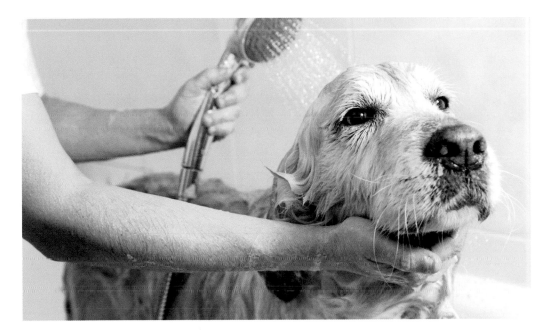

Use a damp washcloth instead of shampoo to get your dog's face clean. When it's time to rinse, don't douse your dog with water or hold his head under the faucet, just pour clean water over his coat. Or consider a pet shower sprayer attachment , which can help your dog can also help him feel more comfortable because it allows you to adjust water pressure to his comfort level and doesn't require you to hold him beneath a faucet with running water. You can take the water to him instead. In any case, hold his head upward so there's no risk of water running into his nose or eyes.

What if your dog still hates baths or is fearful, anxious, or stressed during them? Maybe he runs away when bath time is imminent. He's not being stubborn or bad; he's afraid. Here are some tips to help make baths more enjoyable and less of a struggle for both of you.

Give the experience a name—"Bath"—and help him form a positive association with the word. For a puppy, associate the Bath cue with a brief splash in the water—in, fun splashing, and then done. For an adult dog who has already formed negative associations with the experience, work on desensitization. This may involve asking him to come into the bathroom, giving him a special treat, and then letting

Did You **Know?**

If you don't want your dog to shake during his bath, this one simple trick will put the kibosh on it. All you have to do is gently place one finger on top of his nose and one below it, in sort of a horizontal peace symbol. It prevents him from getting his head turning in that whipsaw motion that's integral to the shake. Once you're ready and have him in a suitable spot, you can let him shake all he wants. (Avoid this technique with dogs who are sensitive about having their muzzle touched.)

—*Dr. Marty Becker*

him leave. Gradually work toward getting him to come into the tub or shower stall, receive a treat, and then leave. Work gradually up to an actual bath.

Keep a snack jar in the bathroom to sweeten the deal. Hand out treats for calm behavior, for all four feet in the tub, or for no splashing. Post-bath, give him a favorite food puzzle or long-lasting treat to occupy him while he dries in his crate.

CHOOSING A GROOMING SALON

When you get your hair or nails done, we're guessing that you appreciate a salon where they offer you coffee, tea, or a glass of wine when you come in; play upbeat music; give you a little neck or shoulder massage with your shampoo; and never burn you with the blow dryer or flat iron. If your dog could articulate what he likes in a salon, we bet he would go

for pheromones diffused into the air, calming music, nonskid mats in the sink, treats (of course!), and gentle but assured handling that lets him know he's in good hands and doesn't have to worry about clipper burn, quicking, or other unpleasantries.

If you're starting with a puppy, now is your chance to help him learn to love going to the groomer. Of course, you have been teaching him to accept combing, brushing, and other grooming care from you at home, but twelve weeks of age is a good time to introduce him to a professional grooming session.

Tour the grooming salon yourself before making an appointment. It's best if dogs are not groomed out in the open, where they are under the eye of every passerby. Ask the groomer about doing a practice visit that doesn't involve any actual grooming. It should simply involve driving to the clinic, walking in the door, getting a treat from the staff, undergoing the experience of being lifted onto and off of the grooming stand, and hearing the sounds of clippers or dryers. Give plenty of treats throughout the visit to associate a trip to the groomer with good things.

Fearful, anxious, or stressed dogs may require some different steps. If your dog pants, whines, drools, trembles, or even vomits during a trip to the groomer, that's not relaxing at all. He may have a clean coat and a precise trim afterward, but if he's exhausted and traumatized, it's no good for anyone—yourself, the groomer, and especially your dog.

With a fearful, anxious, or stressed dog, practice at home first. When a dog is groomed, the groomer handles sensitive areas, such as the muzzle, eyes, ears, paws, tail, and groin—a lot. We've discussed previously how important it is to accustom your dog to this type of handling. One way to do this is to pair a predictor word, such as "Tail," with a gentle touch at that area. Follow up with a treat.

Some dogs are particularly sensitive to being touched in certain areas. Try starting away from that area and gradually working your way to it. For instance, if your dog doesn't like having his paws touched, start at the shoulder and slowly move down. Always do this type of training at a time when your dog is relaxed. After a meal or a long walk might be a good time to schedule it. If your dog is aggressive, seek the help of a veterinary behaviorist.

Maybe your dog doesn't like going to the groomer because it involves a car ride. Talk to your veterinarian about medication for motion sickness to see if that helps reduce his anxiety and discomfort. Using pheromone sprays and

counterconditioning techniques may also help him relax and enjoy the ride.

Work with the groomer to identify specific aspects of grooming that your dog dislikes or is afraid of. Simple changes, such as placing a nonskid mat on the grooming table or using facial wipes instead of running water over his head may solve the problem. Dogs who are sensitive to loud noises may benefit from products that help decrease aural stimuli. Maybe the water temperature needs to be adjusted or he doesn't like the scent of the shampoo. Experiment with these types of changes to help him become more comfortable with the grooming process.

Don't be afraid to use a muzzle for fearful or aggressive dogs. It protects the groomer from a possible bite and protects your dog from the negative consequences of delivering a bite. Even if your young pup isn't aggressive or fearful, it makes a lot of sense to muzzle-train him now. He may need to wear one for any number of reasons in the future, and if he's already accustomed to it, he won't be afraid of the experience.

Taking these types of preventive measures can help address a dog's fear, anxiety, or stress before it escalates into aggression. Most important, if your dog's fear of the groomer is debilitating, talk to your veterinarian. There are many medications that he or she can prescribe that will help your dog relax.

Regular, thorough grooming is one of the best and most inexpensive ways to keep tabs on your dog's physical condition. The bonus is that you have a clean, beautiful dog you can show off with pride.

DOGS AND KIDS: BUILDING A FEAR FREE FRIENDSHIP

A dog is often a child's first best friend. A toddler grasps his dog's fur as he takes his first unsteady steps. They both have endless supplies of energy for never-ending games of fetch or sandlot baseball. They snuggle up together to read a book or watch television. And they share secrets, the child secure in the knowledge that a dog never tells.

Few things are as special as a loving, positive, healthy bond between child and dog. Any parent who has known the love of a dog wants to share that special relationship with his or her child.

For a child, loving a dog involves empathy: learning to pet a dog gently and not to pull

tail, ears, or fur. Dogs learn the valuable lesson that children must be treated gently—no putting teeth or paws on them. For both, social skills and experiences include play, sharing, companionship, and caring.

But that kind of relationship doesn't just happen organically. You have to lay the foundation for it with both child and dog. In this chapter, we'll address how to do that with normal dogs as well as how to ensure safe interactions between kids and dogs who may be fearful, anxious, or stressed.

How do you build that perfect relationship? Like all friendships, it takes work and practice

Dog on **Patrol**

Some dogs aggressively patrol the fenceline, barking and snarling when people walk by. Many times they seem to save their ire for kids. It's not unusual for kids to tease dogs by running sticks along the fence, throwing things over the fence at them, or making barking noises at them.

Often, the simplest solution is to keep your dogs indoors when you know kids are on their way to or from school. You can also make the effort to meet the kids and ask them not to tease your dog, explaining that it makes your dog fearful, anxious, or stressed. You may even discover that the kids are afraid of your dog. Give your dog treats whenever the kids walk by to create positive associations with them. This can have your dog looking forward to seeing children walk by.

from all parties: parent, child, and dog. And even if you don't have children yourself, your dog is likely to encounter them throughout his life. There will be kids in the neighborhood who want to pet him or nieces, nephews, or grandchildren coming to visit. Here, we'll discuss how to manage introductions and interactions successfully, whether your dog is normal or is fearful, anxious, or stressed when he comes in contact with kids.

GROWING UP TOGETHER

If you have a dog and will be giving birth or adopting a baby in the next few months, congratulations! Your dog's relationship

with the new baby starts now. The introduction of a new baby into the home can be stressful for all involved, but with proper precautions and training, it can go smoothly and safely.

Don't wait until the last minute. As soon as you know you are pregnant, it's time to start easing your dog into his new life. In fact, it's a good idea to prepare a dog for kids in his life even if their advent is a couple of years away. For instance, prepping pets for unintentional pokes or grabs is important. When she was pregnant with her daughter, Reagan, Mikkel Becker started preparing her Pugs, Bruce and Willy, for the upcoming change in their lives well before the birth. Without hurting them, of course, she began to accustom them to kid-style tail grabs, heavy pats, and unexpected touches—all of the experiences that a dog may encounter when living with a toddler. The practice sessions help him learn that if this type of handling does occur, it's not such a big deal.

However, if you have a dog who is fearful, anxious, stressed, or aggressive, it's essential to go slowly and carefully with this type of training, always keeping it positive. Seek professional guidance from your veterinarian to avoid a possible bite. Even more important, when your baby or toddler does interact with a dog, hold his or her hand so you can guide where it goes and what it does.

Always **Supervise!**

Remember that young children need constant reminders about how to behave around dogs—not crowding them, not patting too hard, not playing with the dog's toys. They don't have a good sense of empathy yet or an understanding of cause and effect. They can't predict how their behavior is going to affect the dog. And babies who have begun to crawl may draw growls or bites from dogs who are startled when they get crawled on or over.

For these reasons, always supervise young children and pets when they are together. The majority of dog bites to children are caused by a dog that the child knows while an adult is present. Use baby gates or crates when you can't keep an eye on their interactions.

Always practice proactive supervision; this means actively watching the child and the dog. Any dog can becomes startled and scratch or bite a child. Even if you have to leave the room for less than a minute, take your child or your dog with you just to be safe.

BENEFITS FOR CHILDREN

Having a dog can increase children's physical activity, getting them outside to play or go for walks. Scientists have even discovered health benefits. Exposure to pets during a child's first year is associated with reduced risk of developing allergies to dogs and cats by as much as half, according to a study published in June 2011 in the journal *Clinical and Experimental Allergy*.

MANNERS MAKE THE DOG

Accustoming a dog to new or unusual types of touches is just one aspect of preparation. Other factors to consider are whether a dog has fear or aggression issues or needs manners training.

Dogs who are fearful, anxious or stressed often express their feelings by guarding important resources, such as food bowls, toys, and beds. They may react aggressively when approached by people or seem fearful of children or toddlers. Often these dogs dislike having certain areas of their bodies, in particular the mouth, ears, feet, and tail, touched. If you notice any of these behaviors, talk to your veterinarian about getting a referral to a

board-certified veterinary behaviorist or a certified applied animal behaviorist to help you.

Your dog may not be fearful, anxious, or stressed, but his manners might need a tune-up. A dog who jumps up on people is a safety hazard to a new parent holding a baby or, later, to a toddler just learning to walk. Teaching your dog to sit before anyone greets him or to jump in your lap only when invited are preemptive measures that can prevent injury to yourself or your baby.

Loose-leash walking is another must for a child-friendly dog. Have him practice walking nicely next to a stroller as well. By the time your baby makes his or her appearance, a stroller should be a normal part of your dog's life. If necessary, use an aid, such as a front-clip harness or head halter, to prevent pulling.

If he doesn't already know it, teach your dog the Leave It or Drop It cue. It will come in handy when he decides that one of the baby's toys makes a good chew.

BECOMING MORE INDEPENDENT

You will always love your dog, but when a baby comes along, it's just a fact of life that you will need to spend more time tending to your baby and less time interacting with your dog. You can and should start to prepare your dog for that change in his lifestyle before the birth.

Help him become used to less attention from you by introducing food puzzles—or

What Does **Supervision Mean?**

Supervision is more than just being in the same room with a dog and child. It means directly watching them, guiding their interactions, and intervening when necessary. If you're watching television or cooking, for instance, your attention is divided, even if they're playing right in front of you. Things could go bad in a matter of seconds if you miss warning signs, such as your dog freezing or staring if baby gets too close or in his face, escalating to a growl, snap, or bite before you realize what's happening.

Your dog and child should interact only when you are right next to them and have your eyes on them the whole time. When you can't do this, give your dog a place to settle that is off limits to kids, such as a bed placed on a high piece of furniture, such as a chair, or, for a small dog, the back of the sofa if it's against a wall. Behind a baby gate or in another room works, too. These sanctuary areas allow your dog to have a private space where he can't be bothered. They give him the choice of interacting only when he willingly moves off or away from the area.

—*Mikkel Becker*

The First **Meeting**

When we brought Reagan home from the hospital, I waited outdoors with her while my husband brought our two Pugs, Willy and Bruce, out to meet her. They approached calmly as I was kneeling down.

Even though we'd previously had them around other babies to get them used to youngsters, they had shown little interest, but as soon as they could smell Reagan, they became visibly excited and focused solely on her. Willy, in particular, who never wagged his tail, had it ticking back and forth in a frenzy, and I swear I saw a smile on his face. Both were so excited and accepting that I'm convinced they understood what was going on: that Reagan was our baby and part of the family.

—*Mikkel Becker*

a comfortable pet bed for his new sleeping quarters. A baby or pet gate with vertical bars will help keep your dog out of the baby's area when you aren't available to supervise.

When you look at how your dog behaves before the baby arrives, you might worry that he will never be able to adjust to his new housemate. He just seems so rowdy! Bear in mind, though, that not only are you starting early to prepare him, he will also have at least six to eight months to get used to the baby's presence before she starts to becomes mobile. This gives you time as well to continue your dog's "child" training. If possible, borrow a friend's older children who can help him learn to be around children, starting at lower levels of activity and gradually increasing the noise and activity levels. If your dog is fearful of kids, seek professional help.

INTRODUCTIONS IN PRACTICE AND REALITY

You don't need to wait until the baby arrives to accustom your dog to having one around the house. Play recordings of babies crying, cooing,

adding new ones—to help him stay busy while you're decorating the nursery, attending showers, or just taking a nap because your energy is drained. Whatever you do, don't go the opposite route and lavish attention on him because you're feeling guilty about the upcoming change in his life. That will make the contrast all the more stark once you bring the baby home.

This is also the time to rethink where your dog sleeps. Letting him on the bed may no longer be a good choice if the baby will be next to the bed in a bassinet or cosleeper. Ideally, he is already crate-trained and can move back to his crate at bedtime, starting now. If he's not, consider starting crate training or setting up a dog-proofed area with

Tolerance Level

Your dog may be bombproof when it comes to your kids. He lets them hug and kiss him, pull his ears, and use him to pull themselves up to a standing position. That's wonderful, but it doesn't mean you should allow your children to do those things—your dog might not turn on them, but what if they repeat that behavior with a less tolerant dog?

A child who learns to hug a tolerant dog will think that it's OK to do that with any dog. The reality is that lots of dogs don't enjoy being hugged or kissed, and they will respond with a bite.

If a child—yours or someone else's—wants to hug your friendly dog, give her an alternative. Say, "A hug can make dogs feel trapped, but they love showing off and getting treats. Why don't you ask him to sit, and then you can give him this treat. Be sure you hold your hand flat with the treat on it so he can slurp it up." (Of course, you should do this only if your dog already has nice treat manners.) This usually makes a child giggle, and you've averted the desire to hug while giving the child new information about dogs.

and making other noises. Start with the sounds at a low level and pair the noise with tasty treats to help your dog associate it with good things.

You can also use a doll to mimic activities, such as diapering, feeding, and bathing. Your dog can learn to stay calm and respect the "baby's" space when you do these things.

When the baby is born, have a family member bring home a piece of clothing or bedding that bears the baby's scent. He or she should let the dog sniff it and then give him a really special reward, such as a piece of turkey hotdog—anything that he loves and doesn't get every day. Take away the item and then present it for another sniff and reward. Before you and the baby come home, your dog will already associate the new arrival with good things.

When you bring the baby home, keep the meeting low-key. Don't push the baby into the dog's face or force the dog to smell the baby; this is a dangerous practice. If you brought home a blanket, the dog will have smelled his scent already. The husband or partner should carry the baby to give the dog the opportunity to greet the mother, who has been in the

hospital for a few days. Spend a bit of time with the dog, doing some tricks or playing.

Once baby is home, find ways to include your dog in your baby's care. Let the dog hang out in the room while you are diapering, for instance, and talk to him while you clean the baby and fold and fasten the diaper. Your dog will love

Copy **Right**

Kids imitate almost everything their parents do. We've all heard a child repeating something that his or her parents wish the child hadn't overheard. Children like to do things exactly the way Mom or Dad does them. That includes how the parents treat the dog. You can tell your child multiple times not to push the dog off the sofa or yell at him, but if you do it yourself, your child is going to treat the pet the same way. That's one of the reasons we like to use positive-reinforcement techniques. There's little risk of fallout, and it's a great way for the dog to learn manners around the child as well.

being part of the experience, and your child will benefit from hearing you talk.

Try not to scold the dog in the baby's presence. You don't want him to associate being yelled at with the baby. Instead, make the baby's presence desirable by giving him a chew or a favorite toy while you're nursing or caring for the baby in other ways.

RESOURCE GUARDING

Protecting valuable items from intruders is a "dogly" thing to do. We're not talking Grandma's silver or your new flat-screen TV. We mean the dog's prized possessions: his favorite chew toy, his food, his bed.

When your young child wants to investigate those objects or simply stumbles and falls near them, the first reaction of many dogs is to guard their belongings. That's why we recommend giving chews, for instance, when the dog is in a sanctuary room, a doggie playpen, or his crate—anyplace that the child can't invade, even accidentally. Think of it as the dog's down time, when he can really relax and enjoy his chewie, puzzle toy, or meal in peace.

Another source of tension between child and dog can occur when the dog takes a

Creature Comfort

I worked with a family whose Labradoodle was increasingly uncomfortable in the presence of children. The mother took the dog with her every day when they walked her young child to the school bus stop, and the kids there often hugged and kissed him, even if he tried to move away.

I began by suggesting that, at his current level of discomfort, the walks to the bus stop were too much for him to handle. He would likely be more comfortable if left at home and walked at another time.

Next, we worked on exercises to help him become comfortable greeting people, including children. He was conditioned to both a head halter and a front-clip harness to take the place of a flat collar, which didn't offer directional control.

The owner asked children not to hug or grab the dog. In return, she would have the dog do tricks that he enjoyed, such as Shake and Touch. These became his go-to behaviors when meeting children.

In a perfect world, uncomfortable touches would be avoided altogether; instead, we taught him gradually to tolerate pinches, tail and ear pulls, paw touches, and mouth grabs so that, if they did occur, they wouldn't be a big deal.

The dog became much happier, and it showed in his body language in the presence of children. Now, he gladly accompanies his family to the bus stop. Rather than letting him lead the way and leaving him open to unwanted approaches from children, his family learned to give directions to children and provide their dog with predictable interactions. This resolved the problems they were having.

—*Mikkel Becker*

child's beloved stuffed animal. A dog can't always differentiate between a child's toy and his own toys. In this instance, teach your child to always come to you for help. He or she should never try to take the toy away from the dog. Tell your child, "If the dog takes your toy, come and get me." This is one of those cases where it's important for your dog to respond immediately when you say "Drop it," "Leave it," or "Give it." Offer the dog one of his own toys in exchange. This is a good way to help reduce the risk of a bite.

Be aware that a dog who guards resources is one who is likely to have an incident with a child at some point. Ask your veterinarian for a referral to a qualified veterinary behaviorist who can help you resolve or manage the problem.

HUGS AND KISSES

Children love to show their affection for dogs, but they often do it in inappropriate ways. We see photos all over the Internet of young children hugging dogs, kissing them on the face, or lying on top of them. Dogs aren't people in fur suits, and they are uncomfortable with that kind of behavior. While these behaviors make cute photos, they are a bite waiting to happen from a dog trainer's or veterinary behaviorist's perspective.

Dogs are amazing creatures. In most cases, they tolerate a lot of mishandling and give a number of warning signals before they move on to a growl, snap, or bite. It's essential for you—and your child, if he or she is old enough—to know what those signals are. They

Oreo's Story

We moved to Seattle when Reagan was four and a half. One day, we were outside in our new yard when a young Papillon named Oreo came by. Oreo started barking and looked upset at the sight of Reagan. I talked to the owner and showed her some exercises to help Oreo be more comfortable in Reagan's presence. The dog learned that approaching Reagan meant getting to do tricks and receive treats. Soon they were friends, and Oreo wanted nothing more than to play with Reagan. Without that preparation, though, Oreo could have become even more fearful of children. Oreo's owner continued working with her, and the dog became much more sociable with people.

—Mikkel Becker

can include the dog's looking away or leaning his body back. His mouth may be closed tightly, sometimes with the lip just starting to curl up. The eyes may darken with excitement or the whites of the eyes show—resembling a whale eye. The body, including the tail, looks rigid or stiff. Sometimes the tail is curled beneath the dog or drooping low. This "tail talk" can indicate insecurity, uncertainty, or fear. This is a dog who needs a way to cope with or escape a situation.

Conversely, a comfortable dog leans in and isn't actively trying to get away. His body is relaxed; his tail has a nice, loose wag; his eyes have a calm expression; and his mouth is open.

Body language is the only way a dog can communicate to a child to back off because the child is hurting him (maybe he's arthritic) or making him uncomfortable by invading his space. A dog doesn't have the freedom in most cases to come and go as he pleases, so he can feel trapped by a child's hug. It's your responsibility as a parent not to take a picture to post on social media but to make sure that your dog doesn't have to defend himself from an overly affectionate child.

As your child gets older, you can teach him or her how to read and respond appropriately to dog body language. This will be important information as the child starts going to parks or other people's homes. The more your child learns from you about dog behavior, the safer he or she will be when encountering dogs elsewhere.

ENHANCING THE RELATIONSHIP

As your child grows, he or she can learn about canine behavior and how to help care for the dog. Begin with structured, age-appropriate activities. For instance, young children can help to fill a dog's food bowl or wash and refill a water bowl. More important, this reinforces the lesson

Meeting a **Loose Dog**

As soon as your child is walking and has a basic understanding of language (approximately eighteen months old), teach him or her what to do if a strange dog approaches or chases him or her. Kids like to pretend, so have your child practice "being a tree." That means to stand still, cross the arms over the chest, and look down, never at the dog.

If it's possible for the child to get out of the situation by backing away slowly, still not looking at the dog, he or she can do so. Otherwise, the child should stay in place until the dog loses interest or an adult intervenes.

My Dog Doesn't Like My Child

Dogs are individuals, and they can have distinct likes and dislikes. Not every dog is going to love children. Not even if he's a Golden Retriever or a Saint Bernard or some other breed that is supposed to be naturally good with kids. That doesn't make him a bad dog, but it can mean that he's not the right fit for your home. Sometimes, the best thing you can do for that dog is to place him in a loving home where he doesn't have to live with kids for the rest of his life. If you are unsure of how to live peacefully with a child and a fearful dog, see a veterinary behaviorist immediately.

CHILDREN AND FEARFUL, ANXIOUS, OR STRESSED DOGS

Whether your dog likes kids or is fearful of them, never force him to interact with them. Too often, people think they are "socializing" their dog to children when in fact they are confirming and worsening a dog's fears by holding him in place and letting children pet him or pick him up.

If a dog is growling, backing up, or otherwise trying to get away, he doesn't want to be petted. Forcing him causes fear, anxiety, and stress and can lead to a bite.

With the help of a board-certified veterinary behaviorist, dogs who are highly reactive toward children can be helped by changing their underlying emotion—fear, anxiety, or stress—to feelings of calm or even happy anticipation in situations that previously made

that dogs need food and fresh water daily. Other ways to include a child in the dog's care are to have him or her help stuff a puzzle toy, teach him or her how to gently brush the dog, or have him or her give the dog a chewable parasite preventive.

Responsibility can grow along with the child. Older children can learn to walk the dog on leash once they have learned what to do if another dog approaches or a friend wants to pet the dog. All of these things are part of long-term, successful pet care that children need to learn and are among the first steps toward taking on adult responsibilities.

Finally, take training classes together as a family. It's a great opportunity for everyone to learn consistent training techniques from a qualified professional. Don't stop at puppy kindergarten or basic obedience class. Attending other classes, such as canine sports or good citizenship, helps maintain and strengthen the bond between dog and family members and reinforce the dog's skills.

them uncomfortable. This is done by changing how they feel about kids approaching.

One such strategy is to have the sight of a child be the cue for your dog to spin toward you and sit. In the home, with no distractions, practice having the dog turn toward you and sit. Do this by saying his name and then taking a step backward while learning forward slightly. This encourages the dog to turn and look at you. Immediately give the Sit cue and then reward it. Once you've practiced this enough that it's second nature for him to spin and sit when you say his name, you can start to practice in public.

MUTUAL ENJOYMENT

We want both dogs and children to enjoy the experience of being together. Sometimes, the dog is having a great time, but the child is not, or vice versa. We've talked about how dogs can be uncomfortable with hugs and kisses.

On the other side of the fence, a dog may be having a wonderful time jumping up on a kid or nipping at his heels. A child's high-pitched voice and quick movements can encourage a dog to jump up on or chase him or her. A child who screams or tries to push the dog away seems to be instigating an exciting game—one that can

BooBoo's Story

BooBoo, a 10-pound Maltese mix, turned into 10 pounds of furry fury when he saw children running or moving quickly. He would attack doors, nip at their feet, or bark and look scary when children were running or walking out a door. He hadn't broken skin or made marks with his nips, but his behavior was frightening to the family's children, and other kids didn't like to come over.

I worked with the family, and we put in place several procedures to help manage BooBoo's baleful behavior:

- He had several safe places where he could go to get away from the children.
- When guests came over, he wore a harness and dragline or was placed in one of his sanctuary spaces.
- He was brought out only when children were being calm.
- Kids became his ticket to playing the training games he enjoyed, such as puppy push ups, performing sits and downs, and targeting objects.
- He learned the waiting game: waiting at the food bowl and waiting at doors, for instance.
- His owners practiced having him around children, wearing a harness and leash held by an adult.
- The children moved slowly and turned to go out the door while BooBoo waited and was then rewarded for calm behavior.
- BooBoo was most reactive at the front door, so the owners separated him from the door with a baby gate, which reduced much of his reactivity and allowed him to settle down and get rewarded from across the gate. The children's rambunctious behavior, such as running and wrestling, was limited to the playroom or outdoors or while BooBoo was in his sanctuary room.
- BooBoo learned to heel on walks. The owners practiced jogging with him to teach him that faster speeds meant he should move with them at their side rather than biting at feet.

—Mikkel Becker

Treat Him **Right**

Children love to give treats to dogs, but not all dogs are experts at receiving treats. They grab at them, with teeth grazing skin, or they jump up in an attempt to get treats, with the potential of knocking the child over.

Tell children, whether they are your own or visitors, to ask before giving any dog a treat. Show them how to offer a treat on the flat of the hand, below the dog's mouth, instead of holding it above him and encouraging him to jump and bite at it.

Require the dog to sit before the child offers a treat. Reinforcing the habit of sitting in greeting can help your dog stay calm and focused.

If your dog doesn't have nice treat manners, children can still give him rewards by tossing treats on the ground or offering peanut butter on a wooden spoon. These methods make it less likely that a dog will scare or nip a child by excitedly grabbing a treat.

escalate quickly. The dog has no idea that the child is not enjoying the game and is instead terrified. That's one of the reasons it's so important to teach a dog to sit when he greets people.

A similar instance might involve a child's trying to take one of his or her own toys away from a dog. The dog is pulling, and it becomes a tug of war, which is fun for the dog. For the kid, however, not so much.

We must reiterate the importance of supervision and recognizing what's going on. The vast majority of dog bites occur when the adults in charge aren't paying attention. It only takes a moment when they've stepped out of the room to answer the phone or take something out of the oven.

If you're ever in doubt, don't hesitate to make use of baby gates, crates, or sanctuary rooms for pets. None of us have eyes in the back of our heads, so using these tools allows us to keep our children and dogs safe.

Foster the friendship between your child and dog by supervising, teaching, and modeling appropriate interactions. Kids aren't born knowing how to treat a dog kindly, and dogs aren't born knowing how to treat kids gently.

Providing structure and predictability helps dogs become and stay comfortable in the presence of children. The bottom line is that your dog needs to know that he can trust you, the adult, for relief when he's being bombarded by a child throwing blocks at hime, bonking him on the head, or falling on top of him. When the adults in charge take a proactive and vigilant role, your dog and child can get on with the business of being best friends.

ENRICHMENT:
PLAY, GAMES, AND ADVANCED **TRAINING**

Have you been hearing the term "enrichment" thrown around when it comes to dogs? It's considered an essential aspect of living with a dog. Simply, enrichment is providing mental, physical, and environmental stimulation to improve a dog's overall well-being. A dog who is challenged mentally and physically is not only happy, he's tired. And we all know the adage that a tired dog is a good dog.

Think about it. A century ago, dogs lived active lives. They worked on farms herding livestock, helped people hunt for food, pulled carts for butchers, drove cattle to market, or had jobs in shops as ratters or watchdogs. As family companions, they may have walked the kids to school or played outdoors with them or sauntered around the neighborhood on their own during the day.

Few dogs these days can claim such a lifestyle. We live in different times, and technology and lifestyle changes mean that dogs spend most of their time at home, snoozing the day away. They don't have to find their own food or seek out a safe space to sleep or avoid predators. Roaming the streets would put them in danger of being hit by a car. But they still have clever brains and the same amount of energy to expend. It's our job to help them find outlets for their natural behaviors and need for physical activity instead of leading lives of quiet — or sometimes not so quiet—desperation.

Enrichment can sometimes be a coping method to help alleviate tension or increase a dog's physical or mental distance from whatever is causing fear, anxiety, or stress. Techniques, toys, and tricks in this chapter are among the strategies that may help you live successfully with a fearful, anxious, or stressed dog.

ENRICHMENT 101

If your dog seems to do nothing but sleep, has little interest in his surroundings, and doesn't give favorite toys a second glance, there are two things you need to do. The first is to take him to the veterinarian for a checkup. He may have a broken tooth or some other physical ailment that's causing pain and reducing his joy

in life. If he gets a clean bill of health, though, try giving him a good dose of enrichment—stimulating pursuits that will give all his senses a boost. Here are some things to try.

REVERSE BRAIN DRAIN

"I don't have time to exercise my dog more," you may be thinking. You don't necessarily need to add more physical activity. Giving your dog a regular mental workout can often be just as tiring as taking him for a 3-mile run. Games, puzzle toys, and training sessions are all good ways to exercise his little gray cells.

You can combine mental stimulation and physical activity by using puzzle toys that dispense kibble or treats when dogs push or roll them. We're big proponents of having your dog work for his meals. Instead of plopping down a food dish in front of him, fill a treat-dispensing gadget with some of his daily allotment of food and let him have at it. Now he has something to occupy his time while you're at work or running errands. Filling a hollow hard rubber toy with peanut butter and treats or kibble will add in some taste and texture fun. If your dog is aggressive over food or bones, be sure to give him these types of toys in his own space, behind a baby gate or closed door. When you need to take the item, call him out of the space, go inside, close the gate or door with him on the outside, and pick up the item.

ADD ENVIRONMENTAL INTEREST

You may wonder why your dog needs enrichment when he has a nice fenced yard to play in. But just as kids have swing sets, sandboxes, and play houses outdoors, dogs need equivalent motivation to run, jump, and play. Depending on their interests and instincts,

Play's **Benefits**

Play is how puppies learn the social signals they need to get along with other dogs. Dogs who play are also less likely to engage in nuisance chewing, digging, and barking caused by lack of stimulation.

Play also reinforces good behavior. If your dog loves playing fetch or tug, ask him to perform a trick or obedience command before initiating the game.

Play helps keep dogs out of trouble. By nature, they are hunters, scavengers, and roamers. While most of our dogs can't live out that canine dream life, they can approximate it with play that wears them out and prevents frustration or inappropriate play such as chewing up your shoes, digging holes in your garden, or mouthing your arm to get your attention.

Play strengthens the human-animal bond. When we play with our dogs, they associate us with good times. That's the best benefit of all.

ignite their passion for play with one or more of the following:

- A digging pit—the canine equivalent of a sandbox—studded with toys.
- A mini agility course with weave poles, jumps, a teeter-totter or A-frame, and a tunnel.
- A soft rope hung from a tree branch, tied tightly enough that your dog can tug or swing on it but not pull it down
- A plastic wading pool filled with water so he can splash or lounge
- Frozen ice molds made with chicken broth and treats

POWER OF TOUCH

Dogs enjoy pleasant touches as much as anyone. Treat him to petting, massage, and grooming. You can take a class to learn how to massage your dog or make grooming a special part of the day.

Pay attention to how your dog likes to be touched. If his ears go back and he ducks his head or tries to nip when you reach for him, he might dislike being patted on his head. Give him a scratch on the chest or beneath the chin instead.

SOUND HOUND

Anyone who has heard a dog howl along with his shower-singing owner or seen one rock a freestyle competition knows that dogs enjoy and respond to music. To provide your dog with some aural stimulation when you're away from home, tune the radio to an easy listening or other pleasant channel. Choose the station carefully. One study showed that classical music calms dogs while heavy metal revs them up.

You can instead leave the television on, tuned to a nature channel. That not only gives your dog something to watch and listen to, it also helps to dampen sounds from outdoors that may cause him to bark excessively.

A white noise machine blocks sound more consistently than television or radio, which can have highs and lows or moments of silence. Another option is a fan or air purifier. The constant droning sound acts as a buffer against noises the dog may hear coming from outside the house. Playing music as well provides a double layer of helpful sound to combat disruptive noise that causes dogs to bark or become anxious or fearful.

WALKING THE DOG

Walks are more than just chances for your dog to potty and burn off a little energy; they offer socialization and mental stimulation. Don't look at walks as chores to be completed as quickly as possible. Instead, consider them opportunities to provide enrichment for your

Enjoy Every
Smell

What kind of smells can interest a dog? You name it. When a dog sniffs a spot, he is figuring out the history and current state of the area: who has been there, what they were doing, and where they went.

We may not understand what's so intriguing about certain scents, such as animal droppings in the grass, but finding such smells is part of being a fulfilled dog. Allowing your dog to sniff provides mental stimulation and can even calm him in the process. Not all walks are appropriate for long sessions of sniffing, but providing some opportunities for your dog to stop and smell the roses—or fire hydrants—is important.

—Mikkel Becker

dog and relaxation for yourself. A good walk has the power to positively affect a dog's emotional state, behavior, and ability to bond with people. Here are some ways to unleash the full potential of your dog's walk.

Make them "scentsational." Sniffing is how dogs learn about their environment. Think of it as "nosebook" and "pee-mail." You can't always let him amble along at his own speed, but, whenever possible, it's a great idea to combine physical and mental stimulation on a walk by building in plenty of sniff time. We like to think of it as a "dog's choice" walk.

Instead of pulling him along, let him choose the direction and go at his own pace, stopping to sniff for as long as he'd like. This is an especially good option for senior dogs or those with limited mobility. They get environmental stimulation without having to cover much ground. Even if you give him free sniffing time for only a few minutes at the beginning or end of the walk, it's a chance for him to make some of his own decisions and catch up on the neighborhood news.

If a brisk walk is important to you, teach your dog a verbal cue that lets him know when he should continue walking without breaks. For instance, you can say "Let's Go" when you want to walk at a normal pace and "Free Time" when it's OK for him to have a sniff break so he can slow down and check out the area.

Be present. If your dog doesn't pay attention to you on walks, maybe it's because you don't pay attention to him. If you are always on your cell phone, have your earbuds in, or concentrating on a problem at work, your dog can pick up on your inattention. If he gives you eye contact or moves closer to you, and you miss the chance to make that connection with him, those rewarding and "rewardable" moments may occur less frequently.

Being present with your dog, free of distractions, helps to strengthen your relationship. It's also important for paying attention to your surroundings so you can see any approaching distractions or dangers, such as a loose dog, kids on skateboards, or someone operating a motorized toy car that your dog might want to chase.

When you engage with your dog during walks, you can reward moments of focus and attention, such as when your dog looks at you or pays attention to which direction you're going. To get his attention, use a word such as "Turn," "Left," or "Right" to indicate that you're changing direction. When he catches up to

Seniors Need Enrichment, Too

Just because your dog is getting on in years is no reason to quit doing things with him. He might be too arthritic to chase a ball, but he may enjoy going for a ride in a stroller or child's wagon. That kind of outing gives him a chance to see, sniff, and hear interesting things, not to mention the pleasure of the breeze ruffling his fur. Along the way, let him get out and walk around or sniff. When you provide your golden oldie with stimulating experiences, you're sure to notice a spring in his step and a sparkle in his eye.

When my Shiba Inu entered her mid-teens and became arthritic with limited mobility, I did something I never thought I would do: I purchased a stroller for her. It allowed us to still do the things she enjoyed but made them much easier for her. She would walk until she was tired. When she slowed down, I would plop her in the stroller, and she would rest while I pushed her around. I could clearly see that she enjoyed the outing. She would sit or lie down, but her head was up and she was looking around, clearly still interested in the sights and sounds we encountered.

The outings were also helpful in reducing her signs of cognitive decline. Often, she would pace late into the evening, but she would sleep deeply after a stroller ride.

The stroller allowed my senior dog to live the last few years of her life being able to enjoy fun activities, be with us, be social, and take in the rest of the world. Little Bonsai lived to be seventeen years old.

—Dr. Wailani Sung

you, slowly turn and reward him. Additionally, reward any moment that he is looking in your direction or giving eye contact. That adds interest to the walk for him, gives you chances to interact with him, and increases his desire and willingness to check in with you.

Add an exercise routine. Adding physical challenges to a walk not only helps slim your dog's waistline, it also provides a mental challenge and an outlet to release excess energy. Before adding an exercise routine, talk to your veterinarian about your plans, especially if your dog is a puppy, is a senior, or has physical limitations.

Some things to try:

- Tackle hills and stairs that you encounter on your walks for an aerobic workout. Walking on an incline also works your dog's muscles in a different way.
- Walk on sand to add resistance.
- Vary your normal walking pace with speed-walks or jogs.
- Throw in some puppy push-ups: a series of sits, downs, and stands (for a nice reward, of course).
- Have your dog jump on or over benches, walls, stumps, logs, large rocks, or

Get Social **Safely**

Walks are ways to keep up your dog's social skills, but not in the way you might think. It's not necessary or advisable to let him greet every person and dog along the way. It's not good dog manners, and it's time consuming to boot. But letting your dog see, smell, and walk by other people and dogs provides ongoing experience with how to read body language and respond to others.

If you do want social time for yourself and your dog on a walk, invite a friend and his or her dog to go with you, or join a dog-friendly walking group. For dogs who love human interaction, scout out a pet-friendly store or restaurant that you can both visit.

—Mikkel Becker

playground equipment. These are great ways to build coordination, balance, and strength.

- If your dog needs an additional challenge, ask your veterinarian if it's OK for him to do some weight training—not bicep curls, but carrying or pulling some extra weight. A canine backpack, weighted vest, or joring harness attached to a weighted item can add extra oomph to a workout for a dog who is already strong and super-fit.
- Do something new. In some ways, dogs like routine, but it can become boring and restrictive on walks. Try taking a different route or going to another neighborhood once in a while. Change up your walks by going in the opposite direction than normal or going down a street that you usually pass by. Throw in a field trip with a visit to a dog-friendly shopping center, park, trail, or beach. New sights, smells, and sounds are healthy ways to stimulate your dog's mind.

GAMES DOGS PLAY

Walks, hikes, and playtime are all wonderful ways to enrich your dog's life. They don't cost anything, you don't need a training class to learn how to do them, and you can work them into your schedule at any time.

But maybe you want to do something more with your dog because of his brains, athletic ability, or drive. Sometimes the very things that make a dog interesting can also make him a handful to live with if he doesn't have an outlet for his interests and energy. If you want to bring out your dog's full abilities, or if you want to build the confidence of a fearful, anxious, or stressed dog, consider taking up a dog sport that plays to his natural talents or behaviors. Here are some to consider.

Agility. If your dog can leap a fence in a single bound, crawl on his belly in the space behind the sofa, and fly through the park at light speed, he might be a candidate for this canine version of track-and-field events. Agility dogs — guided through the course by their handlers— must negotiate a series of obstacles, such as A-frames, tunnels, jumps, teeter-totters and weave poles. You can do it just for fun or compete for titles.

Flyball. This relay race involves four hurdles and a tennis ball. The twist? The dogs operate the equipment that delivers the tennis ball. A flyball team has a minimum of four dogs and five people per team. Two teams race each other in relay fashion over a 51-foot course lined with four jumps. At the end of the course is a spring-loaded box that ejects a tennis ball when the dog hits it with his paw. When the ball flies out, the dog must catch it and race back over the hurdles, crossing the starting line before the next dog goes. The first team to run the course without errors wins. Dogs earn points toward flyball titles based on their team's time.

Freestyle. Often nicknamed "dancing with dogs," this activity might sound silly, but it requires real talent on the part of both dog and owner. If your dog is good at walking

on his hind legs, backing up, spinning, and sidestepping, he'll be a freestyle star.

Lure coursing. Dogs who are built for speed can't get enough of lure coursing. No bunnies or other animals are harmed in this high-speed sport, which involves chasing a white plastic bag—the lure—along a twisting, turning course. Dogs are judged on enthusiasm, speed, agility, and endurance. The kings of the sport are the sighthounds, but other breeds are starting to take it up. Jack Russell Terriers think it's great fun, and even Cavalier King Charles Spaniels have been known to give it a go and do quite well indeed.

Nosework. Does your dog love to sniff? He'll adore nosework, in which he'll learn to seek out and identify a particular odor — birch, anise or clove — and alert his handler to the find by sitting, looking at the person, or giving some other indication. It can be played indoors or outdoors on all types of surfaces and in all conditions, including rain and snow. Nosework leaves dogs large and small happily exhausted after working to find scent in a container, room, outdoor area, or vehicle. Like agility, you can play it for fun or compete for titles.

The other advantage to nosework is that it was created for reactive or fearful dogs. Whether in class or at a trial, dogs participate one at a time, while other dogs are crated out of sight and hearing range. For this reason alone, nosework is the best sport for fearful dogs.

Rally. In this sport, dog and handler complete a course with ten to twenty stations. At each station, the team must perform a designated skill, such as Sit, Down, Turn, Heel, and more. The goal is to complete the entire sequence correctly.

Treibball. Got a herding dog but no ducks, sheep, or cattle for him to work? Treibball is the sport for you. Dogs use their noses or shoulders to direct eight balls into a goal. It's perfect for herding breeds, but any breed or mix can play.

Old Dog, **New Tricks?**

It's an old wives' tale that senior dogs can't learn new things. One recent study found that dogs are capable of learning well into their golden years. The three-year study tested learning, memory, and problem-solving in ninety-five pet Border Collies ranging in age from five months to thirteen years. All of the dogs were capable of learning, although the older dogs took longer to reach the same level of proficiency as younger dogs. Older dogs performed better than younger ones in reasoning ability, and once they learned something, they remembered it over the long term. So train away: it will help your old dog's brain stay flexible.

—*Dr. Marty Becker*

TRICK AND TREAT?

Who doesn't love a dog who can jump through a hoop, shake hands, or twirl on his hind legs? Teaching tricks is a wonderful way to engage your dog's mind, exercise his body, and give him an entertaining outlet for interacting with people.

Dogs can learn to sit up on their hind legs, turn their head left or right, wave, roll over, wrap up in a blanket, and much more. Some people even teach their dogs such useful skills as picking up and putting away their toys or dirty laundry or closing cupboard doors. If he's tall enough, you can send your dog over to turn off the light that one of the kids left on.

Learning tricks isn't going to magically cure a dog who is fearful, anxious, or stressed, but it can have benefits for him. This type of training can build confidence, add structure to the

Important to Note

dog's life, and encourage him to turn to you for guidance in situations that make him nervous. Teaching your dog to respond to certain cues when he is unsure about a person or situation may play a role in moderating his response to situations that cause fear, anxiety, or stress. Performing a cue he knows well followed by the reinforcement of a food reward or praise can help distract him from a person or situation that is causing fear, anxiety, or stress.

We'll get you going with these six tricks. To learn more, look for a trainer in your area who offers trick classes or see the books we recommend in the appendix.

ADVANCED TRAINING

Tricks are more than just fun and games. They can be fabulously functional. The ability to focus on performing a particular behavior or trick can help your dog calm down in exciting or stressful situations. It can help redirect him from unwanted behaviors, such as barking or jumping, to desirable behaviors, such as being quiet or sitting.

Teaching your dog some simple behaviors that are usually thought of as tricks can help you successfully manage some real-life situations. For example, a dog who likes to chase children, people on bicycles, or other animals can be distracted by performing a series of active tricks such as Sit, Roll Over, and Spin. This can create a diversion until the "chasee" is no longer in sight. Here's how you can use tricks to help your dog relax in stressful situations or cooperate without fear during veterinary exams, grooming, or other instances that require handling or management.

Go to Your Place

As we've mentioned, teaching your dog to go to a specific place, such as his bed, crate, or mat, is helpful in many different situations. To teach this behavior, start by tossing treats toward or onto the mat to engage your dog's interest in it. When he puts a paw on the mat, say "Yes" or click and toss a treat onto the mat. Repeat. Once he's on the mat, ask for a Down (if he knows that command) or wait until it occurs naturally and say "Yes" or click and treat. When your dog goes onto the mat reliably, add a verbal cue, such as "Mat." Reward him intermittently for resting on the mat; he should never be able to figure out a pattern or time frame for treats. Gradually introduce distractions and longer stays on the mat.

Play Dead

This is a simple and entertaining way to calm an anxious dog. If your dog is upset, excited, or just needs a break, ask him to play dead. Most dogs don't like being turned on their sides, but it will be less stressful for them if you have generously rewarded this behavior in the past.

The Play Dead trick begins with the dog in a Down. Hold a treat in front of his nose and use it to guide the head toward the tail. Once the dog has his head turned toward the back, start to move the treat toward the middle of the back. Reward any movement that involves the dog resting his shoulder on the ground. Once the shoulder is on the floor, use the treat to get the dog to move his nose out and forward. Give lots of treats during this process; a high reward rate for small successes will help keep your dog interested and thus less likely to jump up.

Now use the treat to guide the head so it's facing forward. The dog's muzzle will probably be in line with the ground. Reward your dog for staying in place: side resting on the ground and face on the ground. At first, you may need to keep your hand full of treats next to the dog's nose, but begin to move the hand farther away each time while still rewarding the dog for remaining in place. If the dog gets up, lure him back into position and start over.

When your dog understands what you want, fade the lure. Use an empty hand to guide him into position, but continue to reward him once he achieves it. Add a verbal cue, such as "Play Dead" or "Bang!"

To get your dog used to being examined while in this position, touch him briefly and reward him for remaining in place. Gradually extend the length of time you ask him to play dead, and keep those rewards coming. Once he responds reliably to the cue, fade the treat

as soon as possible, but continue to reward him for his efforts. Remember that he will continue to offer only rewarded behaviors.

Roll Over

This trick is a natural progression from Down and Play Dead. You may be lucky enough to have a dog who performs this behavior on his own. If so, simply capture the behavior and give it a name as described for the Down cue. Otherwise, the following technique should have your dog rolling over in no time.

Start with your dog in a Down. Holding a treat in your hand, move it to the side so his head turns. If he hasn't shifted onto one hip, choose whichever direction you prefer. If he has shifted onto one hip, lure his head in the opposite direction of the hip that's tucked under. In other words, if the dog is resting on his left hip, use the lure on his right side so the head turns in that direction and he flops more in the direction of his hip and shoulder. The most important thing is for him to have plenty of room to roll over.

At first, reward small head turns. Gradually increase the difficulty by having him turn his head farther in the direction toward the floor. Once his shoulder is down, continue the roll over by luring the head farther so the dog's body weight begins to shift and the body starts to twist. When he flips all the way over, give him a big jackpot of treats. As your dog begins to understand what you want, fade the lure. Use an empty hand to guide him into position, but continue to reward him once he achieves it. Then a new signal such as a circled finger can be used, followed by the hand gesture to elicit the behavior. Or make the rollover signal smaller and smaller until it becomes the cue. You may need to ask the dog to lie down first before asking for rollover.

Hand Targeting

Teaching your dog to follow your hand or other target has many uses. A dog who jumps on people in greeting can learn instead to touch his nose to a visitor's hand. It's also a simple way to move your dog off a piece of furniture, get him onto the scale at the veterinary clinic, or direct his focus away from food or objects he's not allowed to have. Following and touching a target can help reduce a dog's fear of an object, such as a stethoscope or nail clippers.

To teach hand targeting, present two fingers or an open palm a few inches in front of your dog's nose and slightly to the side. You can also use a wooden spoon or a stick, such as a bird perch. If he looks at your hand or even just moves his eyes toward the target, click and treat. You can put a soft treat, such as peanut butter or cream cheese, on the end of the target to increase his interest, if necessary, but use it only the first few times. Repeat.

If he touches your hand with his nose, click and treat the instant his nose touches your

fingers or hand. Each time you're successful, move the target out of sight (behind your back, for instance) and then present it again. If he doesn't seem to notice it, remove it and try presenting it in a different area. The goal is for him to walk toward the target and touch his nose to it.

Another way to do this if you're using a stick or spoon is to lay the object on the ground with treats around it to pique your dog's interest. Mark and reward any movement toward it or any time your dog touches it with his nose, mouth, or muzzle.

When your dog readily touches his nose to your hand or the target, add a cue such as "Touch!" To create an association between the word and the behavior, say the cue just before or just as your dog moves toward the target. As he begins to respond to the verbal cue, start moving your palm farther away from him, using it to indicate where you want him to go. With practice, your dog should progress from moving a couple of inches to touch the target to following the target even if you're holding it a few feet away. Eventually, he will learn to move onto or off an object to get to the target.

Here's another way this can help your fearful,

anxious, or stressed dog. Maybe he doesn't like the appearance of people in uniform (or on bicycles or wearing hats). Any time you see a police officer, delivery person, or anyone else in a uniform, give your dog the "Touch" cue. He turns to you, touches your hand, and gets rewarded. The presence of a person in uniform becomes a source of good things, not an object of fear.

Shake

This trick is useful for greeting people and having nails trimmed or paws examined. It's a fun way to help boost a dog's confidence.

Your dog can be sitting or standing when he learns this. Have a treat or toy in your hand, and use it to entice him to reach for it with a paw. For even a slight paw lift, mark it with a "Yes!" or click and then reward with a treat. Repeat. The goal is for him to raise his paw all the way off the ground and touch your hand. Try moving the toy or treat higher if needed.

Once your dog understands that the pawing motion is what gets him the treat, decrease the movement of the toy or treat until you are getting a paw swipe just at the sight of it. Gradually move your hand over the toy or treat so it's less noticeable and the paw is touching the hand instead. Start to reward only when the paw touches the hand.

When your dog reliably touches your hand with his paw, remove the toy or treat from the equation and simply hold out your closed hand. As your dog becomes proficient at touching it, slowly open your hand until he's touching your open palm as if giving you a high five. Now you can start to add a verbal cue such as "High Five," "Put 'er There, or "Shake." Begin to say it before your dog puts his paw up and just as your hand stretches out.

GIVE IT A TRY!

Enrichment—and its sidekicks play and training—are important in a dog's life. They build confidence and reduce fear. Dogs who live enriched lives are less stressed, have fewer behavior problems, are more physically fit, have improved social skills and have a stronger bond with their people. Enrichment alone doesn't replace daily exercise or having a job to do, but it sure does enhance them and help to prevent boredom.

Dog sports and tricks are real confidence builders for dogs. Who doesn't love getting smiles and applause from an audience? Use these activities to promote positive interactions, and see how well your dog responds.

Whatever you choose to do with your dog, whether it's an organized competitive activity or special time at home, you'll be building a bond with your beloved pet. Have fun out there!

DOG **PARKS**

One of the most dismaying aspects of living with a fearful, anxious, or stressed dog is the prospect of taking him out in public, especially to a place that's supposed to be fun, like a dog park. When you get a puppy, you envision playing with him at the park or watching him play with other dogs there. Then you discover that your dog wants nothing to do with the dog park because he's afraid of other dogs. He behaves aggressively, requiring you to figure when the dog park is likely to be empty so that you can let him run without fearing that he'll pick a fight with another dog. In this chapter, we're going to talk about ways to navigate public spaces, such as dog parks, and when to use or not use them.

FEAR AGGRESSION

Why do dogs behave fearfully (cowering or trying to run away) or aggressively (snarling or lunging) when they see dogs they don't know? The behavior can have several possible causes, or it might result from a combination of causes.

It's not unusual for dogs to become apprehensive of unknown animals as they enter adolescence, especially if they have received insufficient socialization before they are four months old. Aggressive displays resulting from fear can begin anywhere from eight weeks to two years of age in males and females of any breed or mix. Behavior modification may help, but it should begin as early as possible.

If you have a fearful dog who wasn't socialized, or you don't know his socialization history, don't "flood" him with new experiences or meetings with strange dogs in an attempt to make up for past lack of socialization. That will send his fear levels into overdrive.

Certain dogs may have a genetic predisposition to fearfulness. Socialization and behavior modification may help them deal with their fears, but these methods are not silver bullets.

Some breeds have a naturally protective and suspicious nature. If you bought a guardian-breed puppy with the idea that socialization would ensure that he loved everyone, you are probably discovering the extent of your mistake. Early and extensive socialization is important for guardian breeds because it helps them respond appropriately in a wide variety of situations to many different types of people, but they are never going to be "hail fellow, well met" kind of dogs at a dog park.

Some dogs are fearfully aggressive because they have suffered trauma. They take on the best-defense-is-a-good-offense strategy because they are so scared. Many dogs were friendly toward other dogs until they were attacked at the dog park or the dog beach or even in their own neighborhood. This is a common cause of fear aggression toward other dogs.

Finally, some dogs may be fearful or aggressive as a result of a combination of these factors. Our goal in this chapter is to help you understand how to recognize and respond to your dog's fearful, anxious, or stressed behavior in an appropriate and beneficial way. Whatever your dog's issues at the dog park, it's a good idea to enlist the services of a board-certified veterinary behaviorist or certified applied animal behaviorist who can help you identify triggers and map out a solution.

Don't Make
Matters Worse

One of the biggest concerns I have as a trainer is seeing dogs who are forced into going to a dog park. They become overwhelmed and overloaded—and set up for failure.

Many dog lovers live with the unspoken rule that "good dogs go to dog parks" and "good people take their dogs to dog parks." The negative connotation of his or her dog not being a good fit for a dog park often causes an owner guilt and shame. For that reason, despite a dog's hesitance or involvement in negative incidents, people frequently take their fearful, anxious, or stressed dogs to the park in hopes of making them more social. With most dogs, when a park is used to "fix" social issues, the behavior only becomes worse.

—*Mikkel Becker*

WHICH DOGS DO BEST?

Just as not every person enjoys cocktail parties or fraternity or sorority life, not every dog is cut out for the dog-park circuit. The dog park is a canine version of those social situations. It's unpredictable because of the variety of canine personalities that can gather there, and that makes it a no-go for some dogs.

Don't be frustrated by your dog's reluctance to be a social butterfly at the dog park. It's something that may literally be in his genes. Some dogs have been bred for generations to have personality traits that make them unsuited to interacting with other dogs.

Other dogs have fear-based reactions. They may become pushy from excessive arousal,

Legal Repercussions

Taking a fearful, aggressive, or otherwise unsuitable dog to a dog park can have greater costs than you might realize. If your dog bites another dog or a person, and that dog's owner or person reports the bite, he may have just become labeled a dangerous dog. In some cities or counties, a single bite leaves a dog with a record that has the potential to be fatal depending on the locale's laws. Others may have a "first-bite" warning that's followed by a dangerous-dog designation on the second bite. Additionally, many people risk losing their homeowner's insurance or being sued. If your dog has a bite history or is aggressive, do not bring him to a dog park. One owner of an aggressive dog gives this advice, learned through sad experience: Do not do anything that you couldn't defend in front of a judge. If your dog has bitten someone or even growled, what defense would you have in front of a judge for bringing the dog to a dog park? None. You would lose. It doesn't matter if your dog was defending himself from bullying by another dog or if he accidentally bit a person who was trying to break up a dog fight. The dog who bites is the one who gets labeled.

When your dog bites another person or dog, you may be responsible for medical, veterinary and legal bills. A court may order your dog to wear a muzzle in public or, in the worst case, be euthanized.

All of these reasons are why it's essential to make sure your dog is ready for the increased risks and stimulation that come with going to a dog park. If you have any doubt about your dog's comfort level at a dog park, seek the advice of a board-certified veterinary behaviorist or a veterinarian working in tandem with a positive-reinforcement trainer.

—Mikkel Becker

causing unpredictable interactions or even aggressive encounters.

Dogs are individuals. Just because your neighbor's dog loves going to the dog park doesn't mean your dog will. And if that's the case, it doesn't mean that there's anything wrong with your dog. Your dog may prefer playdates in a familiar area with dogs he already knows. Dogs who are fearful of other dogs or who just prefer human companionship do best with activities, such as training sessions or scentwork, that are done one-on-one.

Prime candidates for dog parks are energetic adolescent dogs from six months to four years old. They tend to have the highest activity levels and a greater desire for play than older dogs. As they mature, energy levels and the desire for play often begin to decrease. They may become less social and have less tolerance for getting along with other dogs at the park.

Here's a checklist to help you decide if you should take your dog to an off-leash park:

- Is my dog comfortable interacting with other dogs?
- Does my dog greet other dogs appropriately?
- Does my dog come when called consistently and without hesitation?
- Am I able to distract and redirect my dog if play gets out of control?
- Is my dog possessive of balls, flying discs, sticks or other items?

Helpful **Cues**

I recommend teaching dogs Look, Turn, and Touch cues. Practice greetings with calm dogs by allowing the dogs to sniff for one to two seconds. Then, instead of applying pressure on the leash, work on teaching the dogs to back off by asking them to "look" or "turn" toward you or come toward you for a "touch." This keeps initial introductions short and sweet. If the first brief meeting goes well, they can go back for round two.

Think of the initial meeting as being similar to a handshake. I like to shake a person's hand twice before I let go. If a person holds my hand for longer than two pumps, it makes me uncomfortable. Dogs may feel the same way about extended greetings. If they are uncomfortable, we need to teach them how to disengage.

—*Dr. Wailani Sung*

The other issue with dogs being on leash during meetings is that dogs are highly sensitive to human emotions. If you are walking your fearful dog into the park on leash and another dog approaches, your automatic instinct is to tense up because you're worried that your dog will behave aggressively. Your anxiety travels right down the leash into your dog's brain, the same way lightning flashed down Ben Franklin's kite string, striking the key on the end and giving old Ben a shock. Your dog senses your anxiety and becomes anxious himself, especially if you pull back on the leash. He feels threatened not only on his own behalf but also on yours. His hackles rise, he lets out a low growl, and the other dog responds in kind. Boom! You have a situation, whether it's defensive posturing or a flat-out fight.

PARK MEET AND GREETS

Should your dog be on leash when he meets other dogs at the park? It seems like that would be a no-brainer, but there are good reasons to let meetings occur with dogs off leash. Here's why.

Being on a leash makes a dog—especially a fearful dog—feel restrained and vulnerable. He knows there's no way he can escape if the other dog attacks (whether or not that's likely). This is why fearful dogs often react defensively to the sight of an approaching dog, even if that other dog is also on leash. And chances are, the approaching dog is feeling the same internal conflicts about your dog. The same thing can happen when a leashed dog meets an unleashed dog.

Instead, take a cue from surfers and scuba divers and spend a few minutes surveying the scene before you jump into the dog-park waves. Look around to see which dogs are there, how they're interacting, and whether other owners are paying attention and seem to be in control of their dogs. If you're satisfied, then go into the park, close the gate behind you, unleash your dog, and let him sniff and interact in proper canine fashion, without the restraint of a leash.

Remember that this advice applies only to friendly, well-socialized dogs. If your dog has issues with other dogs, you're not doing him a favor by forcing dog-park visits. Find other ways to get your dog the activity and interaction he needs.

Selective **Fear**

Some dogs are fearful only of certain breeds or dogs of certain colors. For example, I know of a Cavalier King Charles Spaniel who is antagonistic toward German Shepherd Dogs, even though she's never had a bad experience with one. Another dog is afraid of black dogs because he was once attacked by one.

If your dog is fearful, anxious, or stressed around certain types of dogs, condition him to think that seeing that type of dog is the best thing ever. This could involve starting to hand out treats as soon as this type of dog comes into view, ideally before your dog reacts. Another technique is to interrupt an anticipated reaction to the dog's approach by calling your dog to you and giving him a treat or a favorite toy.

—*Mikkel Becker*

AT HOME **AND AWAY**

In most families, travel is a part of every dog's life at some point. Your dog may go with you on road trips in the car or RV or fly cross country to a canine sports event or move with you to a new home. A dog who knows how to get in and out of a carrier, can ride comfortably in a car (or on a boat or plane), and stay politely in a hotel is one who can go anywhere and be welcome.

For some dogs, though, travel may be frightening or stressful. Travel can involve coming into contact with unknown people or dogs, going to unfamiliar places, and walking on busy streets and loud noises, to name just a few of the experiences that can unsettle dogs.

If you must travel with your fearful, anxious, or stressed dog, you can benefit from these helpful hints that we've compiled to help things go smoothly. Or, you may decide that your dog is better off staying home. A boarding kennel or pet sitter may be a better option for him than joining you on the road. Here's how to keep your dog in a zen state during journeys.

PLAN AHEAD

Planning to travel with your dog involves more than just packing a bag with food, medication, and his favorite toy. It involves knowing what fearsome experiences your dog might encounter along the way and being prepared for them.

For instance, if you're staying at a hotel in Anaheim or Orlando, near one of the big theme parks, your noise-shy dog will hear fireworks

Manage Motion Sickness

Your dog may hate travel because he suffers from motion sickness. If you notice that he yawns, pants, whines, drools, or vomits during car rides, on your boat, or during air travel, chances are you have a dog who is motion sick. It's no wonder he's reluctant to go anywhere! The following tips may help to ease his upset tummy.

For mild motion sickness, a couple of gingersnaps before leaving may quell his queasiness. A dog seatbelt or raised car seat may allow him to see out the window; a little fresh air and a view of the horizon can help to minimize carsickness.

Severe cases of motion sickness call for stiffer measures. Ask your veterinarian about anti-nausea medication, which can be useful for all types of travel as well.

every night. Consider staying farther away or packing your dog's compression garment and a good supply of pheromone spray or whatever else helps calm him in the face of loud noises.

You may be visiting an area with more foot or car traffic than your dog is accustomed to. As you walk him, be aware of your surroundings. Watch for the approach of possible fear triggers, such as unknown dogs or people wearing hats, and be prepared to distract your dog. Ask your veterinarian about canine "blinders" that can limit your dog's vision, especially in crowded places such as airports, city streets, or hotel lobbies. On the plus side, some dogs are less fearful in new areas because they aren't on their own territory and don't feel the need to protect it.

Bring familiar items so that every place you go smells like home. Depending on the amount of space you have in your suitcase or vehicle, that could be his bed or blanket, a soft toy, or a T-shirt bearing your scent. Access to his crate or carrier will also give your dog a feeling of security, especially if you have sprayed or wiped it with a pheromone product.

Drug-Free **Flight**

It may seem counterintuitive, but avoid giving your dog tranquilizers before a flight. Drugs can have different effects at altitude. Sedatives or tranquilizers can affect a dog's equilibrium and blood pressure, causing respiratory and cardiovascular problems, especially in dogs with flat faces, such as Pugs, Bulldogs, Boston Terriers, and Pekingese. They can also blunt a dog's ability to pant or to deal with temperature extremes. Stick to pheromone sprays or wipes in the carrier, or ask your veterinarian to recommend other products that can help your dog stay calm without the side effects of sedatives or tranquilizers.

—Dr. Marty Becker

IN THE AIR

For their safety and sanity, we recommend that dogs travel only in the cabin, not cargo. Unless you use a pet transportation service, that limits air travel to puppies and small breeds whose

carriers fit beneath the seats in ever-more-cramped airplanes. A flight can go smoothly if you plan carefully and take some precautions.

Your dog should already be accustomed to riding in his carrier. Make a visit to the airport beforehand to ensure that his carrier fits beneath the seat. Airports have measuring devices that you can use to make sure the bag or crate has appropriate dimensions.

Bring a copy of your dog's rabies certificate (and any other required health information required by your destination) as well as the ticket he was issued when you made the reservation (don't try to fly without it). It's unlikely that anyone will ask to see either document, but you'll need to have them regardless. If you're calm because you have the necessary paperwork in hand, your dog is likely to tune in to your relaxed vibe.

If you have plenty of time before the trip, consider working to desensitize your dog to the sounds of airplanes taking off and landing. You can find recordings of airplanes that will help. Start with the recording at an extremely low volume and gradually increase it as your dog becomes comfortable with the sound. As always, reinforce calm, relaxed behavior.

Reserve a window seat. You'll have slightly more space beneath the seat in front of you than with an aisle seat, and your dog will have less reason to fret about all the people walking by him or the refreshment carts rumbling along.

Help him stay comfortable by providing him with a long-lasting chew. A hard rubber toy filled with tasty treats can keep him occupied for hours. Other ways to help a dog stay calm include canine "headphones" that reduce sound.

STAYING AT HOTELS OR HOMES

Walking into an unfamiliar place, such as a hotel room or a friend's home, can give your fearful dog the jitters. You can take some steps to help him relax.

When you arrive at your destination, take your dog out of the car and let him walk around, giving him plenty of time to take in the smells. Be sure that he empties his bladder in an appropriate spot. If you can get him to defecate as well, so much the better; be sure to clean up afterward.

If possible, leave your dog in the care of your traveling companion while you set up the room or his area with his crate, food and water dishes, and toys. Coming into a room that already has familiar items and scents in it will help your dog relax. Turning on a white noise machine can further reduce sounds from other rooms or people walking down the hall.

Ride with a View

Some hotels have glass elevators. Your dog may take normal elevators in stride but freak out inside a glass one. Don't force him onto it if he's reluctant or fearful. Ask hotel staff to direct you to a different elevator—one that won't have your dog thinking he's plunging into thin air.

Visiting the home of someone who also has a dog? Introduce the dogs outdoors, with each on a long, loose leash so they both feel as if they can escape if need be. Start with them at a distance of 15 to 20 feet from each other and reward calm behavior. Take them for a walk together. Once they seem relaxed together, you can let them have a brief meet and greet. Avoid letting them stare at each other, reward friendly

behavior, and separate them if normal play behavior turns aggressive.

If the dogs remain comfortable in each other's presence, let them get to know each other better in a fenced yard; keep them on the long leashes in case you need to separate them in a hurry. Before you take them indoors, make sure that they do not have access to anything that they might fight over, such as bones, toys, or other resources. Feed them in separate rooms or in their crates, out of each other's sight.

SEEING OTHER DOGS IN PUBLIC

Whether you are around town or on a trip with your dog, you will probably frequently see other dogs being walked. Often, the other people want their dogs to meet yours in a misguided attempt to socialize them or just be friendly. These people may not be familiar with canine body language or behavior, or they think that their dog's friendliness will overcome any fear on your dog's part. Whether your dog is fearful or not, it's best to avoid these types of meetings. It's all too easy for them to go badly, especially if both dogs are on leash or you don't know the other dog. Here are some phrases and techniques that can help you dodge dog-to-dog encounters:

- "My dog is skittish, so it's best not to let them get nose to nose."
- "My dog is fearful of other dogs."
- "My dog doesn't play well with others."
- Avoid eye contact with the person.
- Move off the sidewalk or trail, making it clear you don't want them to meet.
- "We're training right now."
- "Give him space, please."
- Stop, hold your finger (not the middle one) or hand up, and say "No contact."

- To someone whose dog is out of control on an extendible leash, "Reel your dog in now."
- When someone says, "Don't worry; he's friendly," reply "I'm not" or "My dog isn't."
- "The vet says it might be contagious" (no need to specify what "it" is).
- Teach your dog the Leave It cue and reward him with a treat for responding
- Turn around and go a different direction.
- Just say "no."

ALTERNATIVES TO TRAVEL

You may decide that your fearful dog is better off staying home, and that's OK—for you and for him. It doesn't mean that you have to stay home, though. A good boarding kennel, in-home boarding service, or pet sitter can be a best friend to you and your fearful dog. Whichever you choose, the key to finding the right one for your dog is asking the right questions.

An overnight stay in a strange place can be stressful for your dog—no doubt about it. That's especially true if he suffers from fear, anxiety, or stress. A good kennel or pet sitter is prepared to care for dogs with special needs and ensure that your dog's stay is comfortable and enjoyable. Here's what to look for.

BOARDING FACILITY

When you think boarding kennel, you may picture the old-style places with banks of side-by-side chain-link runs. These still exist, but other kennels resemble resorts, with daily hikes, massage, swimming pools, and more. Your dog may have a television in his room or even have the option of sleeping on a caretaker's bed at night. You may be able to check in on him any time of day or night via webcam. A good boarding facility provides opportunities to engage a dog's mind and body in different ways, such as puzzle toys, walks, and playtime with staff and—if appropriate—other dogs.

To determine if a kennel is right for your dog, don't let a fancy website with beautiful pictures sway your decision. Make at least one unannounced visit before you make a reservation for your dog. A tour will allow you to evaluate cleanliness as well as the comfort of the dogs currently boarding. Cross off your list any place that doesn't permit tours. Here's what you should find out with regard to boarding a dog who is fearful, anxious, or stressed:

- What experience do you have caring for dogs who are fearful, anxious, or stressed?
- How do you meet the needs of a fearful dog?
- What types of interactions will my dog have during his stay?
- How do you provide dogs with mental and physical stimulation during their stay?
- Will my people-oriented dog receive individual attention from kennel staff during the day? Does it cost extra?
- Is the kennel staffed at night? (Most are not, but emergencies can occur after hours, and it's best if you can find a kennel that has someone on the premises 24/7 as well as a veterinarian on call. This is also important for dogs with severe separation issues.)

- What are your sanitation measures? (The facility should be disinfected daily, with proper ventilation to promote airflow and discourage odors.)
- If you allow group play, is someone always there to supervise, and are dogs separated by size and temperament? (A small but game terrier can easily and quickly injure or kill a gentle toy breed before the supervisor can step in.)
- How do you provide this stimulation if my dog can't interact with other dogs? Where does my dog stay if he can't interact with other dogs?
- Do you have references from clients and veterinarians?
- Do you offer daycare as well? (This gives you the option of boarding your dog at a place with which he's already familiar.)

If you are satisfied with the responses, bring your dog to visit the facility. Note how staff members interact with your dog. Do they give him time to relax, and do they wait for him to approach them?

Pay attention as well to your dog's behavior. Dogs who have been adopted from shelters may be fearful in a kennel situation. If your dog trembles, pants or whines at the sights, sounds, or smells of a kennel, he may do best with in-home boarding or a pet sitter who comes in to care for him.

IN-HOME BOARDING AND PET SITTERS

Instead of leaving your dog in a kennel or home alone with a pet sitter who comes in several times a day, you may be able to find pet sitters who care for pets in their home. Some pet sitters do this instead of coming to your home, or they stay in your home overnight.

The benefit to having a pet sitter come in is that your dog gets to stay in his own familiar home while you are away. A pet sitter may come by a few times a day to walk, feed, and play with your dog or may stay overnight. The primary drawback to the former is that your dog will be alone most of the time, but he may already be used to that if you work outside the home. And for a fearful dog, that may be

preferable to staying in a boarding kennel. He won't be stressed by new sights, sounds, and smells or the presence of unfamiliar dogs. An ideal solution is the pet sitter who stays overnight. Your dog is in the environment where he feels most secure, and he's not alone at night.

Whether you go with in-home boarding or pet-sitter visits, your first choice should always be a professional pet sitter who knows how to give medication, takes care to prevent escapes, and keeps the pets' safety foremost. If your dog will be staying at the pet-sitter's home, evaluate it carefully. Are the home and yard thoroughly pet-proofed? Is there some kind of double-gate setup to prevent dogs from sneaking out? Are fences and gates sturdy, tall, and in good repair?

Watch how the pet sitter interacts with your dog during the interview visit. He or she should always allow your fearful dog to make the first approach. The pet sitter may ask what your dog likes best and come prepared with

Remember:

When it comes to traveling with your fearful dog or leaving him at home in the care of a responsible business or person, there is no right or wrong choice—only what's best for your dog.

his favorite treats or toys, sitting on the floor during introductions so he or she seems less threatening. Choose someone who has the patience to observe your dog and wait for your dog to come to him or her.

Ask the pet sitter the same types of questions you would ask a boarding kennel: what is his or her experience with fearful dogs, emergency response plan, training in giving medication, and so on. Check references. Hire the person who understands your dog's needs and finds out as much as possible about him before you leave so that he or she will be prepared for any eventuality.

BUILDING
A FEAR FREE LIFE

Building a Fear Free life is a team effort involving family members, veterinary staff, pet-care professionals, and others with whom your dog interacts. As a dog owner, you can build your pet's behavior and work with those who care for or meet your pet, ideally as a team, or at least by guiding them with information on what works best for your pet. You do have options and can make requests.

You and your dog will come into contact with many caregivers throughout your lives: veterinarians, veterinary technicians, dog trainers, and groomers, to name just a few. In this chapter, we'll help you learn how to find

and, if necessary, "train" the people who care for or work with your dog.

GETTING HELP FROM A VETERINARY BEHAVIORIST

Throughout this book, we've recommended seeking the help of a board-certified veterinary behaviorist. We're not just trying to drum up business—honest. In cases involving aggression, anxiety, compulsive disorders, cognitive decline, or behavior disorders rooted in neurotransmitter dysfunctions, we believe that board-certified veterinary behaviorists are

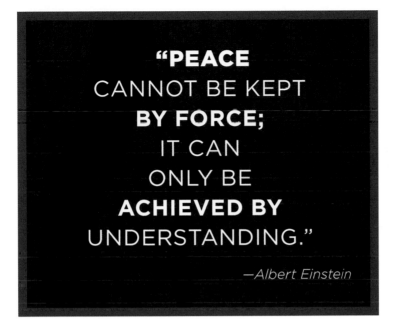

> **"PEACE** CANNOT BE KEPT **BY FORCE;** IT CAN ONLY BE **ACHIEVED BY** UNDERSTANDING."
>
> —*Albert Einstein*

the most effective and experienced choice to diagnose and address your dog's issue. As trained veterinarians, they know which medical problems may cause or worsen behavior problems. They are licensed to prescribe medication, if needed, for behavioral issues, and they know if or how that medication could affect any physical problems the dog has. They can help with a range of problems, including aggression toward people or other animals, fear of thunderstorms, noise phobias, and compulsive disorders, such as excessive chewing, licking, or tail chasing.

WHAT VETERINARY BEHAVIORISTS KNOW

Veterinary specialists of all stripes have advanced training, called a residency, in their particular field. During this training program, veterinary behaviorists dive into subjects such as behavioral genetics, psychology of learning, behavioral physiology (brain-behavior relationships), psychopharmacology (how drugs affect mood, sensation, thinking, and behavior), and more.

Training for a veterinary behavior specialty requires an additional three to five years beyond veterinary school. During this time, residents treat hundreds of cases under supervision, write case reports, and submit their own research for publication in peer-reviewed journals. Residents are mentored by board-certified veterinary behaviorists who can share their in-depth knowledge, experience, and research. To finally achieve certification as a veterinary behaviorist, the candidate must pass a sixteen-hour exam over a two-day period.

A veterinary behaviorist's background and training gives him or her the know-how to interview pet owners and evaluate dogs to diagnose behavior problems and follow up with treatment plans that take into account not only family-pet dynamics but also possible health problems.

WHAT VETERINARY BEHAVIORISTS DO

Either in his or her office or at your home, a veterinary behaviorist's job is to put your dog on the metaphoric couch and analyze his behavior. This includes evaluating his living arrangements; looking at how he interacts with different people in the family as well as outsiders; examining whether he's getting appropriate levels of exercise, training, and social intection; determining whether certain family dynamics or life changes may be causing fear, anxiety, or stress; and even whether he's getting a balanced, nutritious diet. A veterinary behaviorist obtains detailed information from the family through specific questions about the dog's body language and the how the owners interact with and manage the dog.

Once the behaviorist gathers a dog's comprehensive medical and behavioral history, he or she will write up a plan to address the problem. A treatment plan might include behavioral treatments, environmental/ management changes, medication, or a combination of methods.

WHEN TO SEEK A BEHAVIORIST'S HELP

Does your fearful, anxious, or stressed dog always need the services of a veterinary behaviorist? Not necessarily. If your young puppy is having accidents in the house, you need better housetraining skills, not a behaviorist. If your normally well-behaved adult dog suddenly starts stealing food, he may have an endocrine imbalance. Take him to your primary care veterinarian.

Other times, behavior issues are learned through opportunity. For example, your dog discovers that if he stands up on his hind legs, he can easily take food left out on a counter or table. Sometimes, though, you could use a little help from your veterinary behaviorist friends. The following list illustrates instances in which you and your dog may benefit from a veterinary behaviorist's advice.

- Your dog is aggressive. If his behavior puts you, family members, or other people and pets at risk, don't mess around.
- Your dog has a problem that causes him to have significant fear, anxiety, or stress that affects his quality of life. A veterinary behaviorist can help you figure out the root cause of your dog's fear, anxiety, or stress and how to help him cope.
- Your dog has a behavior problem that requires medication. Medication isn't always necessary for behavior problems, but in certain instances it can help a dog

relax enough for behavioral therapies or environmental changes to take effect; when used correctly, medication won't turn your dog into a zombie. A dog trainer can't prescribe medication, and your primary care veterinarian may not necessarily have the behavior expertise to use it in the way it's intended.

- Your dog's behavior problem is really… different. He sucks his sides until they're raw, fixates on the ceiling fan, or growls at magazine ads featuring supermodels (true story). Chances are, your dog's not unique, and a veterinary behaviorist can help sort out the serious from the superficial. (The supermodel thing? Just a weird dog. She got over it.)
- Your dog is injuring himself or destroying your home. Fearful, anxious, or stressed dogs can jump out windows, gnaw through doors, and devour furniture. In the process, they can also hurt themselves. Behavioral therapies, environmental changes, and sometimes medication can help.
- You've been trying to deal with your dog's fear, anxiety, and stress and aren't seeing any progress. The time, money, and effort you're expending could be better spent consulting an expert.
- Your dog's physical health complicates matters. A veterinary behaviorist is trained to navigate the sometimes rocky shoals when a dog must be treated for both a physical ailment and a behavioral one.
- Your dog's life is at risk. You're at your wit's end, and you think euthanasia is the only answer. A veterinary behavior expert may be able to offer you a different option.

FINDING A FEAR FREE FACILITY

Your dog may not need the services of a veterinary behaviorist, but it can be helpful for

What Does "Behaviorist" Mean?

Anyone, including dog trainers or Joe Smith down the street, can use the term "behaviorist." There's no statute requiring that people calling themselves behaviorists have specific qualifications to back up their claim.

Earlier in this chapter, we described the training of a veterinary behaviorist. A veterinarian with those qualifications is said to be "board-certified." That's who you want to look for when you need help.

To find a diplomate of the American College of Veterinary Behaviorists (DACVB), visit the website of the American College of Veterinary Behaviorists (www.dacvb.org) and search for one in your area.

If there's not a DACVB in your area—and there are fewer than 100 in the United States and Canada—you may benefit from a consultation with a certified applied animal behaviorist (CAAB) who works in partnership with a veterinarian. A CAAB has a doctorate in psychology, biology, or zoology with an emphasis in animal behavior, plus at least five years professional experience. They have apprenticed with veterinary behaviorists or other CAABs and have met other requirements for certification set by the Animal Behavior Society. An associate CAAB (ACAAB) has a master's degree with an emphasis in animal behavior and at least two years experience in applied animal behavior.

him to go to a clinic where the veterinarians and technicians are trained in Fear Free techniques. It's especially wonderful if you have a new puppy because the right handling can help him start life off on the right paw, thinking that veterinary visits are grrreat!

More and more veterinarians and their staff are becoming certified in Fear Free methods of handling and interacting with animals. You can look for one in your area by searching online at FearFreePets.com.

If you can't find a Fear Free-certified clinic in your area, talk to your veterinarian about how you'd like him or her and the clinic's staff to handle your dog. He or she may well be open to learning some kinder, more effective methods that will make it easier to examine your pet for all involved.

DOG GROOMERS

Other pet professionals are jumping on the Fear Free bandwagon as well. For instance, some groomers play soothing music, dim the lights, burn scented candles, and treat dogs to a warm bubble bath followed by a deep relaxation massage. Heck, we'd go for that ourselves, but there are other things to look for as well in a Fear Free grooming salon.

Pet groomers who take a Fear Free approach try to achieve a low-stress experience with a space designed to help dogs feel secure and calm.

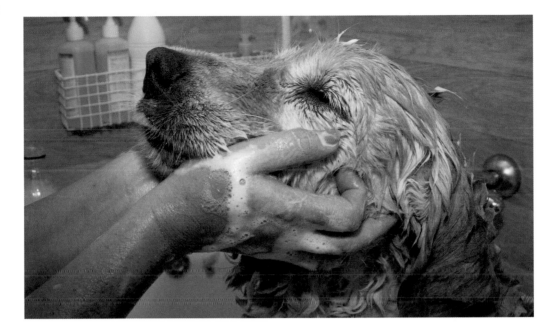

They observe dogs from start to finish to see if they are showing any signs of fear, anxiety, or stress or if they have certain areas that are sensitive to touch. They've learned techniques that allow them to desensitize dogs to loud noises or the blast from a dryer. They may use a hoodie or other device to muffle sounds. They give praise or a treat to associate grooming procedures such as nail trims with good things, and they reinforce calm behavior. Taking such simple extra steps can make the experience less stressful for the dog—and the groomer.

TRAINERS

Working with a dog trainer is a normal part of every pet owner's life, and it's an important one. The trainer you choose can either set up or set back your dog's training success. A skilled dog trainer can help you strengthen the bond between your dog and family, restore harmony in the home, and build the foundation for a successful life together.

Finding a trainer who is best suited to work with your dog takes careful research. Anyone can claim to be a dog trainer, and different trainers can have vast differences in methodologies, credentials, education, skills, and experience. Here are factors to consider.

Methods. Punitive training methods escalate a dog's level of fear, anxiety, and aggression and will only temporarily inhibit unwanted behaviors. The problem behavior might go away for a time, but it will come back sooner rather than later. Self-proclaimed "balanced" trainers who combine force-based methods and reward-based training can set up dogs for confusion and anxiety because of the unpredictable methods used.

Reward-based training builds on trust and improved communication. It teaches and reinforces desired behaviors in a preventive way. Rewards used include treats, toys, attention, and other privileges. Non-force techniques, such as ignoring unwanted behavior or removing rewards when unwanted behaviors occur, may be used. The trainer helps the owner set up management and routine structures to channel the dog's activity and prevent misbehavior. Over the long term, reward-based training is safer and more effective.

Equipment. Ask about the type of equipment the trainer uses and recommends. Avoid trainers who use corrective "choke," prong, or electronic collars. These types of collars can create unintended negative associations and increase a dog's level of fear, anxiety, or stress.

Education. Look for a trainer who has a solid knowledge of dog behavior combined with an educational background in the principles of training and behavior modification, and attends regular continuing-education classes.

Credentials. As we've noted, anyone can hang out a shingle and go to work as a dog trainer, whether or not he or she has an appropriate educational background or certification. Certification by a governing body with specific standards and minimum requirements for training, hours of

experience, and continuing education is one way to know if a trainer has a certain skill level. Among the reputable organizations that oversee trainer certification and practices are the Karen Pryor Academy for Animal Training and Behavior, the Certification Council of Professional Dog Trainers, Jean Donaldson's Academy for Dog Trainers, and the International Association of Animal Behavior Consultants. All have their own specific requirements for minimum hours of training and experience, references, testing, and continuing education.

Experience. Trainers may focus on specific areas: building basic manners, preventive training, resolving minor behavior issues, dog sports, or therapy certification. Some work primarily in behavior counseling and have qualifications that enable them to work with in-depth issues.

Training options. Training needs vary from dog to dog. Depending on your personal situation and your dog's issues, you may work in a class setting, with private lessons, or with in-home training sessions. Some training approaches involve the trainer working with the dog and then teaching the owner how to maintain the behaviors. Other methods involve coaching the owner to do the training himself or herself. Letting someone else train your dog has some benefits, including faster progress and less frustration for many pet owners, but it can lead to backsliding if the owner doesn't successfully maintain what the dog has learned. The best recipe for success is a combination of training by the trainer, training of the owner, and guidance during the transition.

Collaboration. Some issues are best addressed with the guidance of a veterinarian or veterinary behaviorist. A partnership of a veterinary behaviorist, veterinarian, and reward-based trainer is sometimes the best

Advanced **Training**

It's not only veterinarians who may specialize in behavior. Some veterinary technologists specialize in this field as well after meeting rigorous educational and experience requirements. That's not surprising, since a large part of their job involves dealing with animals who may be aggressive or fearful. A knowledge of behavior can go a long way toward helping them gain an animal's trust and prevent bites—to themselves or others. Vet techs with a specialty in behavior work to improve the relationship and communication between people and pets and lessen the likelihood of a pet's death because of behavior disorders.

A vet tech who specializes in behavior may assist a veterinarian or veterinary behaviorist with consultations and treatment plans; help identify a dog's trainability, anxiety, and aggression levels; and teach clients how to employ behavior therapies. At veterinary clinics or animal shelters, they may identify animals with behavior problems that require management or modification; educate pet owners, volunteers, or the public about behavior; or run a behavior hotline.

choice for addressing certain behavioral issues. Ask your veterinary team for a referral to a trusted trainer, or look for a trainer who works with a veterinarian and makes referrals when appropriate.

Insurance. Trainers should have insurance coverage for any potential incidents.

Guarantees. Guarantees may sound good, but they can have ethical and legal drawbacks as well as loopholes that work in the trainer's favor.

SPREADING THE FEAR FREE MESSAGE

As Fear Free veterinarians, behaviorists, and trainers, our goal is to spread the philosophy of the importance of a dog's well-being and mental health so that it becomes a part of everything that touches an animal's life. Whether we are treating a broken leg, pulling rotten teeth, treating diabetes, helping resolve a behavior problem, or teaching new skills, we want to create better experiences for the animals—and humans—involved. It's not only kinder, it also allows us to provide better care. We get more accurate results because we've worked with the owner in advance to make

sure that the animal arrives at the clinic in a more relaxed state, and we work to keep him that way during the exam and treatment. Even better, we are able to follow up because we've removed the barrier that was preventing the dog from receiving health care.

As our fellow Fear Free colleague Dr. John Talmadge says, "Together, we are all celebrating the pet bond that exists, and that makes everyone, including the pet, smile!"

Appendix

COUNTERCONDITIONING YOUR DOG TO HANDLING
What you'll need:
- Some type of smearable food (baby food, squeeze cheese, peanut butter)
- A plate or a squeeze tube

What to do:
- Make a list of the ways or places your dog dislikes being touched (e.g., top of head, ears, having lips lifted for mouth examination) as well as his responses (e.g., growls, tucks tail, pulls away).
- Place food in the tube or smear it on the plate.
- Place the tube or plate on the floor where your dog can see it.
- When your dog shows interest and begins licking the food, briefly touch him, for no more than one second to start, on the areas where he's sensitive. Remove your hand and then take the plate or tube away.
- Over many sessions, gradually increase the amount of time your hand touches your dog. Do not progress until you've had three complete, consecutive (they can be on different days) sessions during which your dog shows no negative reaction to your touch.
- Any time your dog responds fearfully or aggressively, remove your hand immediately and then take away the plate or tube.

Note: *Be aware of your dog's body language. Negative body language is anything, such as head down or tail tucked, that is not relaxed and happy.*

What Is Calm Body Language?
A calm dog's face is relaxed, his mouth closed or slightly open, his tail and ears held normally, and his body balanced on all four legs.

COUNTERCONDITIONING YOUR DOG TO BEING GROOMED WHILE WEARING A MUZZLE
For this exercise, your dog should already be accustomed to wearing a muzzle.

What you'll need:
- The same supplies as described in the section on counterconditioning a dog to handling, plus a basket muzzle
- A helper who can be in charge of adding food to the muzzle as needed (optional, but a good idea)

What to Do:
- List the types of grooming your dog dislikes (e.g., having his ears combed or his nails trimmed) and his reactions to each.
- Begin by smearing food inside the basket muzzle. Put the muzzle on your dog.
- While your dog is licking the muzzle, briefly touch the areas where he's sensitive, for no more than one second.
- If he stops eating, move your hand away and wait for him to begin eating again, at which point you can repeat the brief touch (it's all right if you aren't able to touch him for more than one second at a time).
- Repeat the process many times. Wait until you've had at least two complete sessions of only happy and relaxed body language before you gradually add time. Remove your hand if he stops eating.

Special Diets
For dogs on restricted diets, you can use the canned version of their regular food as a treat or you can use small pieces of the same protein source (lamb, venison, etc.) as in his regular food.

COUNTERCONDITIONING YOUR DOG TO VETERINARY VISITS

If your dog shows signs of stress or fear, you may need to use other behavior modification techniques. You can also try to distance your dog from the person or object that frightens him; this may help decrease the intensity of his fear.

What you'll need:
- High-value treats, such as rotisserie chicken or deli turkey that your dog gets only during veterinary visits
- A standard nylon or leather leash (no retractable leashes)
- An assistant who can help with check-in and check-out procedures and ask questions (optional)

What to do:
- Give your dog a few treats in the parking lot when you arrive. If he seems fearful, anxious or stressed in the car, give treats there first.
- If you know from experience that your dog is able to wait calmly in the lobby, bring him in. As you wait, give treats intermittently as long as he displays calm body language. If your dog is already muzzle-trained and can relax on his mat for fifteen to thirty minutes, you can bring his mat into the lobby.
- Give treats more frequently if a veterinary technician or veterinarian walks by. Continue giving treats until the person is far away or out of sight and then slow the rate of reinforcement (repeat this for anything that makes your dog afraid.) This should help your dog to remain calm.
- Give treats on the way to the exam room and intermittently once you are inside it. Give treats more frequently when the technician or veterinarian enters the room.
- During the exam, give treats continuously. You may need to stop giving treats during certain parts of the exam, such as when the veterinarian is listening to the heart through a stethoscope, but you can still hold treats within view to keep your dog focused. When the exam is over, give treats less frequently.
- Give treats as you leave, all the way out to the car. You don't need to give them at the same frequency as you did during the exam.
- If possible, schedule one or more mock visits that don't involve an exam. Schedule mock visits for times when the veterinary clinic isn't very busy and has an exam room available for practice. Follow the steps above as if it were a real visit.

Note: *Some dogs are unable to remain calm in the lobby. In this case, ask beforehand or send in your helper to ask if you and your dog can wait in the car or parking lot until the exam room is ready. Alternatively, you can use your cell phone to call from the parking lot to let the receptionist know you have arrived and will wait outside until your dog can go directly to the exam room.*

TEACHING YOUR DOG TO HAND TARGET

Targeting involves teaching the dog to touch her nose to an object—in this case, an outstretched hand. For shy or fearful dogs, hand-targeting can be especially helpful in building confidence, because it provides a predictable way for them to interact with people.

Pick a quiet time and a quiet place to begin this training. Keep the training sessions short, no more than two to three minutes.

What you'll need:
- Plenty of training treats (pea-sized pieces of food items your dog really likes)

What to do:
- Place a small treat in your hand and form a fist. Have your fist dangle loosely by the side of your body at the level of your dog's nose. You may need to kneel slightly if you have a short dog.
- Allow your dog to sniff your fist. As soon as your dog touches your hand with her nose, immediately open up the fist and offer the treat.
- Repeat the sequence several times: treat in fist, dog touches, hand opens and offers treat.
- After five to ten repetitions, begin to add a cue word ("Touch" or "Target") when you offer your fist. Continue to repeat the process of giving a treat whenever your dog touches your hand with her nose.
- As your dog becomes more reliable, start to hold your hand out in locations that are a little more challenging, such as out to one side and then the other.

- Switch hands so your dog learns to touch either hand
- Try variations of "touch" so that your dog learns to target the hand no matter what position it is in:
  - A loose fist
  - Two fingers sticking out
  - Open palm facing the dog
  - Open palm turned away from the dog
  - Open palm facing up
  - Open palm facing the ground (but elevated above the dog's head)
  - Begin practicing in different locations, gradually moving to places with various distractions present.

Note: *If your dog becomes frustrated, take a break! Practice a few simple cues that your dog already knows well and reward him for performing those fun activities. Every dog varies in how long it takes to make the connection that touching his owner's hand makes a treat appear, so be patient.*

CRATE TRAINING

Some dogs dislike being in a crate. They may have negative associations from a previous bad experience, and treats may not outweigh their dislike or fear of being alone in a confined area. There may be an element of separation anxiety related to their distress. We're going to address how to teach a normal dog to stay happily in a crate as well as ways to retrain dogs who suffer from crate anxiety.

What you'll need:
- Crate
- Plenty of small high-value treats and/or smearable food

What to do (with a normal dog):
- Place the crate in a common area of the home, with the door open or the top off.
- Hide treats inside the crate for your dog to find.
- When he enters the crate, or any time you see him in it, say "Crate," "Kennel," or some other verbal cue to help your dog associate that word with entering the crate.
- Once your dog is comfortable going into the crate, keep him occupied with a special treat, such as a chew toy stuffed with goodies, and then slowly touch the kennel door and move it an inch toward the closed position. If he turns to look at you, toss him a treat as long as he remains calm and does not appear stressed.
- Over subsequent sessions, slowly work toward moving the door to the closed position. Close the door for one second, then immediately open it before your dog gets upset. Work up to closing the door and leaving your dog inside the crate for brief periods with a favorite toy or treat.
- Don't let your dog out of the crate if he is barking or whining. Wait for a pause in his vocalizations before opening the door. Gradually build up to longer stays in the crate. Note: Dogs with confinement anxiety will panic inside the crate. If this occurs, let him out and talk to your veterinarian about treatment.

What to do (with a fearful dog):
- Make a video of your pet when he's home alone and show it to your veterinarian. He or she can either rule out separation anxiety or give you guidance about how to deal with it. If your dog does show signs of separation anxiety, he may do better if left uncrated; a sanctuary room or puppy playpen can be an option.
- If separation anxiety isn't the problem, and depending on your dog's reaction to the crate, your veterinarian may recommend the assistance of a certified professional dog trainer or a board-certified veterinary behaviorist. Consistent training and, if necessary, medication can help a dog learn to stay calmly in a crate. The following steps are for owners who have been given the green light to retrain their dogs to the crate.
- Get the right crate, preferably one that is different from the one your pet has used in the past. If choosing a wire crate, be sure to pick one with narrow spaces so your dog can't stick his leg through the wire and injure himself.
- Let your dog get used to the crate at her own pace. For instance, you can begin by teaching him to enter a crate with the top removed. Once he's comfortable doing that, practice having him enter the crate with the top on and eventually with the door closed.

- Use rewards to teach your dog to go into the crate. Place his food bowl just outside the crate at mealtimes. With each meal, move the dish slightly farther toward the back of the crate.
- If your dog remains relaxed, close the door once he's inside the crate and offer treats through the slats before immediately reopening it.
- Eventually, you can close the door for longer periods of time and give your dog a long-lasting chew to distract him.
- Place the crate in a well-trafficked area that's not socially isolated, such as next to you while you watch TV. You can leave the crate door open and allow your dog to choose whether she wants to go inside. As soon as she does go into the crate, praise her and drop treats inside it.
- You should also toss treats into the crate throughout the day to encourage your dog to venture inside often to check for goodies. Another trick is to spritz the crate with a pheromone spray that mimics the "at ease" feeling puppies experience when nursing.
- Avoid crating your dog for longer than three or four hours at a time, unless it's overnight. If you plan to be gone for extended periods of time, consider looking into a day care program or a pet sitter or dog walker who can let your pet out of the crate for a break.
- With proper training, your dog's view of her kennel can go from a place of fear to one of relaxation.

Note: *Other ways to help your dog associate the crate with good things are to feed him in it, place a treat trail leading into the crate, or smear peanut butter or cream cheese on the back wall of the crate for him to lick off.*

FOUNDATION TRAINING

Knowing some basic cues will help your dog successfully navigate everyday life. He should know Sit, Stay, Relax, Focus, Turn, Come, Place, Give, Leave It, and Find It. With these ten cues, the two of you can begin the lifelong process of communication that will make you best friends.

Work on each behavior daily if possible or at least once or twice a week. Limit the length of training sessions; they can be as brief as two minutes but no longer than 15 minutes. Cut the session short if you or your dog become frustrated or upset. Try to end on a positive note.

During a training session, you can work on a single cue or multiple cues. If you work on multiple cues, limit each one to one to three minutes.

Use a marker, such as a click or a verbal "Yes" or "Good" to let your dog know his action is what you want. Immediately follow the marker with a food reward.

Rewards should be tasty and tiny, no larger than a pea. Give treats within one to three seconds after using the marker sound or word. The faster you reward correct behavior, the stronger the behavior will become.

Aim for an 80 percent success rate in each behavior before you increase the level of difficulty. For example, your dog should perform correctly in four out of five or eight out of ten tries.

Increase the level of difficulty by having your dog perform the behavior in a different room, in the backyard, in front of the house, or on a walk.

SIT-STAY-RELAX

This sequence of exercises is intended to teach your dog how to calm down, listen, and learn to be patient. Whenever your dog appears upset, agitated ,or anxious, get his attention and help him focus on familiar exercises (e.g., Sit, Down, Look) to redirect his nervous energy into more appropriate, calm behaviors. Remember that the goal of these exercises is relaxation, not obedience.

> **Signs of Relaxation**
> Notice when your dog is relaxed: ears forward, making eye contact, mouth closed. A closed mouth allows deeper breaths, which slow down his breathing, reduce his heart rate and drop his blood pressure. Ears forward and eye contact indicate attentiveness.

Start by asking your dog to sit. When he does, wait for him to look at you with a relaxed expression. If necessary, whistle to get him to move his ears forward or wait for him to close his mouth to swallow. Sometimes lowering your hand slightly may encourage him to close his mouth in anticipation of receiving the reward. Once your dog's eyes are on you, his mouth is closed, and his ears are forward, mark the behavior and give the reward.

To work on Stay for an extended period, ask your dog to sit and stay behind a gate, inside an exercise pen or on his bed. Combine a verbal cue—"Stay"—with a hand signal (hand up with palm facing him). Take one step away from him and then return, release him from the Stay with a specific word ("Okay" or "Free"), and reward him.

Repeat the exercise, gradually increasing the distance you move away from him.

If your dog breaks the Stay or appears overly anxious, go back to a shorter distance from him and proceed more slowly. Work up to being able to walk around the room without your dog getting up.

Progress to moving out of the dog's line of sight and build up to more time spent out of sight: start with one second, repeat several times; then two seconds, repeat several times; and so forth, gradually working up to having your dog sit in one location for fifteen minutes both with you in the room and with you out of sight.

WATCH (OR LOOK OR FOCUS)
Use a food lure to teach your dog to make eye contact with you on cue. When your dog looks at you, mark the behavior with a click or a word and then follow with a reward. Practice five to ten times, with your hand holding the treat directly in front of your face. Then move the hand with the treat an inch away from your face. Use the marker when your dog stops looking at the treat and looks you in the eye. Repeat five to ten times and then move your hand farther from your face. Keep repeating the process, moving farther and farther from your face, and eventually you should be able to hold your hand out to your side with your dog looking into your eyes instead of at your hand.

TURN
Use a treat to lure your dog into a 180-degree turn to the right. As he turns, say "Turn." Once he is facing 180 degrees from the starting point, praise him and give a food reward. Practice ten to fifteen times and then begin to withhold the treat and have him follow your hand only. Once he's facing the correct direction, give praise and a treat.

COME
Start by putting a long leash on your dog and letting him drag it around. Next, have friends or family members stand about 5 feet apart in a loose circle. Each person should randomly call your dog to come and give him lavish praise and food rewards when he responds.After each person has called your dog to come at least twice, everyone should take a step back and repeat the exercise. If your dog tries to run out of the circle, step on the leash to keep him inside it. Go back to a smaller circle and repeat the exercise.

Initially practice in situations with no distractions. Practice Come in different parts of the house, in different areas of the yard, and outside in securely enclosed areas.

GO TO MAT/PLACE (TARGET LOCATION)
Teach your dog to go to a designated location on cue by calling him over to the designated area, which can be a mat, his bed, or some other place that you choose. It's helpful to have a visual aid, such as a small blanket, towel, or mat, which can also become a portable relaxation spot for your dog that can be used anywhere.

Start by pointing your hand toward the mat and dropping a handful of tiny treats onto it. As soon as your dog places one or two paws onto the mat to eat the treats, say "Target," "Mat," or "Place." Repeat ten to fifteen times until your dog immediately steps onto the mat when you point your hand down. Then reward him with treats.

As your dog responds more reliably, wait until all four paws are on the mat before giving the reward. When your dog starts to respond more quickly to the cue, ask him to sit on the mat. Offer him a delicious, long-lasting treat, such as a small chew or rawhide. It should be something that will keep him happy and focused on staying in that location. If he takes the item away from the mat, carefully take the item away and place it back on the target location. After he learns to sit on the mat, progress to Down and Stay. Once he stays on the mat reliably, gradually start moving away from him.

The goal is to be able to have him go to his mat, sit or lie down, and wait for further instructions from you. Going to his special location should always be associated with wonderful treats and plenty of praise.

GIVE (DROP IT)

To teach your dog a Give or Drop It cue, offer him a tasty treat when he has an object in his mouth. As he opens his mouth to take the treat, say the cue word as the object falls from his mouth. Repeat five to ten times.

Next, give him the object, say the cue word, and wait for him to drop the object before offering him the reward. Repeat five to ten times. Gradually progress to practicing with more highly valued objects.

If you are working with a dog who is aggressive about his possessions, avoid the potential for a bite by tossing the treats instead of handing them to him. Lay a trail of treats, Hansel-and-Gretel-style, to lead him away from the object you want to take.

LEAVE IT

Use this cue when you want your dog to ignore a person, other animal, or object.

Place a handful of treats in your left hand, fist closed. Use your right hand to give the treats.

Let your dog sniff at the closed fist. Once he looks away or backs off, meaning that his nose is no longer touching your hand, offer him a treat with your right hand. Repeat this exercise several times. Once your dog understands that he must look away or move back to get a treat, you can use the cue Leave It. Repeat the exercise several times until he is reliable.

The second part of this exercise is to place the treats on the floor and use your left hand to cover them. Tell your dog to leave it. As soon as he looks away or backs away, give him a treat. Repeat this exercise several times.

Uncover the treats and give him the cue. Be ready to cover the treats with your left hand or use a bowl to cover them in case your dog tries to eat the treats on the floor. If he looks away, give him a food treat. Repeat this exercise until you can gradually increase the amount of time that your dog ignores the uncovered treats.

FIND IT

Toss a handful of tasty treats on the ground right in front of your dog's face.

As he sniffs and starts to eat the treats, say "Find It." Repeat three to five times.

Start tossing the treats in a wider area away from your dog so that he has to search for the individual treats. Repeat three to five times. Eventually, scatter treats farther away from your dog, praising him as he finds and eats them.

Glossary

anxiety: anticipation that something harmful will happen when there is no clear threat present.

behavior: the way in which an animal or person responds to a particular situation or stimulus.

classical conditioning: a technique for altering behavior that works by establishing associations between previously neutral events and involuntary responses. The classic example is Pavlov's dogs, who began to salivate at the sound of a bell because they associated it with food.

counterconditioning: pairing something good with something scary or stressful in order to change the dog's emotional state and eventually change his response to the scary stimulus to a more relaxed response.

cue: a verbal (such as "Sit" or "Down") or hand signal indicating to a dog which behavior he should or should not perform. If the behavior after the cue is rewarded, the dog will become more likely to offer the behavior in the future. A cue can also be a physical action by a person that a dog has learned will initiate a particular event, such as picking up the leash to go for a walk or going into the kitchen at night to get bedtime treats.

desensitization: gradual exposure of a dog to the thing that frightens him, beginning at such a low level that he doesn't react at all and slowly increasing the level of exposure without provoking a stress response, with the goal of reducing or eliminating fear, anxiety, or stress.

fear: an emotion aroused by pain, danger, or some other unpleasant situation.

flooding: exposing a dog for a prolonged period to the thing that frightens him without attention to the dog's stress level.

marker: that acts as a bridge between a desired behavior and the resulting reward that follows.

phobia: a persistent, abnormal, irrational, out-of-context fear of a specific situation or object.

positive reinforcement: rewarding a dog for a desired behavior, with the goal of increasing that behavior in the future.

punishment: a consequence that represses a behavior by adding or removing something to make the behavior less likely to occur. Positive punishment, for instance, involves adding a consequence, such as yelling, jerking on the leash, or using a shock collar. Negative punishment involves taking away something the dog wants, such as attention or play.

reinforcement: anything that increases or strengthens the likelihood that a behavior will occur.

reinforcer: anything a dog will work for, such as praise, treats, toys, petting or play.

reward: something desirable given to an individual directly after a desired response. The reward increases the probability that the behavior/response will be repeated. The reward can be food, praise, attention, or anything else the animal finds pleasing.

sensitization: increasing the strength of a reaction to a stimulus through repeated exposure to it. For instance, a dog who at first loves car rides but then is taken only to the veterinarian's office in the car may gradually come to dislike car rides.

socialization: exposing a puppy to positive experiences with people, other animals, places, objects, sights, sounds and experiences.

stimulus: any object or change in the environment that elicits a response.

Resources

Academy of Veterinary Behavior Technicians
www.avbt.net
Veterinary technicians who become certified as behavior specialists are trained in scientific and humane techniques of behavior health, problem prevention, training, management, and behavior modification. They are essential members of a veterinary behavior team and are important in building, maintaining, and strengthening the bond between human and animal.

American College of Veterinary Behaviorists
www.dacvb.org
The members of this professional organization are veterinarians who have completed advanced studies in animal behavior. They are board-certified, meaning that they have fulfilled specific education, research, and practice requirements and passed a rigorous exam. Board-certified specialists are known as diplomates. Their goal is to help people manage a pet's behavior problems and improve that animal's well being. They may work with pet owners; other animal professionals, including general-practice veterinarians; or facilities that care for animals.

American Veterinary Society of Animal Behavior
www.avsabonline.org
This group of veterinarians and researchers seeks to develop a thorough understanding of animal behavior. It promotes low-stress handling techniques and positive conditioning for veterinary exams. The organization's goal is to improve animal quality of life and to strengthen the human-animal bond.

Animal Behavior Society
www.animalbehaviorsociety.org
The mission of the ABS is to promote and encourage the study of animal behavior under both natural and controlled conditions. Membership is open to anyone interested in the study of animal behavior.

Certification Council for Professional Dog Trainers
www.ccpdt.org
The CCPDT is an independent testing and certification resource for dog trainers and behavior professionals using humane, science-based techniques. Professionals certified by CCPDT have been tested for knowledge and skill, must earn continuing education units to maintain their designations, and must follow a code of ethics. We recommend trainers who have achieved the designation CPDT-KA. The letters KA stand for "knowledge assessed," which means that the person has a broad range of knowledge and skills in ethology, learning theory, and dog-training techniques; has at least 300 hours of experience in dog training within the last three years; has a reference from a CCPDT certificate holder or a veterinarian; has signed the code of ethics; and has passed the CPDT-KA exam.

International Association of Animal Behavior Consultants
www.iaabc.org
The goals of the IAABC are to standardize and support the practice of companion animal behavior consulting and provide resources for pet owners who need advice. It has more than 1,000 members worldwide who help people manage and modify a pet's problem behaviors through least intrusive and minimally aversive methods.

Karen Pryor Academy
www.karenpryoracademy.com
This organization's professional dog-training curriculum teaches force-free methods and a solid knowledge of the science behind learning. Graduates must demonstrate technical excellence and hands-on skills. A searchable online database can help you find one of more than 550 KPA-certified trainers in the United States and Canada.

Society of Veterinary Behavior Technicians
www.svbt.org
The SVBT's goal is to promote scientifically based techniques of training, management, and behavior modification.

Index

Dr. Marty Becker, "America's Veterinarian," has spent his life working toward better physical and emotional well-being for pets, which led him to create and launch the Fear Free initiative: an educational certification program to train veterinarians in easing the fear and anxiety of their patients and clients. Dr. Becker was the resident veterinary contributor on *Good Morning America* for seventeen years and is currently a member of the Board of Directors of the American Humane Association. He currently lives in northern Idaho and serves as an adjunct professor at his alma mater, the Washington State University College of Veterinary Medicine, and practices at North Idaho Animal Hospital.

Board-certified veterinary behaviorist **Dr. Lisa Radosta** graduated from the University of Florida College of Veterinary Medicine and later completed a residency in behavioral medicine at the University of Pennsylvania. She has owned Florida Veterinary Behavior Service since 2007. Dr. Radosta lectures nationally and internationally and has written textbook chapters, scientific research articles, and review articles. She is the section editor for *Advances in Small Animal Medicine and Surgery* and has been interviewed for numerous magazines, newspapers, and television shows as well as Steve Dale's *Pet Talk*. She serves on the Fear Free™ Executive Committee and the AAHA Behavior Management Task Force.

Dr. Wailani Sung has a passion for helping owners prevent or effectively manage behavior problems in companion animals, enabling them to maintain a high quality of life. Dr. Sung obtained her master's degree and Doctorate in Psychology, with a special interest in animal behavior from the University of Georgia. Upon completion of these graduate programs, she obtained a Doctorate in Veterinary Medicine from the University of Georgia College of Veterinary Medicine, then board certification in veterinary behavioral medicine. Dr. Sung practiced veterinary behavioral medicine in dogs, cats and birds in the greater Seattle area for the past 10 years. She is a frequent contributor to the *Healthy Pet* magazine and the websites Vetstreet.com and PetMD.com. Dr. Sung currently practices veterinary behavioral medicine at the San Francisco SPCA. Dr. Sung enjoys spending her free time with her husband and their family of two dogs, a senior cat, a red-bellied parrot and a citron-crested cockatoo.

Mikkel Becker is a Certified Behavior Consultant Canine (CBCC-KA), Certified Professional Dog Trainer (CPDT-KA), and Certified Dog Behavior Counselor (CDBC) through IAABC. She specializes in reward-based training with a specialty in preventing and addressing fear issues using calm, trust, and communication. Mikkel graduated from the San Francisco SPCA Dog Training Academy, the Karen Pryor Academy, and the Purdue Dogs and Cats Course and has completed internships at Tufts Animal Behavior Clinic and Jungle Island, where she specialized in orangutan care. Mikkel is the animal trainer for Vetstreet.com and resident trainer for Dr. Wailani Sung as well as the co-author of five books and a regular contributor to national publications. She is also the lead animal trainer for FearFreePets.com.

FEAR FREE
HAPPY
HOMES

Helping pets live happy, healthy, full lives

It's easy for pet lovers to feel more than a little guilty when it comes to the "balance sheet" with their beloved pets. Our dogs (and cats) give us unconditional love, limitless affection and to-die-for loyalty and with our hectic lives often getting in the way, we give them the time we can spare and the love we can share. We can give them the basics of food, water, shelter and veterinary care, but there is so much more we can do for the ones we love to keep their minds sharp and their bodies healthy.

We now know that pets also need to have enrichment activities to keep their bodies moving, minds sharp and for them to be able to showcase their amazing genetic gifts to hunt for their food, even if that involves a non-lethal hunt involving rubber prey inside a high-rise apartment or suburban home.

To help your pet live a happy, healthy, full life, check out the amazing resources at FearFreeHappyHomes.com, where hundreds of the world's top experts in animal behavior, medicine, nutrition and enrichment share cutting-edge education courses, tactics and tips to help prevent problems, improve behaviors and ensure that your pets have optimal physical and emotional wellbeing.

Using the resources at FearFreeHappyHomes.com, your pet can actually look forward to trips to the veterinarian and groomer, enjoy car travel, walk on a loose leash, stop excessive barking, and not cower during thunderstorms and fireworks. You'll find amazing deals on products not available anywhere else, as well as help pets in need.

FEAR FREE
Taking the pet out of petrified.